STUDY GUIDE

Volume II: Since 1500

The Earth and Its Peoples

A Global History

STUDY GUIDE

Volume II: Since 1500

The Earth and Its Peoples

A Global History

STUDY GUIDE

Volume II: Since 1500

The Earth and Its Peoples

A Global History

THIRD EDITION

Richard W. Bulliet / Pamela Kyle Crossley / Daniel R. Headrick /
Steven W. Hirsch / Lyman L. Johnson / David Northrup

Michele G. Scott James

MiraCosta College

HOUGHTON MIFFLIN COMPANY   BOSTON   NEW YORK

Senior Sponsoring Editor: *Nancy Blaine*
Editorial Associate: *Annette Fantasia*
Editorial Assistant: *Trinity Peacock-Broyles*
Manufacturing Manager: *Florence Cadran*
Senior Marketing Manager: *Sandra McGuire*

Del and Jacob, All my love, MSJ.

Printed in the U.S.A.

ISBN: 0-618-427724

123456789-POO-08 07 06 05 04

Contents

To the Student vii

CHAPTER 16 - The Maritime Revolution, to 1550 1

CHAPTER 17 - Transformations in Europe, 1500–1750 23

CHAPTER 18 - The Diversity of American Colonial Societies, 1530–1770 50

CHAPTER 19 - The Atlantic System and Africa, 1550–1800 78

CHAPTER 20 - Southwest Asia and the Indian Ocean, 1500-1750 101

CHAPTER 21 - Northern Eurasia, 1500–1800 130

CHAPTER 22 - Revolutionary Changes in the Atlantic World, 1750–1850 158

CHAPTER 23 - The Early Industrial Revolution, 1760–1851 187

CHAPTER 24 - Nation Building and Economic Transformation in the
Americas, 1800–1890 213

CHAPTER 25 - Africa, India, and the New British Empire, 1750-1870 243

CHAPTER 26 - Land Empires in the Age of Imperialism, 1800-1870 270

CHAPTER 27 - The New Power Balance, 1850–1900 295

CHAPTER 28 - The New Imperialism, 1869–1914 323

CHAPTER 29 - The Crisis of the Imperial Order, 1900–1929 350

CHAPTER 30 - The Collapse of the Old Order, 1929–1949 383

CHAPTER 31 - Striving for Independence: Africa, India, and Latin
America, 1900–1949 415

CHAPTER 32 - The Cold War and Decolonization, 1945–1975 441

CHAPTER 33 - Crisis, Realignment, and the Dawn of the Post-Cold War
World, 1975–1991 470

CHAPTER 34 - Globalization at the Turn of the Millennium 499

To the Student

Welcome to world history. Whether this is your first history course or you are a history major, you will enjoy the vast scope and quick pace of world history. You will be learning a great deal about the earth and its peoples in one class. Because there is a large amount of information, it helps to be organized right from the beginning. Part of your study system should be the completion of this *Study Guide*.

HOW TO USE THIS STUDY GUIDE

Read the chapter objectives in *The Earth and Its Peoples: A Global History;* then read the entire chapter.

Highlight or underline important facts or words. Do *not* underline too much of the text; underline only key words and phrases so that you can find them when you review.

Fill in the blank *outline* provided for you in the *Study Guide.* Included are the large subject headings to keep you on track. You may not need to fill in all the lines, or you may find yourself adding lines. That's okay. The outline is designed to help you learn the structure and important themes of the chapter.

Then fill in the *identifications* section. It contains the key terms listed at the end of each chapter, plus a few additional terms, names, and concepts that you need to learn in order to master the material. To answer an identification question, define the term; provide relevant date or dates; and tell why the term is significant. If you leave out any of this information on a test, you will probably not receive full credit, even if what you have written is correct.

Next, test yourself with the *multiple-choice questions.* Many professors like to test a student's recall of facts and so will use multiple-choice questions. However, even if your professor does not give multiple-choice tests, you will find that if you do well on this section, it will improve your overall performance.

The *short-answer questions* resemble the identifications in that you should define the term, event, or concept, then give a date, and explain the significance. Three to five sentences are usually sufficient to answer such a question.

Essay questions are probably the most difficult type of question that students must deal with. The key to answering them successfully is to be organized. First outline the major themes that you will use to answer the question. Then assemble the details, including dates, that you will need to support your themes. When you have them all together, you can begin to write your essay. Write formally, using complete sentences, good grammar and style, and correct spelling. Always reread your essays, both to make any needed corrections and to ensure that you have answered the question completely.

Comparison charts allow you to make comparisons between societies, time periods, peoples, and philosophies. Be guided by the chart title and chapter content for hints on how to complete each chart. Fill in all the blank areas that you can. These charts will aid you in class discussions, essays, and perhaps even term papers.

The *Diversity and Dominance* sections allow you to critically examine a primary document created by people who lived in the past. The *Study Guide* contains some questions that supplement those in the text. By reading the primary documents and answering the questions, you will have a unique ability to see the past through the eyes of individuals who lived long ago.

The *Internet Assignment* section will allow you to view at least two relevant images from each chapter. Use your favorite browser to look up the keywords listed and then analyze each image. Questions are provided to help you interpret what you are viewing. Your instructor has a list of the images, and may use them in class discussion or in assignments or tests. Here, as well as in your research assignments, you may want to rely on college or university sites (these often contain "edu" in the address) and well-established sites such as PBS.org or Discovery.com. Some of the images may be found in the *History WIRED* image library on the Bulliet, *The Earth and Its Peoples* web site. To locate the Bulliet home page, begin at the Houghton Mifflin college site (http://college.hmco.com) and select "history" from the available disciplines. Once you have located the history homepage, select *The Earth and Its Peoples* from the books listed to visit *History WIRED*, as well as a wealth of other resources.

Internet Exploration offers some less conventional web sites and keywords designed to stretch and challenge the boundaries of history and the teaching of history. Many keywords and sites will lead you to virtual tours, games, and sites containing controversial theories. History is constantly changing, and new theories rise all of the time. Using the keywords and web sites listed in each chapter will expose you to new ideas, and to things you may never have thought of as history.

Maps help you visualize the geographic region in which the historical events you are studying took place, thus increasing your understanding of these events. Because many professors give map quizzes or include geography questions on tests, the *map exercises* at the end of each chapter will help you prepare to answer such questions. Feel free to use different colors and patterns to shade in regions and plot map points on the blank maps provided with the exercises.

TEN QUICK TIPS FOR DOING WELL IN YOUR WORLD HISTORY CLASS

1. Attend all the classes and take careful notes.

2. Read your textbook chapter attentively. Remember that many professors require students to read the text before class. Don't get behind on the reading and don't put off catching up until late in the term.

3. Complete your *Study Guide*.

4. Spend some quiet, uninterrupted time each week really learning the material, not just reading over the text.

5. After you finish each chapter, read over your lecture notes and *Study Guide* outline.

6. Get together with your classmates and form study groups.

7. Get enough sleep and eat a good meal before your test.

8. Don't cram before an examination. If you like, you can read over your notes just before a test, but don't try to learn new material. Instead, concentrate on the material you already know.

9. Relax, word hard, and do your best.

10. History is fun—so enjoy yourself!

WHY STUDY HISTORY?

Each of us walked with Lucy at Hadar. Each of us was a soldier in Napoleon's army, a Chinese princess, an artist painting the walls of the cave at Lascaux, an Olmec astronomer, a follower of the Buddha, a pilgrim traveling with Mansa Kankan Musa, a suffragist marching for the vote of women, and a Polynesian navigator. Since we are all each of these people, history belongs to us; it is our participation in the human experience.

We study history because it teaches us about the nature of humanity. Studying history is not merely learning what we have done in the past; it is studying who we are. It leads us to understand and cherish the vast range of human experience and so helps us recognize the value of diversity. It encourages us to look up from our daily lives toward a larger world and to appreciate the role we play in that world—the role we play in history.

CHAPTER 16

The Maritime Revolution, to 1550

LEARNING OBJECTIVES

After reading Chapter 16 and completing this study chapter, you should be able to explain:

- In what ways the period from 1400 to 1550 represents a departure from earlier global expansion.

- Through what motives and methods Europeans gained global dominance.

- How the peoples of Africa, Asia, and the Americas reacted to European dominance.

- Why European empire building was more effective in the Americas than in either Africa or Asia.

CHAPTER OUTLINE

In the outline below include important themes, concepts, and details in the blank spaces provided. If you find fewer points than you have space for, leave lines blank. If you find more points, add as many lines as necessary.

I. *Introduction*
    A. *Magellan's Voyages*
        1. _____

        2. _____

        3. _____

    B. *Completing the voyage*
        1. _____

        2. _____

        3. _____

    C. *This was the end of an era in which influences tended to move from east to west*
        1. _____

        2. _____

        3. _____

II. *Global Maritime Expansion Before 1450*
    A. *The Pacific Ocean*
        1. *Peoples from Malay settled Southeast Asia*
            a) _____

            b) _____

            c) _____

        2. *Peoples from Fiji settled Polynesia*
            a) _____

            b) _____

            c) _____

        3. *Some scholars think they couldn't have done it except by accident—now we know it was planned*
            a) _____

            b) _____

            c) _____

    B. *The Indian Ocean*
        1. *Other Malayo-Indonesians*
            a) _____

            b) _____

            c) _____

        2. *The rise of Medieval Islam boosted Indian Ocean trade*
            a) _____

            b) _____

            c) _____

        3. *China and the Ming dynasty*
            a) _____

            b) _____

        c) _____

        d) _____

   4. *Zheng He (1371–1435) and his voyages*
        a) _____

        b) _____

        c) _____

        d) _____

        e) _____

        f) _____

   5. **Delegations from Africa**
        a) _____

        b) _____

        c) _____

   6. **Opposition to voyages**
        a) _____

        b) _____

        c) _____

C. *The Atlantic Ocean*
   1. *The Vikings*
        a) _____

        b) _____

        c) _____

        d) _____

   2. *Southern Europeans, Mediterranean, and the Atlantic Coast*
       a) _____

       b) _____

       c) _____

   3. *African voyages of exploration into the Atlantic*
       a) _____

       b) _____

       c) _____

       d) _____

       e) _____

   4. *Amerindians from South America*
       a) _____

       b) _____

       c) _____

       d) _____

III. *European Expansion, 1400–1550*
   A. *Motives for Exploration*
       1. *Motives*
           a) _____

           b) _____

           c) _____

       2. *Methods*
           a) _____

           b) _____

           c) _____

B.   *Portuguese Voyages*
   1.   *Attack on Ceuta—1415*
        a)   _____

        b)   _____

        c)   _____

   2.   *Prince Henry the Navigator*
        a)   _____

        b)   _____

        c)   _____

        d)   _____

   3.   *Technology*
        a)   _____

        b)   _____

        c)   _____

        d)   _____

        e)   _____

   4.   *Voyages*
        a)   _____

        b)   _____

        c)   _____

   5.   *Sailing far and returning*
        a)   _____

        b)   _____

        c)   _____

d)   _____

6.   *The Order of Christ*
a)   _____

b)   _____

c)   _____

C.   *Spanish Voyages*
1.   **Columbus**
a)   _____

b)   _____

c)   _____

2.   *Amerigo Vespucci explored American mainland*
a)   _____

b)   _____

c)   _____

3.   *1454—Treaty of Tordesillas with Portugal*
a)   _____

b)   _____

c)   _____

4.   *Balboa and Magellan*
a)   _____

b)   _____

c)   _____

IV. *Encounters with Europe, 1450–1550*
    A.   *Western Africa*
        1.   *Gold Coast—eager for trade with the Portuguese*
            a) _____

            b) _____

            c) _____

        2.   *Early contact mixed commercial, military, and religious interests*
            a) _____

            b) _____

            c) _____

        3.   *Benin—near the peak of its power when first encountering the Portuguese*
            a) _____

            b) _____

            c) _____

        4.   *Kongo*
            a) _____

            b) _____

            c) _____

            d) _____

    B.   *Eastern Africa*
        1.   *1498—Malindi*
            a) _____

            b) _____

            c) _____

2. *Christian Ethiopia*
   a) _____

   b) _____

   c) _____

3. *African encounters with the Portuguese before 1550 varied considerably*
   a) _____

   b) _____

   c) _____

C. *Indian Ocean States*
   1. *1498—da Gama arrived at Malabar Coast*
      a) _____

      b) _____

      c) _____

   2. *Portuguese wanted a private "Portuguese Sea"*
      a) _____

      b) _____

      c) _____

      d) _____

      e) _____

   3. *Portuguese power grab and resistance*
      a) _____

      b) _____

      c) _____

      d) _____

e) _____

D.   *The Americas*
1.   *Territorial rather than trading empire*
a) _____

b) _____

c) _____

2.   *Aztec leader Moctezuma II*
a) _____

b) _____

c) _____

d) _____

e) _____

3.   *Inca leader Atahualpa*
a) _____

b) _____

c) _____

E.   *Patterns of Dominance*
1.   *European dominance more complete in Americas due to many factors*
a) _____

b) _____

c) _____

d) _____

2.   *Less successful in Old World*
a) _____

b) _____

    c) _____

    d) _____

V. *Conclusion*
  A. *Century between 1450 and 1550 a turning point in world history—modern age*
    1. _____

    2. _____

    3. _____

  B. *Degree of conquest similar to some that had gone before*
    1. _____

    2. _____

    3. _____

  C. *European empires lasted longer and had a bigger impact*
    1. _____

    2. _____

    3. _____

IDENTIFICATIONS

Define each term and explain why it is significant, including any important dates.

          Identification   **Significance**

Zheng He

Arawak

Henry the Navigator

	Identification	Significance

caravel

Gold Coast

Treaty of Tordesillas

Bartolomeu Dias

Vasco da Gama

Christopher Columbus

Ferdinand Magellan

Kongo

Malindi

Christian Ethiopia

Malacca

	Identification	Significance
conquistadors		
Hernán Cortés		
Moctezuma II		
Francisco Pizarro		
Atahualpa		

MULTIPLE-CHOICE QUESTIONS

Read the entire question, including *all* the possible answers. Then choose the *one* answer that best fits the question.

1. The *Victoria*'s successful return to Spain in 1522 was
    a. the signal that the Spanish were not to be the dominant force in the Americas.
    b. the crowning example of the Europeans' new ability and determination to make themselves masters of the oceans.
    c. the end of the first expedition led by the English.
    d. the final glory of Spanish dominance in Asia.
    e. confirmation of Magellan's failure.
2. The Polynesian migrations were
    a. obviously accidental since Polynesians lacked navigational devices to plot their way.
    b. obviously from the Americas as Thor Heyerdhal proved in 1947.
    c. the result of a planned expansion.
    d. really a small and unimpressive achievement.
    e. probably really Phoenicians blown off course.
3. Why did the Viking settlements of Greenland and Vinland go into decline after 1200?
    a. The bubonic plague broke out.
    b. Those colonies seceded.
    c. The Vikings' attention was drawn to continental affairs.
    d. The mainland Vikings became Christians, but the island Vikings did not, causing a breach between the two groups.
    e. The weather changed.

4. Which of the following did *not* contribute to the Iberians' decision to begin making the voyages of exploration?

    a.   the revival of urban life and trade
    b.   to find a route to the Americas
    c.   a struggle with Islamic powers for dominance of the Mediterranean
    d.   growing intellectual curiosity about the outside world
    e.   an alliance between merchants and rulers

5. The new anti-Muslim Crusades of 1396 and 1444 were launched by the Europeans because

    a.   of a renaissance in European Christianity.
    b.   the Europeans had finally made contact with the elusive Prester John, and he was going to help reclaim the Holy Land.
    c.   the expansion of the Ottoman Turks disrupted trade routes.
    d.   they felt the need to compete with the Chinese in their voyages of exploration.
    e.   the Ottoman Turks defaulted on their debt to Spain.

6. Which of the following was *not* one aspect of the Portuguese attack on Ceuta in 1415?

    a.   a plundering expedition
    b.   a religious crusade
    c.   a military tournament
    d.   a diplomatic overture
    e.   an information gathering expedition, particularly to gain knowledge about African caravans

7. Columbus finally persuaded Queen Isabella and King Ferdinand to finance his voyage to the East Indies by

    a.   impressing them with his command of geography.
    b.   offering a money-back guarantee.
    c.   proving his theory by using a ninth-century Arab map.
    d.   sheer persistence.
    e.   threatening to sail for France.

8. Why did Columbus call the native people of the Americas "Indians?"

    a.   He thought that he had landed on an island in the East Indies.
    b.   He thought that he had landed in India.
    c.   "Indian" means foreigner.
    d.   "Indian" means savage.
    e.   "Indian" means "beloved of God."

9. The Treaty of Tordesillas (1494)

    a.   split the world between Spain and Portugal.
    b.   legalized African slave trading.
    c.   protected Amerindians from Spanish abuses.
    d.   was vetoed by the pope.
    e.   prevented Brazil from being claimed by Portugal.

10. When the Portuguese first encountered African kingdoms, they

    a.   found nothing of interest there.
    b.   were equal in power, or even less powerful than their African counterparts.
    c.   easily dominated them.
    d.   found that Africans had no interest in trade.
    e.   found that Africans were eager for trade.

11. What finally kept Portugal and Ethiopia from making a permanent alliance?
    a. The Portuguese were afraid to make an alliance with a Muslim kingdom.
    b. Ethiopia needed military assistance that the Portuguese were unwilling to give.
    c. Ethiopia was led by a Queen, and Christian countries were never led by female monarchs.
    d. Ethiopia refused to transfer Christian affiliation from the patriarch of Alexandria to the pope in Rome.
    e. The Portuguese discovered that the Ethiopians were plotting against them.
12. The Portuguese were able to assert control over the Indian Ocean because
    a. of the superiority of Christianity over indigenous beliefs.
    b. the constant warfare in the region allowed the disruption of traditional trade systems.
    c. Portuguese trade goods were vastly superior to anything to be found in the region.
    d. of the temporary alliance they were able to make with the Ethiopians.
    e. of the superiority of their ships and weapons over the smaller and lightly armed merchant dhows.
13. How did the Arawaks respond to the Spaniards' ever-increasing demands for more gold?
    a. They gladly provided more of their plentiful gold.
    b. They told Columbus exaggerated stories about gold in other places to persuade him to move on.
    c. They ran away.
    d. They held Columbus for ransom in order to get gold from the Spaniards.
    e. They attacked Columbus's fort.
14. Which of the following factors did *not* contribute to the success of the Spanish in creating a vast land empire so quickly in the Americas?
    a. Spaniards immigrated in great numbers to the American colonies.
    b. The long isolation of the Americas made its inhabitants vulnerable to European diseases.
    c. The Spanish had superior military technology.
    d. The Spaniards' no-holds-barred fighting style learned at home against the Muslims.
    e. The Spaniards had gained a psychological edge from use of the muskets and cannon.

SHORT-ANSWER QUESTIONS

Answer each question in one short paragraph, giving the definition, dates, and significance.

1. Why did the Ming voyages of exploration end?
2. What kind of technology was employed by the Portuguese, and later other Europeans, to facilitate their voyages of exploration?
3. What did Afonso I hope to gain by his relationship with the Portuguese and how did the situation get out of his control?
4. Why did Ethiopia need Portuguese help and under what conditions would Portugal grant it?
5. Describe the career, motivation, and impact of Prince Henry the Navigator.
6. Briefly explain why the century between 1450 and 1550 was a major turning point in history.

ESSAY QUESTIONS

Make an outline of each question, listing the major points you want to discuss. Then write your practice essay, following your outline carefully and making sure that you do not skip any of your major points. At this time you will want to add the relevant dates and details that will make your essay persuasive and accurate.

1. Briefly describe the non-European patterns of expansion before 1450. What were the goals in these expansions and what methods were used to achieve them?

2. What were the Europeans' motives and methods in their voyages of exploration?

3. Compare and contrast three responses to European exploration.

4. Describe the role of the Portuguese in the Indian Ocean trading network. What methods did they use and how successful were they in achieving their goals?

5. Why were Europeans so much more successful in establishing territorial empires in the Americas than in Africa and Asia?

COMPARISON CHARTS

Using information gathered from the text, fill in the blank areas of each chart with the relevant data pertaining to the regions and categories listed. (Not all blank areas will necessarily be used.)

Chart 16.1

PATTERNS OF EXPANSION

	Dates	Regions	Goals	Technology	Impact
Spanish/Portuguese					
Mongol					
Chinese					
Muslim					
Malayo-Indonesian					
Amerindian					

Chart 16.2

EUROPEAN IMPACT IN ASIA AND AFRICA VERSUS IMPACT IN AMERICA

	Asia/Africa	America
Motives		
Methods		
Response by Local Peoples		

DIVERSITY AND DOMINANCE

After reading "Diversity and Dominance: Congo's Christian King" in your text, answer the following additional questions.

How do you think people respond to unfamiliar and frightening cultures? Put yourself in the place of Moctezuma; how would you see the Spanish?

Why is it so important that Juan Ginés de Sepúlveda need to demonstrate the barbarity of the Amerindians? Do you see similarities between the two cultures?

INTERNET ASSIGNMENT

Keywords: **"Psalter world map"**

                        "Henricus Martellus map" or "Cantino world map"

Maps are valuable tools we use to locate streets, schools, and vacation spots. But maps can also be used to learn about the people who created them. Use the above keywords to locate web sites about the Psalter world map, Henricus Martellus map, and the Cantino world map. You might want to consult the *History WIRED* image library on the Bulliet, *The Earth and Its Peoples* web site (refer to the preface of this study guide for information on how to locate the Bulliet home page).

The first keyword is for a map from the Middle Ages, and the second set of keywords is for maps from the early Renaissance period. What do you notice about the map from the Middle Ages? What is missing? How do the Renaissance maps differ in style and geography from the medieval maps? What seems to be the major concern of each map? What do you think of the geographical accuracy of these maps? How does each map reflect the outlook of the people who created them?

INTERNET EXPLORATION

Today with modern jets, satellites, and transatlantic conference calls, it's hard to imagine that long, dangerous voyages were once the only way to see the world. But in the sixteenth century the only way to travel was on wooden oceangoing vessels with uncertain navigational techniques. To learn something about how we used to travel use the keywords "Spanish caravel." Would you like to have been alive in those days, sailing into unknown lands? What adventures and perils might you have encountered?

MAP EXERCISES

On Outline Map 16.1, plot the routes of the following:

Voyages of Zheng He

Polynesian voyages

Malayo-Indonesian voyages

African voyages

Prince Henry the Navigator's ships

Christopher Columbus

Vasco Da Gama

Amerigo Vespucci

Ferdinand Magellan

On Outline Map 16.2, use shading to differentiate the following:

Aztec Empire

Inca Empire

Arawak homeland

Arawak voyages

Carib voyages

Andean voyages

Outline Map 16.1

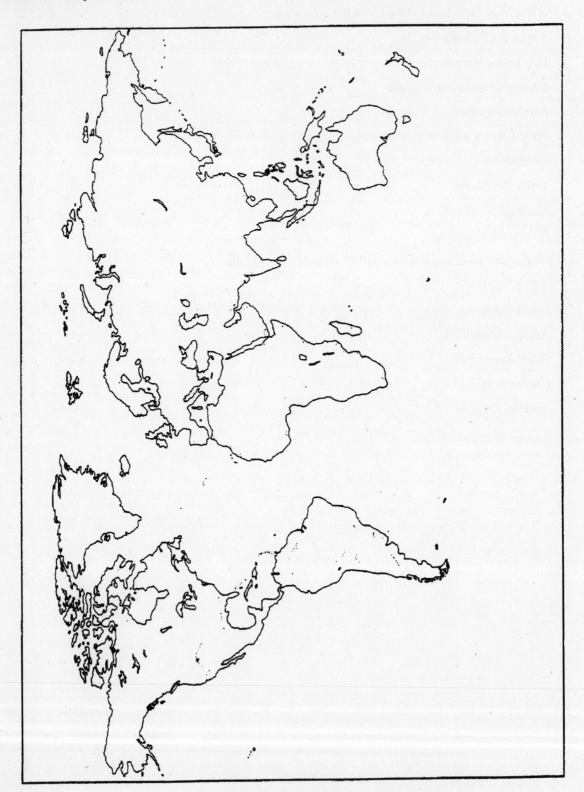

Outline Map 16.2

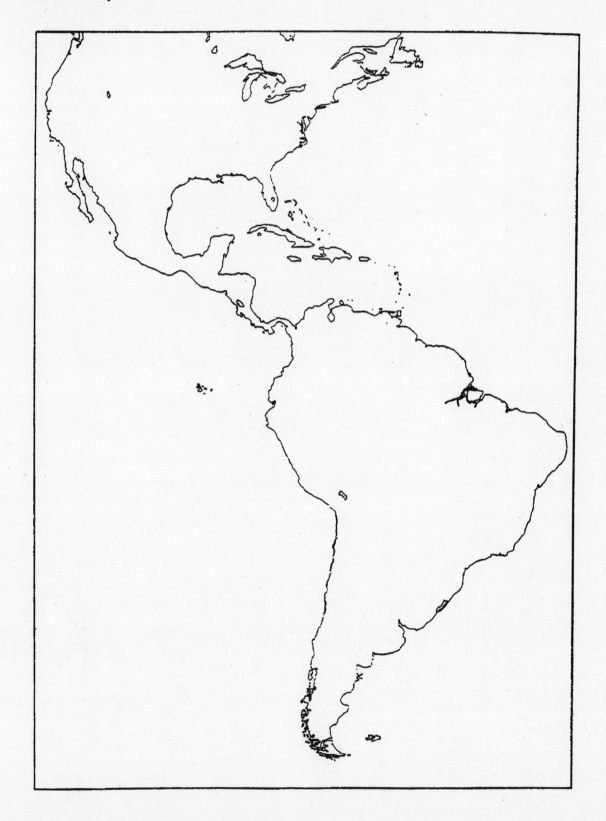

ANSWERS TO MULTIPLE CHOICE QUESTIONS

1. b   p. 418
2. c   p. 420
3. e   p. 423
4. b   p. 425
5. c   p. 425
6. d   p. 425
7. d   p. 430
8. a   p. 430
9. a   p. 430
10. e   p. 431
11. d   p. 433
12. e   p. 433, 434
13. b   p. 436
14. a   p. 440

CHAPTER 17

Transformations in Europe, 1500–1750

LEARNING OBJECTIVES

After reading Chapter 17 and completing this study chapter, you should be able to explain:

- How the Protestant and Catholic Reformations changed the face of Europe.

- How different nation-states were built and how the various governments promoted trade and economic institutions to help in this effort.

- How the new politics and economics affected urban and rural life, and the environment. You should also become aware of how they affected families in the different classes in society.

- What role the Scientific Revolution and the Enlightenment played in European technology, politics, society, and outlook.

- How the nobles, clergy, and monarchs struggled for supremacy during this period of transformation.

CHAPTER OUTLINE

In the outline below, include important themes, concepts, and details in the blank spaces provided. If you find fewer points than you have space for, leave lines blank. If you find more points, add as many lines as necessary.

I. *Introduction*
    A. *Loys Le Roy's retrospection 1575*
        1. _____

        2. _____

        3. _____

    B. *Europe's accomplishments*
        1. _____

        2. _____

        3. _____

    C. *Accomplishments outside of Europe*
        1. _____

2. _____

3. _____

D. *Turning point—ascendancy of the West*
1. _____

2. _____

3. _____

II. *Culture and Ideas*
A. *Religious Reformation*
1. *State of the Catholic Church—prestige and corruption*
a) _____

b) _____

c) _____

d) _____

e) _____

f) _____

2. *Martin Luther and the Protestant Reformation*
a) _____

b) _____

c) _____

d) _____

e) _____

f) _____

3. *John Calvin and further reforms*
a) _____

b) _____

c) _____

d) _____

e) _____

f) _____

4. *The secular and political aspects of the Reformation*
   a) _____

   b) _____

   c) _____

   d) _____

5. *The Catholic Reformation, the Jesuits, and religious wars*
   a) _____

   b) _____

   c) _____

   d) _____

   e) _____

B. *Traditional Thinking and Witch-Hunts*
   1. *Catholics and Protestants held many beliefs in common*
      a) _____

      b) _____

      c) _____

   2. *It was believed that natural events could have supernatural causes*
      a) _____

      b) _____

c) _____

3. *The witch-hunts (sixteenth and seventeenth centuries)*
   a) _____

   b) _____

   c) _____

   d) _____

   e) _____

   f) _____

4. *Modern historians on the witch-hunts*
   a) _____

   b) _____

   c) _____

   d) _____

C. *The Scientific Revolution*
   1. *Aristotle and Pythagoras*
      a) _____

      b) _____

      c) _____

      d) _____

      e) _____

   2. *Copernicus, Brahe, and Kepler*
      a) _____

      b) _____

      c) _____

d) _____

e) _____

3. *Galileo*
   a) _____

   b) _____

   c) _____

4. *Critics*
   a) _____

   b) _____

   c) _____

   d) _____

5. *Religious condemnation*
   a) _____

   b) _____

   c) _____

   d) _____

   e) _____

   f) _____

6. *Mathematics and Newton*
   a) _____

   b) _____

   c) _____

   d) _____

7. *Scientific discoveries and revealed religion not in conflict*
    a) _____

    b) _____

    c) _____

D. *The Early Enlightenment*
    1. *The beliefs of the Enlightenment encouraged by the Scientific Revolution*
        a) _____

        b) _____

        c) _____

    2. *Non-Scientific Revolution influences*
        a) _____

        b) _____

        c) _____

        d) _____

        e) _____

        f) _____

    3. *Changes to society?*
        a) _____

        b) _____

        c) _____

        d) _____

        e) _____

III. *Social and Economic Life*

    A.   **The Bourgeoisie**

        1.   *The creation and use of wealth*

            a) _____

            b) _____

            c) _____

            d) _____

            e) _____

        2.   *Bourgeois enterprise in the Netherlands*

            a) _____

            b) _____

            c) _____

            d) _____

            e) _____

        3.   *Amsterdam and ships*

            a) _____

            b) _____

            c) _____

            d) _____

            e) _____

            f) _____

        4.   *Joint-stock companies and stock exchanges*

            a) _____

            b) _____

c) _____

d) _____

e) _____

f) _____

5. *Business and government, a close association*
   a) _____

   b) _____

   c) _____

   d) _____

   e) _____

6. *Wealth and status*
   a) _____

   b) _____

   c) _____

B. *Peasants and Laborers*
   1. *Serfdom*
      a) _____

      b) _____

      c) _____

   2. *Condition of average person worsened between 1500 and 1750*
      a) _____

      b) _____

      c) _____

3. *Wood and coal*
    a) _____

    b) _____

    c) _____

    d) _____

    e) _____

    f) _____

    g) _____

4. *The results of deforestation*
    a) _____

    b) _____

    c) _____

5. *The rural poor and urban poor*
    a) _____

    b) _____

    c) _____

    d) _____

    e) _____

    f) _____

    g) _____

C. *Women and the Family*
    1. *A woman's class and wealth defined a woman's position in life more than her sex*
        a) _____

        b) _____

         c) _____

   2.   *Marriage*
         a) _____

         b) _____

         c) _____

         d) _____

         e) _____

   3.   *Sex and the underprivileged*
         a) _____

         b) _____

         c) _____

         d) _____

         e) _____

   4.   *Bourgeois education*
         a) _____

         b) _____

         c) _____

         d) _____

         e) _____

         f) _____

IV.   *Political Innovations*
   A.   *State Development*
     1.   *Dreams of pan-European empire frustrated*
         a) _____

b) _____

c) _____

2. *Charles V and the Holy Roman Empire*
   a) _____

   b) _____

   c) _____

   d) _____

   e) _____

   f) _____

   g) _____

3. *German wars of religion*
   a) _____

   b) _____

   c) _____

B. *Religious Policies*
   1. *Spain and France*
      a) _____

      b) _____

      c) _____

      d) _____

      e) _____

   2. *England*
      a) _____

      b) _____

c) _____

d) _____

e) _____

C. *Monarchies in England and France*
    1.   **Charles I and Parliament (England)**
       a) _____

       b) _____

       c) _____

       d) _____

       e) _____

       f) _____

    2.   **James II and the Glorious Revolution (England)**
       a) _____

       b) _____

       c) _____

    3.   **Estates General and Louis XIV (France)**
       a) _____

       b) _____

       c) _____

    4.   **Effects of Absolutism and its failure**
       a) _____

       b) _____

       c) _____

D. *Warfare and Diplomacy*
   1. *Size of armies*
       a) _____

       b) _____

       c) _____

       d) _____

   2. *Technical improvements*
       a) _____

       b) _____

       c) _____

       d) _____

   3. *England's navy*
       a) _____

       b) _____

       c) _____

   4. *France's frustration and the balance of power*
       a) _____

       b) _____

       c) _____

       d) _____

       e) _____

E. *Paying the Piper*
   1. *The price of war*
       a) _____

       b) _____

c) _____

2. *Spain*
    a) _____

    b) _____

    c) _____

    d) _____

    e) _____

    f) _____

3. *The Netherlands*
    a) _____

    b) _____

    c) _____

    d) _____

    e) _____

    f) _____

4. *England*
    a) _____

    b) _____

    c) _____

    d) _____

5. *France*
    a) _____

    b) _____

c) _____

d) _____

V. *Conclusion*
  A. **Revolution**
    1. _____

    2. _____

    3. _____

  B. **Downside**
    1. _____

    2. _____

    3. _____

  C. **European power**
    1. _____

    2. _____

    3. _____

IDENTIFICATIONS

Define each term and explain why it is significant, including any important dates.

	Identification	**Significance**
papacy		
Renaissance (Europe)		
indulgence		

	Identification	Significance
Protestant Reformation		
Catholic Reformation		
witch-hunt		
Scientific Revolution		
Enlightenment		
Copernicus		
Galileo Galilei		
Isaac Newton		
John Locke		
bourgeoisie		
joint-stock company		

Identification	Significance

stock exchange

Little Ice Age

deforestation

Holy Roman Empire

Habsburg

English Civil War

absolutism

constitutionalism

Versailles Palace

balance of power

MULTIPLE-CHOICE QUESTIONS

Read the entire question, including *all* the possible answers. Then choose the *one* answer that best fits the question.

1. Which of the following were *not* among the complaints Martin Luther had about the Catholic Church?

    a. The way the new indulgences were preached
    b. That kings were more powerful than the pope
    c. The Church's reliance on good work, de-emphasizing faith
    d. The lack of exclusive reliance on the Bible as the sole authority
    e. Too much emphasis on the authority of the pope

2. Calvinists were visually distinguishable by

    a. their beards.
    b. their badges.
    c. their simple black dress.
    d. their reluctance to ride horses.
    e. their wealth.

3. According to most historians, why did the Early Modern European witch-hunts take place?

    a. Labeling older women, especially widows, as witches may have reflected the widespread belief that women not directly under the control of men were likely to turn evil.
    b. The religious disputes of the time produced a religious identity crisis, causing people to look for satanic tendencies in their neighbors.
    c. Witch-hunts tend to arise at times of social stress, and people marginalized by poverty and social suspicion often relish the celebrity that public confession brings.
    d. Backward thinking.
    e. No single explanation can account for the rise in witchcraft accusations and fears.

4. The Copernican universe at first found more critics than supporters because

    a. it directly challenged popular beliefs.
    b. Copernicus was wrong.
    c. Copernicus could not prove his theories empirically.
    d. it challenged the intellectual synthesis of classical and biblical authorities.
    e. most people agreed with Galileo instead.

5. Most Protestant leaders, following Martin Luther,

    a. openly supported the concept of a heliocentric (sun-centered) universe.
    b. awaited the verdict of the Catholic Church about Galileo's theories.
    c. consulted the many Arabic works on the matter of the composition of the universe.
    d. condemned the heliocentric universe as contrary to the teachings of the Bible.
    e. hired Galileo to investigate further.

6. Nearly all Enlightenment thinkers were optimistic that

    a. they could get the Catholic Church banned.
    b. they could get the Protestant Church banned.
    c. they would see improvements in human beliefs and institutions.
    d. they could stop the Industrial Revolution.
    e. they could get Voltaire elected pope.

7. Dutch ships carried what percentage of trade between Spain and Northern Europe in 1700?

    a. Less than 10 percent
    b. About 25 percent
    c. No more than 40 percent
    d. About 60 percent
    e. Over 80 percent

8. When a group of visiting Amerindian chiefs was asked what impressed them most about European cities, they replied,

    a. the beautiful architecture.
    b. the crowds of people, horses, and carriages.
    c. the frightening (and loud) factories.
    d. how people could walk on the filthy streets.
    e. why the poor did not slit the throats of the rich.

9. Why did Francis I openly support the Muslim Turks?

    a. To weaken his rival for the throne of Holy Roman Emperor, Charles V
    b. To help form an alliance against the Protestants
    c. To help him gain the French throne
    d. To undermine their empire by trickery
    e. To increase trade

10. Henry VIII's move to make himself head of the Church in England was probably mostly a move to

    a. radically change the teaching of the Catholic Church, to which he was opposed.
    b. support the Puritan movement, which was condemned by the pope.
    c. change marriage laws in England.
    d. solidify his power over all English institutions.
    e. antagonize his Spanish in-laws.

11. The major obstacle that an absolutist ruler had to contend with was the

    a. Holy Roman Empire.
    b. Catholic Church.
    c. nobility.
    d. representative assemblies.
    e. peasants.

12. What did Louis XIV's palace at Versailles symbolize?

    a. A triumph over the traditional rights of the nobility
    b. The epitome of secular Gothic architecture
    c. The integration of all three Estates into French government
    d. A life of abandonment and pleasure following the plague
    e. The wealth of the French court

13. Prussia was such a powerful nation because

    a. of its plentiful natural resources.
    b. it devoted so many resources to building a splendid army.
    c. of the government's promotion of industrialization.
    d. it was once a part of France.
    e. of its close ties to the Vatican.

14. What is the historical significance of the early modern period in Europe?
    a. It was primarily an age of progress for Europe.
    b. It allowed women to gain equality with men.
    c. Most Europeans became better off with the increase in wages and the decrease in prices.
    d. It was a time when European technology was outstripped by Chinese technology.
    e. The balance of power had shifted in the Europeans' favor.

SHORT-ANSWER QUESTIONS

Answer each question in one short paragraph, giving the definition, dates, and significance.

1. How did Europe's disunity lead to its growing strength in the world?

2. For what other reasons besides faith did people of all classes follow Martin Luther?

3. How did Oliver Cromwell become the ruler of England?

4. Why was Spain not a lasting world power?

5. Discuss how various financial institutions revolutionized business and economics in seventeenth- and eighteenth-century Europe.

6. How did environmental factors affect European rural life in the seventeenth century?

ESSAY QUESTIONS

Make an outline of each question, listing the major points you want to discuss. Then write your practice essay, following your outline carefully and making sure that you do not skip any of your major points. At this time you will want to add the relevant dates and details that will make your essay persuasive and accurate.

1. How did Martin Luther's beliefs challenge the views of the Catholic Church, and how did the Catholic Church respond to the Protestant Reformation?

2. How did various rulers use religion to further their own (non-religious) ends?

3. Compare and contrast royal absolutism and constitutionalism. Could elements of both appear in the same government? Were they sequential systems?

4. Describe the rise of the Netherlands in the seventeenth and eighteenth centuries, and compare and contrast Dutch policies with those of the other European powers.

5. Discuss the advancements made in military technology in seventeenth- and eighteenth-century Europe. What were their roots, how were they promoted by the government, and what was the impact of this new technology?

6. Discuss the major ideas of the Enlightenment, and describe their impact on European government, education, and society.

COMPARISON CHARTS

Using information gathered from the text, fill in the blank areas of each chart with the relevant data pertaining to the regions and categories listed. (Not all blank areas will necessarily be used.)

Chart 17.1

RELIGIOUS CONCERNS

	Countries where influence was greatest	Relation with Government	Views on Government	Basic Tenets	Methods
Roman Catholics					
Martin Luther/ Lutheranism					
John Calvin/ Calvinism					
Henry VIII					
Puritans					

Chart 17.2

PROBLEMS FOR THE POOR

	agriculture	deforestation	coal/coke	foraging	rural life	urban life	prostitution
England							
France							
Netherlands							

DIVERSITY AND DOMINANCE

After reading "Diversity and Dominance: Political Craft and Craftiness" in your text, answer the following additional questions.

What do you think of Machiavelli's assessment of human nature and loyalty? How does this fit in with his advice about image and actions? How does this justify his assertions?

Do you think that Machiavelli would approve of Queen Elizabeth's speech? Why or why not?

INTERNET ASSIGNMENT

Keywords: **"European witch-hunts" or "Malefice Justice"**

          "Galilei Galileo and telescope"

The sixteenth and seventeenth centuries in Europe were filled with social changes and new technological advances. Among the worse events that took place were the witch trials, and among the most important advancements was the telescope. Using the above keywords, consider how the brilliance of Galileo can be contrasted with the narrow-mindedness and superstitions of the judges at the witchcraft trials. Can you see similarities between the two events? How can one era produce both witch trials and Galileo? For help in locating Internet materials, you might also want to consult *History WIRED* on *The Earth and Its Peoples* web site (refer to the preface of this study guide for information on how to locate the text home page).

INTERNET EXPLORATION

Versailles was the premier palace of France during the age of absolute rulers. It was the site of Louis XIV's court and as such was filled with interesting people, art, gardens, and of course le Roi de Soleil himself (the "Sun King," Louis XIV). To take a virtual tour of Versailles, use the keywords, "Palace at Versailles" or visit http://chateauversailles.fr/ on the world wide web. What political role did the palace and the court play? What would life have been like at Versailles during Louis' reign? Try to imagine yourself there walking through the gardens or attending one of the many costume balls. If you get tired of the splendor and luxury of Versailles, National Geographic's website has an interactive witch trial at http://www.nationalgeographic.com/features/97/salem/.

MAP EXERCISES

On Outline Map 17.1, use shading to mark these:

     Habsburg lands

     Habsburg allies

     Habsburg enemies

     Holy Roman Empire

     Catholic and Protestant spheres of influence in 1555

On Outline Map 17.2, shade in the following:

     Bourbon Empire

     Habsburg Empire

     Holy Roman Empire

     Ottoman Empire

Outline Map 17.1

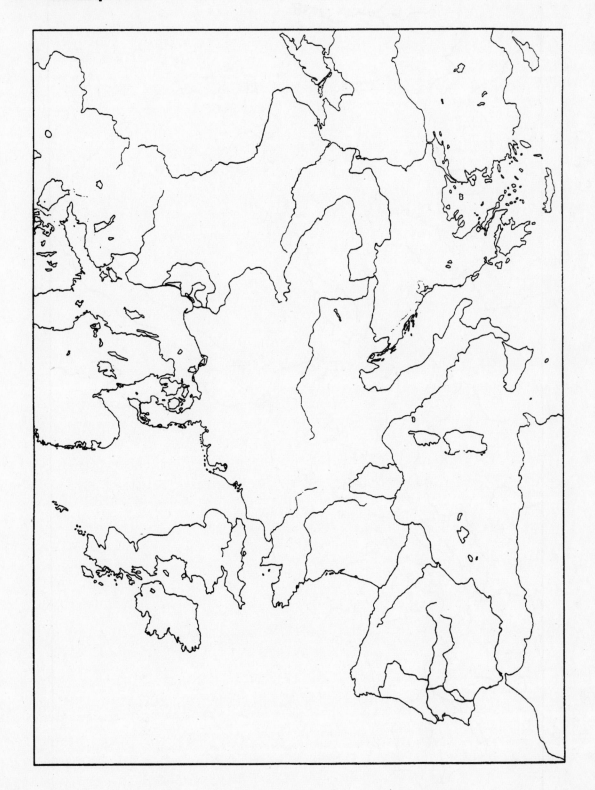

Outline Map 17.2

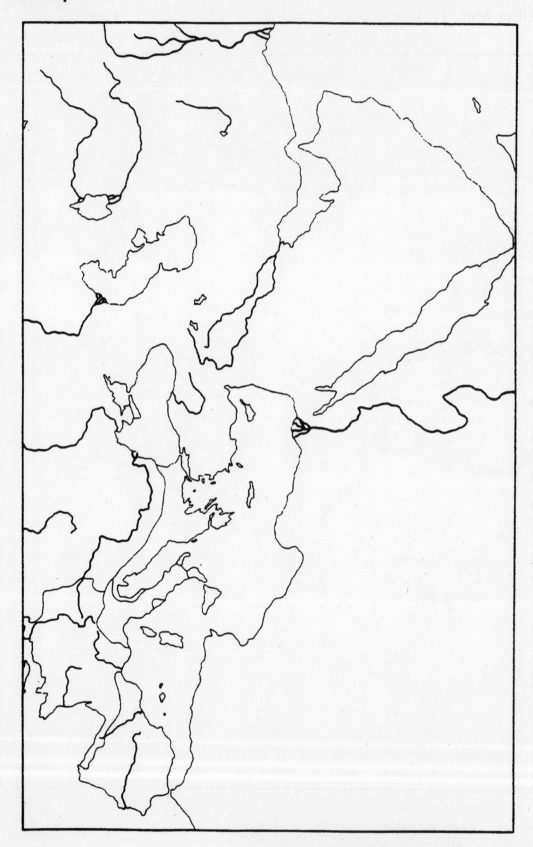

ANSWERS TO MULTIPLE-CHOICE QUESTIONS

1. b p. 450
2. c p. 451
3. e p. 454
4. d p. 455
5. d p. 455
6. c p. 456
7. e p. 457
8. e p. 461
9. a p. 462
10. c p. 466
11. d p. 466
12. a p. 466
13. b p. 467
14. a p. 471

CHAPTER 18

The Diversity of American Colonial Societies, 1530–1770

LEARNING OBJECTIVES

After reading Chapter 18 and completing this study chapter, you should be able to explain:

- How the land and peoples of the Americas changed after contact with the Europeans and what was involved in this process.

- How each colonizer influenced its colony and was in turn influenced by Amerindians.

- Why colonies dominated even by the same European powers could have distinct differences based on race, class, and geography.

- What the Columbian Exchange was and how it influenced both the Old and New Worlds.

- What role the American colonies played in European politics, economics, and outlook.

CHAPTER OUTLINE

In the outline below, include important themes, concepts, and details in the blank spaces provided. If you find fewer points than you have space for, leave lines blank. If you find more points, add as many lines as necessary.

I. *Introduction*
    A. *Choctaw leader Red Shoes (Shulush Homa)*
        1. _____

        2. _____

        3. _____

    B. *Lessons from the Red Shoe episode*
        1. _____

        2. _____

        3. _____

C. *Americas were drawn into global events*
    1. _____

    2. _____

    3. _____

D. *Complex colonial societies*
    1. _____

    2. _____

    3. _____

II. *The Columbian Exchange*
    A. *Demographic Changes*
        1. *Disease and population numbers*
            a) _____

            b) _____

            c) _____

        2. *Diseases in Spanish America*
            a) _____

            b) _____

            c) _____

            d) _____

        3. *How African and American diseases affected Europeans*
            a) _____

            b) _____

            c) _____

        4. *Disease in English and French America*
            a) _____

            b) _____

c) _____

B.   *Transfer of Plants and Animals*
 1.   *Introduction of "Old World" plants to Americas*
  a) _____

  b) _____

  c) _____

 2.   *"New World" plants offer abundance of plants to "Old World"*
  a) _____

  b) _____

  c) _____

  d) _____

 3.   *Introduction of European livestock had a dramatic impact on "New World" environments and cultures*
  a) _____

  b) _____

  c) _____

 4.   *Effect of European livestock on Native Americans: good and bad*
  a) _____

  b) _____

  c) _____

  d) _____

  e) _____

  f) _____

III.   *Spanish America and Brazil*
    A.   *State and Church*
        1.   *Spain tried to control colonies, but was limited by the challenges of communication*
            a) _____

            b) _____

            c) _____

            d) _____

            e) _____

        2.   *Portugal and its colonies in Asia and Africa*
            a) _____

            b) _____

            c) _____

        3.   *Intrusive colonial bureaucracies*
            a) _____

            b) _____

            c) _____

        4.   *The Catholic Church and the spread of Christianity*
            a) _____

            b) _____

            c) _____

            d) _____

            e) _____

            f) _____

5. *The Catholic Church provided Amerindians some protection, and Church beliefs mixed with indigenous beliefs*

   a) _____

   b) _____

   c) _____

   d) _____

   e) _____

   f) _____

B. *Colonial Economies*

   1. *Sources of colonial wealth*

      a) _____

      b) _____

      c) _____

      d) _____

   2. *Gold, silver, and environment*

      a) _____

      b) _____

      c) _____

      d) _____

      e) _____

   3. *Labor systems:* encomienda *and the* mita

      a) _____

      b) _____

      c) _____

d) _____

e) _____

f) _____

4. ***Sugar plantations and slave labor***
    a) _____

    b) _____

    c) _____

    d) _____

    e) _____

    f) _____

    g) _____

5. ***The global and colonial economic impact of silver***
    a) _____

    b) _____

    c) _____

6. ***The growth of Brazil and the attempts to control trade***
    a) _____

    b) _____

    c) _____

    d) _____

C. ***Society in Colonial Latin America***
    1. ***Immigration, nobles,* encomienda, *and creoles***
        a) _____

        b) _____

c) _____

d) _____

2. *Native peoples, native elites, and the blurring of lines*
   a) _____

   b) _____

   c) _____

   d) _____

   e) _____

3. *Blacks: free and slave*
   a) _____

   b) _____

   c) _____

   d) _____

   e) _____

4. *Slave resistance*
   a) _____

   b) _____

   c) _____

5. *Slave lifestyles*
   a) _____

   b) _____

   c) _____

   d) _____

6. *Brazilian differences and similarities*

a) _____

b) _____

c) _____

7. *Manumission, mestizos, and mulattoes*

a) _____

b) _____

c) _____

d) _____

e) _____

f) _____

IV. *English and French Colonies in North America*
   A. *Early English Experiments*
      1. *Newfoundland*

   a) _____

   b) _____

   c) _____

      2. *Roanoke Island*

   a) _____

   b) _____

   c) _____

      3. *Ireland: a model*

   a) _____

   b) _____

   c) _____

B.   ***The South***
   1.   ***Jamestown***
      a)   _____

      b)   _____

      c)   _____

      d)   _____

   2.   ***The development of the Virginia colony and indentured servants***
      a)   _____

      b)   _____

      c)   _____

      d)   _____

      e)   _____

      f)   _____

   3.   ***Colonial government and freedom***
      a)   _____

      b)   _____

      c)   _____

   4.   ***Fur trade and Amerindians***
      a)   _____

      b)   _____

      c)   _____

      d)   _____

      e)   _____

      f)   _____

5.   *The Carolinas*
a) _____

b) _____

c) _____

d) _____

e) _____

f) _____

6.   *Slavery in South Carolina*
a) _____

b) _____

c) _____

d) _____

e) _____

f) _____

7.   *Hierarchy in South Carolina*
a) _____

b) _____

c) _____

d) _____

C.   *New England*
1.   *The Pilgrims and Plymouth Colony*
a) _____

b) _____

c) _____

d) _____

e) _____

2. *The Puritans and the Massachusetts Bay Colony*
   a) _____

   b) _____

   c) _____

   d) _____

   e) _____

   f) _____

3. *The evolution of political institutions in Massachusetts*
   a) _____

   b) _____

   c) _____

4. *The economics of Massachusetts and the southern colonies*
   a) _____

   b) _____

   c) _____

   d) _____

   e) _____

D. *The Middle Atlantic Region*
   1. *New York*
      a) _____

      b) _____

      c) _____

d) _____

e) _____

f) _____

2. *Pennsylvania*
    a) _____

    b) _____

    c) _____

    d) _____

    e) _____

3. *Comparison between Pennsylvania and South Carolina*
    a) _____

    b) _____

    c) _____

E. *French America*
    1. *Early American colonies*
        a) _____

        b) _____

        c) _____

        d) _____

    2. *Fur trade and firearms*
        a) _____

        b) _____

        c) _____

        d) _____

e) _____

f) _____

3. *French missionary efforts*
   a) _____

   b) _____

   c) _____

   d) _____

   e) _____

4. *Comparison between French colonies and others*
   a) _____

   b) _____

   c) _____

5. *The competition between the French and the English, and Native American involvement*
   a) _____

   b) _____

   c) _____

   d) _____

   e) _____

V. *Colonial Expansion and Conflict*
   A. *Imperial Reform in Spanish America and Brazil*
      1. *Philip V reformed Spanish colonies*
         a) _____

         b) _____

         c) _____

d) _____

e) _____

f) _____

2. *Amerindian uprisings and Tupac Amaru II*
    a) _____

    b) _____

    c) _____

    d) _____

    e) _____

    f) _____

3. *Brazilian expansion*
    a) _____

    b) _____

    c) _____

B. *Reform and Reorganization in British America*
    1. *Charles II and James II put colonies under direct control of the British crown*
        a) _____

        b) _____

        c) _____

    2. *Rebellion in the colonies*
        a) _____

        b) _____

        c) _____

        d) _____

e) _____

VI. *Conclusion*
    A. *Similarities among the colonies*
       1. _____

       2. _____

       3. _____

       4. _____

       5. _____

    B. *The effect colonizing countries had on their colonies*
       1. _____

       2. _____

       3. _____

       4. _____

       5. _____

       6. _____

       7. _____

IDENTIFICATIONS

Define each term and explain why it is significant, including any important dates.

	Identification	Significance
Columbian Exchange		
smallpox		

Identification   Significance

Council of the Indies

Bartolomé de las Casas

Potosí

silver

mita

encomienda

creoles

mestizo

mulatto

indentured servant

House of Burgesses

	Identification	Significance

Pilgrims

Puritans

Iroquois Confederacy

New France

coureurs de bois

firearms

French and Indian War (the Seven Years' War)

Tupac Amaru II

MULTIPLE-CHOICE QUESTIONS

Read the entire question, including *all* the possible answers. Then choose the *one* answer that best fits the question.

1.   What was the Columbian Exchange?

    a.   The exchange of New and Old World plants, animals, peoples, and diseases

    b.   The replacing of all New World products with Old World products

    c.   The practice Columbus's crew used to get gold from the natives of Hispañola

    d.   The exchange of New and Old World plants only

    e.   The name of the Spanish stock exchange

2.   The most deadly of the early epidemics brought to the Americas from Europe was

    a.   cholera.

    b.   measles.

    c.   smallpox.

    d.   bubonic plague.

    e.   influenza.

3.   Which of these European animals had the greatest impact on the lifestyle of Amerindians?

    a.   Sheep

    b.   Horses

    c.   Cattle

    d.   Dogs

    e.   Rabbits

4.   What occurrence eventually allowed members of the colonial elite to gain high positions in the colonial bureaucracy?

    a.   A revolt among the creoles in the American colonies forced the Spanish crown to accede to their demands.

    b.   An economic crisis in Spain forced the Spanish crown to begin selling appointments to the highest bidder.

    c.   The colonial elite had always been able to gain these offices.

    d.   The native-born Spaniards held a monopoly on those offices, and that did not change until independence.

    e.   People stopped emigrating from Spain, and so only Creoles were available for offices.

5.   Which of the following became the richest institution of the Spanish colonies?

    a.   The Catholic Church

    b.   The colonial government

    c.   The silver mines

    d.   The military

    e.   The haciendas

6.   The *mita* was

    a.   the indigenous name for "miner."

    b.   the name for the wage-labor system used in the silver mines.

    c.   a pack animal that was also used for wool and meat.

    d.   the sharp blade used to cut sugar cane.

    e.   a system under which one-seventh of Amerindian males were required to work for a time in the mines.

7. The ratio of African slaves to free Europeans arriving in Brazil between 1650 and 1750 was

    a. one to one.
    b. two to one.
    c. three to one.
    d. five to one.
    e. ten to one.

8. Why did colonists in Spanish and Portuguese colonies establish illegal commercial relations with the English, French, and Dutch?

    a. The Spanish and Portuguese governments discouraged imports, wanting instead to develop local industry.
    b. The Spanish and Portuguese policy of monopoly and convoy systems slowed the flow of European goods, keeping prices high.
    c. The merchants used this tactic to withhold sales tax from the government to protest tariffs.
    d. English, French, and Dutch products were far superior to those of the Spanish and Portuguese.
    e. Crafts produced by Amerindians were very popular export items, and so smuggling them proved quite lucrative to the colonists.

9. England's first efforts to gain a foothold in the Americas

    a. produced more failures than successes.
    b. succeeded both financially and socially.
    c. met with frequent defeat at the hands of the French.
    d. succeeded at assimilating Amerindians better than the efforts of any other group.
    e. always antagonized the Amerindians.

10. Which of the following attracted six times as many immigrants as New England in the seventeenth century?

    a. Pennsylvania
    b. Virginia
    c. India
    d. Ireland
    e. New York

11. What event shocked slave owners throughout the South and led to greater repression?

    a. The Seven Years' War
    b. The patio process
    c. The Stono Rebellion
    d. A significant rise in the manumission of slaves
    e. The publication of *Uncle Tom's Cabin*

12. Why did the Pilgrims immigrate to the Colony of Plymouth?

    a. Unlike the Puritans, they wanted to break with the Church of England and practice their religion without persecution.
    b. They, like the Puritans, wanted to create a model of the English church in a new land.
    c. The government deported them because the Pilgrims were Dutch, living illegally in England.
    d. There was no more room in Chesapeake for immigrants.
    e. To escape the smallpox epidemic in England.

13. What factor fueled French settlement in the Americas?
    a. The European market for fur
    b. Religious persecution at home
    c. The wish to create an industrial base in the New World
    d. The French government's desire for a base in the Americas from which to conduct its war against the English
    e. Overpopulation in France
14. What was the ultimate outcome of the French and Indian War (the Seven Years' War)?
    a. France won its bid to build an empire in the Americas without the interference of the English.
    b. A large Amerindian confederation was formed with which later European immigrants had to negotiate.
    c. France finally lost the war to the Spanish.
    d. France was forced to yield Canada to England and cede Louisiana to Spain.
    e. France lost America, but was free to dominate India, which it did.

SHORT-ANSWER QUESTIONS

Answer each question in one short paragraph, giving the definition, dates, and significance.

1. Discuss both the positive and negative impact of the introduction of European livestock into the Americas.
2. Discuss the system of *encomiendas* and explain to what end this system was instituted.
3. How did the arrival of European women affect Amerindian women?
4. Compare and contrast the mid-Atlantic colonies of Pennsylvania and South Carolina.
5. What changes occurred in Amerindian culture due to the introduction of European material goods?
6. How did firearms change the lifestyles of Amerindian groups such as the Sioux, Comanche, and Cheyenne?
7. Discuss the role of silver in the development of the Americas.

ESSAY QUESTIONS

Make an outline of each question, listing the major points you want to discuss. Then write your practice essay, following your outline carefully and making sure that you do not skip any of your major points. At this time you will want to add the relevant dates and details that will make your essay persuasive and accurate.

1. Describe the Columbian Exchange and discuss its impact on both the Old and New Worlds.
2. Discuss how each colonizing country affected the character of its colonial empire in America. For example, how did the policies and attitudes of the Spanish people and government affect Spanish America? Choose two countries.
3. Discuss the racial and social makeup of colonial Latin America. What sphere of influence did each class have, and how did the classes interact?
4. Discuss the role of the Catholic Church in Spanish and Portuguese America. What was its aim, what methods did it employ, and what was the eventual impact on American society?

5.   Compare and contrast the population makeup and the social and economic structure of
      Massachusetts and Chesapeake.

COMPARISON CHARTS

Using information gathered from the text, fill in the blank areas of each chart with the relevant data
pertaining to the regions and categories listed. (Not all blank areas will necessarily be used.)

Chart 18.1

COLUMBIAN EXCHANGE

	Old World	New World
People (Population, Races, Social Status)		
Plants		
Animals		
Diseases		
Social Impact		
Economic Impact		

Chart 18.2

COLONIES AND COLONIZERS

	Region and Date	Government and Private Roles	Products	Economy and Trade	Immigrants	Social Structure	Relation with Environment
Spain							
Portugal							
Britain							
France							

DIVERSITY AND DOMINANCE

After reading "Diversity and Dominance: Race and Ethnicity in the Spanish Colonies: Negotiating Hierarchy" in your text, answer the following additional questions.

What attributes, physical and moral, do Juan and Ulloa assign to the various racial groups? How did they reach their conclusions?

Was there social mobility, and if so, how was it achieved?

INTERNET ASSIGNMENT

Keyword: **"Theodor de Bry"**

Theodor de Bry's engravings of Amerindians are one of the most used sources showing early contact between Europeans and Indians. He is particularly famous for promoting the Spanish "Black Legend." Most scholars feel that engravings of Amerindians from the contact period with Europeans fall into two distinct categories. Using the above keyword, can you find a number of images by de Bry and others depicting early exchanges between Amerindians and Europeans? Do you think that the engravings fall into two distinct categories, and if so, what are they? What perspectives do you see represented in this art? What can scholars learn about perception and viewpoint in these pictures, and do you think that they are accurate representations? For help in locating Internet material, you may also want to consult the *History WIRED* image library on *The Earth and Its Peoples* web site (refer to the preface of this study guide for information on how to locate the text home page).

INTERNET EXPLORATION

Make a list of foods that you think originated in the Americas. Next make a list of foods you think originated in the "Old World." Now compare your lists to the ones on this web site: http://www.mnh.si.edu/garden/history. Study the brief description and history of each entry. For more in-depth information on the introduction of foods between the Eastern and Western Hemispheres, continue exploring using the keywords "Columbian Exchange."

MAP EXERCISES

On Outline Map 18.1, plot the following, differentiating between Spanish and Portuguese land:

      Viceroyalty of New Spain

      Viceroyalty of New Granada

      Viceroyalty of Brazil

      Viceroyalty of Peru

      Viceroyalty of Rio de la Plata

      Audiencia de Chile

On Outline Map 18.2, label each of these regions and color-code by colonizer as of 1755:

      British

      French

      Spanish

      Russian

Then use shading to show changes by 1763.

Outline Map 18.1

Outline Map 18.2

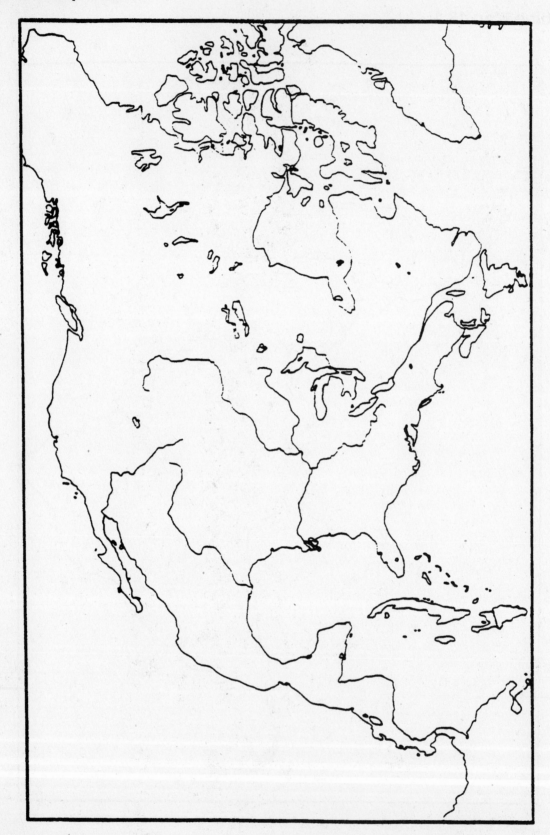

ANSWERS TO MULTIPLE-CHOICE QUESTIONS

1. a p. 474
2. c p. 475
3. b p. 477
4. b p. 478
5. a p. 480
6. e p. 482
7. c p. 482
8. b p. 483
9. a p. 488
10. d p. 488
11. c p. 490
12. a p. 490
13. a p. 493
14. d p. 495

CHAPTER 19

The Atlantic System and Africa, 1550–1800

LEARNING OBJECTIVES

After reading Chapter 19 and completing this study chapter, you should be able to explain:

- How the Atlantic system changed the lives of Africans, Europeans, and Amerindians.

- In what ways the new institutions, technology, and political systems facilitated the rise of capitalism and mercantilism.

- How sugar plantations operated and what impact they had on society and the environment.

- What role Christianity and Islam played in African politics, economics, and society.

CHAPTER OUTLINE

In the outline below, include important themes, concepts, and details in the blank spaces provided. If you find fewer points than you have space for, leave lines blank. If you find more points, add as many lines as necessary.

I. *Introduction*
    A. *The 1694 slave shipment on the Hannibal*
        1. _____

        2. _____

        3. _____

    B. *RAC and methods of the voyages*
        1. _____

        2. _____

        3. _____

    C. *Loss of life and profits*
        1. _____

        2. _____

        3. _____

II.   *Plantations in the West Indies*
   A.   *Colonization Before 1650*
      1.   *Tobacco cultivation and charter companies*
         a) _____

         b) _____

         c) _____

         d) _____

         e) _____

      2.   *Sugar cultivation and slavery*
         a) _____

         b) _____

         c) _____

      3.   *The rise of the Dutch & DWIC*
         a) _____

         b) _____

         c) _____

         d) _____

         e) _____

      4.   *Portugal regained some of its lands*
         a) _____

         b) _____

         c) _____

   B.   *Sugar and Slaves*
      1.   *Barbados*
         a) _____

         b) _____

c) _____

2. *A sharp increase in the slave trade*
    a) _____

    b) _____

    c) _____

3. *Why the switch to African slave labor?*
    a) _____

    b) _____

    c) _____

    d) _____

    e) _____

III. *Plantation Life in the Eighteenth Century*
    A.   *Technology and Environment*
        1.   *Sugar cane production*
            a) _____

            b) _____

            c) _____

            d) _____

            e) _____

            f) _____

        2.   *The environmental repercussions of sugar production*
            a) _____

            b) _____

            c) _____

d) _____

3. *Changes in native plant, animal, and human populations*
    a) _____

    b) _____

    c) _____

B. *Slaves' Lives*
    1. *Many more slaves than whites, and long work hours*
        a) _____

        b) _____

        c) _____

    2. *The division of labor was by gender and age*
        a) _____

        b) _____

        c) _____

        d) _____

        e) _____

    3. *Tasks, punishments, and family life*
        a) _____

        b) _____

        c) _____

        d) _____

        e) _____

    4. *Life expectancy*
        a) _____

b) _____

c) _____

d) _____

e) _____

f) _____

5. *Rebellion and African heritage*

a) _____

b) _____

c) _____

d) _____

e) _____

C. *Free Whites and Free Blacks*
1. *The ranking of free peoples*

a) _____

b) _____

c) _____

d) _____

2. *The dominance of the plantocracy and the cost of a plantation*

a) _____

b) _____

c) _____

d) _____

3. *The power and wealth of the British West Indian planters*
    a) _____

    b) _____

    c) _____

4. *Slave owners, manumission, and maroons*
    a) _____

    b) _____

    c) _____

    d) _____

    e) _____

    f) _____

IV. *Creating the Atlantic Economy*
    A. *Capitalism and Mercantilism*
        1. *The development of capitalism and its spread outside of Europe*
            a) _____

            b) _____

            c) _____

            d) _____

        2. *Banks, joint-stock companies, and mercantilism*
            a) _____

            b) _____

            c) _____

            d) _____

            e) _____

3. *Chartered companies and military force*

    a) _____

    b) _____

    c) _____

    d) _____

    e) _____

4. *Charters revoked and tariffs begun*

    a) _____

    b) _____

    c) _____

    d) _____

    e) _____

    f) _____

B. *The Atlantic Circuit*
    1. *The three legs of the Great Circuit*

        a) _____

        b) _____

        c) _____

        d) _____

        e) _____

    2. *The "Triangular Trade"*

        a) _____

        b) _____

c) _____

3. *Europe dominated and benefited from the system*
   a) _____

   b) _____

   c) _____

4. *Sugar consumption*
   a) _____

   b) _____

   c) _____

5. *The business of transporting slaves and mortality*
   a) _____

   b) _____

   c) _____

   d) _____

   e) _____

   f) _____

   g) _____

V. *Africa, the Atlantic, and Islam*
   A. *The Gold Coast and the Slave Coast*
      1. *Euro-African trade evolved into the slave trade*
         a) _____

         b) _____

         c) _____

         d) _____

2. *African taste for European goods*
    a) _____

    b) _____

    c) _____

    d) _____

    e) _____

    f) _____

3. *Africans had upper hand, and Dahomey*
    a) _____

    b) _____

    c) _____

    d) _____

    e) _____

    f) _____

4. *How slaves were acquired*
    a) _____

    b) _____

    c) _____

    d) _____

    e) _____

B. *The Bight of Biafra and Angola*
    1. *Slaves usually procured by kidnapping in the Bight of Biafra*
        a) _____

        b) _____

c) _____

d) _____

e) _____

2. *The Portuguese and the Congo*
   a) _____

   b) _____

   c) _____

   d) _____

   e) _____

3. *Enslavement and environmental crisis in Angola*
   a) _____

   b) _____

   c) _____

   d) _____

   e) _____

C. *Africa's European and Islamic Contacts*
   1. *Europeans controlled little land, and Muslims controlled most of North Africa*
      a) _____

      b) _____

      c) _____

      d) _____

      e) _____

      f) _____

2. *Morocco and trans-Saharan trade*

a) _____

b) _____

c) _____

d) _____

e) _____

f) _____

3. *Slavery in the Islamic world*

a) _____

b) _____

c) _____

d) _____

e) _____

4. *Bornu*

a) _____

b) _____

c) _____

5. *Muslim notions of slavery and Ayuba Suleiman Diallo*

a) _____

b) _____

c) _____

d) _____

6. *Islam had more influence than Christianity*
   a) _____

   b) _____

   c) _____

   d) _____

   e) _____

7. *Depopulation and its effects in Africa*
   a) _____

   b) _____

   c) _____

   d) _____

   e) _____

   f) _____

VI. *Conclusion*
   A. *Europeans in America*
      1. _____

      2. _____

      3. _____

   B. *Europeans in the West Indies*
      1. _____

      2. _____

      3. _____

   C. *Europeans in Africa*
      1. _____

2. _____

3. _____

IDENTIFICATIONS

Define each term and explain why it is significant, including any important dates.

                                Identification   **Significance**

Royal African Company

Atlantic System

chartered company

Dutch West India Company

plantocracy

driver

seasoning

manumission

maroon

	Identification	Significance
capitalism		
mercantilism		
Great Circuit		
Middle Passage		
Songhai		
Bornu		
Hausa		

MULTIPLE-CHOICE QUESTIONS

Read the entire question, including *all* the possible answers. Then choose the *one* answer that best fits the question.

1. What made possible the expansion of the sugar plantations in the West Indies?
    a. The introduction of a superior strain of sugar cane
    b. A jump in the volume of the slave trade from Africa
    c. Quinine, used to treat malaria, which was endemic among the African immigrants
    d. Massive immigration of Europeans to the West Indies as indentured servants
    e. The failure of the tobacco crops

2. Why were African slaves the form of labor preferred by the operators of sugar plantations?
    a. Africans were better suited to field labor than Europeans.
    b. Africans were better able to withstand disease.
    c. Africans were enslaved primarily because of European prejudice against them.
    d. African already knew how to grow sugar cane.
    e. African slaves were simply more cost effective.

3. Poor Europeans tended to emigrate to North America rather than to the West Indies because

    a. they did not want to be enslaved like the Africans.
    b. the price of land was too high in the West Indies, and they could not afford to buy any after they earned their freedom.
    c. the colonizers of the West Indies forbade whites to immigrate there.
    d. North America was wealthier.
    e. The mortality rate was higher in the Caribbean.

4. Why did Jamaica need to import most of its food in 1774?

    a. Everybody grew sugar instead of subsistence crops.
    b. A terrible famine had destroyed all the wheat.
    c. The population grew so much that it could no longer be supported with domestically grown crops.
    d. It was more lucrative to export the food grown there and to import cheaper food from elsewhere.
    e. The indigenous plants did not appeal to the Europeans or Africans living there.

5. The "great gang" did most of the field work and was comprised mainly of

    a. slave women.
    b. slave men.
    c. slave children.
    d. older slaves.
    e. indentured servants of both sexes.

6. Which of the following did *not* lead to the low fertility among African slaves in the Caribbean?

    a. Time for family life was inadequate.
    b. Many more women than men were imported.
    c. Poor nutrition lowered fertility.
    d. Pregnant women found it difficult to carry their babies to term.
    e. Overwork lowered fertility.

7. Why did European planters try to curtail African cultural traditions?

    a. They viewed the Africans as barbarians and found their traditions distasteful.
    b. Their main goal was to convert Africans to Christianity.
    c. They felt that if Africans learned European languages they would communicate better with their masters.
    d. They thought that slave revolts were led by slaves with the strongest African heritage.
    e. The different African ethnic groups hated each other, and repressing their different cultures was believed to reduce violence.

8. Restrictions on Dutch access to French and English colonies

    a. ensured that the Dutch could not sell enough African slaves.
    b. ensured that the French and English maintained their monopoly on sugar.
    c. provoked a series of wars, which the Dutch lost.
    d. provoked a series of wars, which the French and the English lost.
    e. forced the Dutch to expand their American holdings.

9. Most slave deaths on the Middle Passage were due to

    a. drowning when slaves tried to swim to shore while manacled.
    b. starvation.
    c. disease.
    d. punishment or execution.
    e. suicide.

10. In general, what trade goods were the Africans most interested in importing from Europe?

    a. Gold, salt, and ivory
    b. Porcelain, silver, and guns
    c. Textiles, hardware, and guns
    d. Gold, silver, and guns
    e. Beads, iron kettles, and brass pans

11. How did African kings and merchants obtain slaves for sale?

    a. Most of them were prisoners of war.
    b. Most of them were children sold into slavery by their parents.
    c. Most of them were captured in slave raids.
    d. Most of them were hereditary slaves owned by kings.
    e. Most of them were indentured servants.

12. Female slaves were more in demand than male slaves in the Islamic world because

    a. men were too violent and tended to run away.
    b. women were more popular as commodities for sale to American slavers.
    c. women were intended as wives in depopulated areas inland.
    d. women had many business skills which were valued in the Muslim market places.
    e. women were intended as concubines and servants.

13. The European cultural impact on Africa during the Atlantic system is best described as

    a. vast.
    b. minimal.
    c. non-existent.
    d. equal to that of Islam.
    e. greater than that of Islam.

14. Which areas of Africa suffered the most losses in the slave trade?

    a. The coastal regions
    b. The lands behind the Slave Coast
    c. Both coastal and inland regions
    d. The Cape Colony
    e. Actually, historians today think that the damage to Africa from the slave trade has been overstated.

15. How did European goods such as textiles and metals affect Africa?

    a. They undermined the local artisans.
    b. They were imitated by local artisans.
    c. They were rejected by Africans as inferior goods.
    d. They were intended only for consumption and did not help to develop the economy.
    e. They became highly prized luxury goods.

SHORT-ANSWER QUESTIONS

Answer each question in one short paragraph, giving the definition, dates, and significance.

1. What was the most common reason that slaves worked hard?

2. What role did sugar play in the economy, politics, and diet of Britain?

3. Why was the mortality rate on the Middle Passage so high? How did the crew's mortality rates compare with those of the slaves?

4. How did Africans prevent Europeans from taking over their territories?

5. Describe the process by which African slaves were acquired for the slave trade.

6.   What is the relevance of Morocco's defeat of the Songhai Empire?

7.   How did American food crops such as maize, cassava, and peanuts affect Africa's nutritional base?

8.   Describe the life of runaway slaves.

ESSAY QUESTIONS

Make an outline of each question, listing the major points you want to discuss. Then write your practice essay, following your outline carefully and making sure that you do not skip any of your major points. At this time you will want to add the relevant dates and details that will make your essay persuasive and accurate.

1.   Describe the Atlantic system. How did it operate, what countries were involved, and what were their motivations? Finally, what was the system's legacy?

2.   How did sugar plantations work, and what was their relationship with the environment? Why are they often called sugar factories?

3.   Describe the lifestyle of African slaves in the Caribbean. What were their duties, how much did they work, what were the dangers and rewards of their lives, and did they have any leisure time?

4.   Discuss how the various economic institutions in the systems of capitalism and mercantilism contributed to the development of the Atlantic system and the slave trade.

5.   Compare and contrast Christian and Muslim influence in Africa.

COMPARISON CHARTS

Using information gathered from the text, fill in the blank areas of each chart with the relevant data pertaining to the regions and categories listed. (Not all blank areas will necessarily be used.)

Chart 19.1

THE GREAT CIRCUIT

	Starting Points/Regions Covered	Goods Transported
First Leg		
Second Leg		
Third Leg		

Chart 19.2

SLAVE LIFESTYLES

	Caribbean	North Atlantic
Percentage of Population		
Main Duties/Free Time		
Rate of Manumission		
Occupation		
Life Expectancy		
Culture		

DIVERSITY AND DOMINANCE

After reading "Diversity and Dominance: Slavery in West Africa and the Americas" in your text, answer the following additional questions.

Why do you think that the Muslim scholar Ahmad Baba made a distinction between prisoners taken in a state of unbelief, and those who have become Muslims of their own free will?

What did you think of the treatment Job received at the hands of his master Mr. Tolstoy?

What do you think of the great compassion of many of Job's white acquaintances? How does this compare or contrast with the institution of slavery in which they all participated?

INTERNET ASSIGNMENT

Keywords: **"Africans in America"**

"Thomas Jefferson"

Using the above keywords, explore the differing lifestyles of slaves and plantation owners. Was Thomas Jefferson, usually considered to be a man of the Enlightenment, a typical slave owner? Some historians see in Jefferson a microcosm of the social conflicts of the entire South. Why is this? For help in locating Internet material you might also want to consult *History WIRED* on *The Earth and Its Peoples* web site (refer to the preface of this study guide for information on how to locate the text home page).

INTERNET EXPLORATION

Thomas Jefferson is one of our founding fathers, and as such, he has been elevated to the status of an American icon. However, from Jefferson's lifetime to the present, rumors have circulated that he had a slave lover: Sally Hemings. Recently these allegations have gained credibility due to advances in DNA testing. Use the keywords "Thomas Jefferson and Sally Hemings" to find web sites or read the new findings at http://www.pbs.org./wgbh/pages/frontline/shows/jefferson/. If Jefferson did indeed father children with Sally Hemings, do you think it affects his status as one of our founding fathers? What do you think your parents or grandparents would think?

MAP EXERCISES

On Outline Map 19.1, mark the main sources of African slaves for the New World and the main areas of importation of slaves in the New World in blue; then add the routes used by the slave trade in red.

On Outline Map 19.2, shade in or mark the following areas:

Kingdom of Songhai ca. 1500

Sierra Leone

Hausaland

Bornu

Timbuktu

Outline Map 19.1

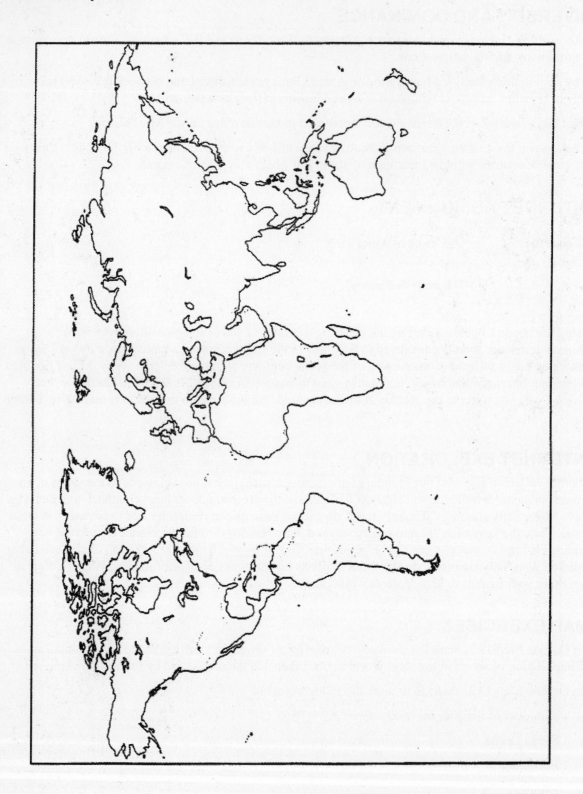

Outline Map 19.2

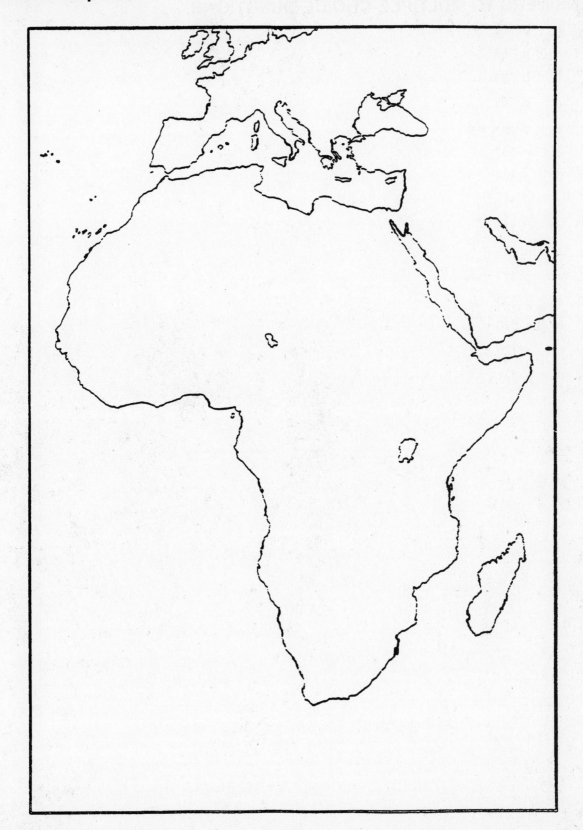

ANSWERS TO MULTIPLE-CHOICE QUESTIONS

1. b   p. 502
2. e   p. 503
3. b   p. 503
4. a   p. 505
5. a   p. 505, 506
6. b   p. 507
7. d   p. 508
8. c   p. 511
9. c   p. 515
10. c   p. 515
11. a   p. 517
12. e   p. 520
13. b   p. 520
14. b   p. 520, 521
15. d   p. 521

CHAPTER 20

Southwest Asia and the Indian Ocean, 1500-1750

LEARNING OBJECTIVES

After reading Chapter 20 and completing this study chapter, you should be able to explain:

- How Islam developed and interacted in three Muslim empires—the Ottoman, the Safavid, and the Mughal.

- In what ways each empire was distinct, yet unified to some extent by Islam.

- How European trading dramatically altered these empires, while also changing Europe's role in the world economy.

- What role the Muslim traders and the Dutch played in the Indian Ocean trade, particularly in Africa and Southeast Asia.

CHAPTER OUTLINE

In the outline below, include important themes, concepts, and details in the blank spaces provided. If you find fewer points than you have space for, leave lines blank. If you find more points, add as many lines as necessary.

I. *Introduction*
    A. *The English attempted to trade with Iran*
        1. _____

        2. _____

        3. _____

        4. _____

        5. _____

    B. *Safavid-Ottoman relations*
        1. _____

        2. _____

3. _____

4. _____

5. _____

C. *Russia and the contest for Central Asia*
    1. _____

    2. _____

    3. _____

    4. _____

II. *The Ottoman Empire, to 1750*
     A. *Expansion and Frontiers*
         1. *The rise of the Ottomans*
             a) _____

             b) _____

             c) _____

         2. *The defeat of Constantinople and the establishment of the borders of the empire*
             a) _____

             b) _____

             c) _____

             d) _____

             e) _____

             f) _____

             g) _____

3. *Suleiman the Magnificent*
    a) _____

    b) _____

    c) _____

4. *More conquests and trade*
    a) _____

    b) _____

    c) _____

    d) _____

5. *Competition with Venice*
    a) _____

    b) _____

    c) _____

    d) _____

6. *Ottoman reaction to Portuguese incursion*
    a) _____

    b) _____

    c) _____

B. *Central Institutions*
    1. *The Janissaries and the* devshirme
        a) _____

        b) _____

        c) _____

        d) _____

e) _____

f) _____

2. ***The languages and peoples of the empire***
    a) _____

    b) _____

    c) _____

    d) _____

    e) _____

3. ***The military and control of the land, and taxes***
    a) _____

    b) _____

    c) _____

    d) _____

    e) _____

4. ***The relationship between the common people and those in power***
    a) _____

    b) _____

    c) _____

C. ***Crisis of the Military State, 1585–1650***
    1. ***The role of the cavalry lessened***
        a) _____

        b) _____

        c) _____

2. *A flood of cheap New World silver*
   a) _____

   b) _____

   c) _____

3. *Islam forbade the raising of taxes, instead used emergency sur-taxes to raise funds*
   a) _____

   b) _____

   c) _____

4. *Revolts between 1590 and 1610*
   a) _____

   b) _____

   c) _____

   d) _____

5. *The Janissaries gain relief from traditional prohibitions*
   a) _____

   b) _____

   c) _____

D. *Economic Change and Growing Weakness, 1650–1750*
   1. *The changing role of the sultan*
      a) _____

      b) _____

      c) _____

   2. *The changing role of the Janissaries and the introduction of tax farming*
      a) _____

      b) _____

c) _____

d) _____

e) _____

f) _____

3. *Izmir (Smyrna) and Ottoman lack of control of trade*
   a) _____

   b) _____

   c) _____

   d) _____

   e) _____

   f) _____

   g) _____

4. *Decline of military power*
   a) _____

   b) _____

   c) _____

5. *Ottomans never made great economic advances, in fact dominated by Europe*
   a) _____

   b) _____

   c) _____

   d) _____

   e) _____

6.   *Downturn*
   a) _____

   b) _____

   c) _____

   d) _____

   e) _____

7.   *While the center suffered, many peripheral areas prospered*
   a) _____

   b) _____

   c) _____

   d) _____

III. *The Safavid Empire, 1502–1722*
   A.   *The Rise of the Safavids*
      1.   *Ismail and the Safavi brotherhood*
         a) _____

         b) _____

         c) _____

      2.   *The adoption of Shi'ite Islam*
         a) _____

         b) _____

         c) _____

         d) _____

         e) _____

B. *Society and Religion*
  1. *A wedge between Iran and its neighbors*
      a) _____

      b) _____

      c) _____

  2. *Differences in language: Arabic versus Persian*
      a) _____

      b) _____

      c) _____

  3. *Artistic developments in Iran, and Turks using Persian*
      a) _____

      b) _____

      c) _____

      d) _____

  4. *Islam provided a link between the cultures*
      a) _____

      b) _____

      c) _____

  5. *The impact of Shi'ism and the Hidden Imam*
      a) _____

      b) _____

      c) _____

      d) _____

      e) _____

6. *Commemoration of the martyrdom of Imam Husayn*
   a) _____

   b) _____

   c) _____

   d) _____

C. *A Tale of Two Cities: Isfahan and Istanbul*
   1. *Differences between the two capitals*
      a) _____

      b) _____

      c) _____

      d) _____

      e) _____

      f) _____

   2. *Similarities between the two capitals*
      a) _____

      b) _____

      c) _____

      d) _____

      e) _____

      f) _____

   3. *Women and family life in the two empires*
      a) _____

      b) _____

c) _____

d) _____

e) _____

f) _____

4. *The dress of men and women*
   a) _____

   b) _____

   c) _____

   d) _____

5. *Public life was the domain of men*
   a) _____

   b) _____

   c) _____

6. *Istanbul and Isfahan had different flavors*
   a) _____

   b) _____

   c) _____

D. *Economic Crisis and Political Collapse*
   1. *Textile production, especially carpets*
      a) _____

      b) _____

      c) _____

2. *Overall, most people lived by farming and herding*

a) _____

b) _____

c) _____

d) _____

e) _____

3. *Military*

a) _____

b) _____

c) _____

d) _____

4. *Cheap silver (late sixteenth century) caused inflation and overland trade declined*

a) _____

b) _____

c) _____

5. *Fall in 1722 and navy*

a) _____

b) _____

c) _____

d) _____

e) _____

IV. *The Mughal Empire, 1526–1761*
   A.   *Political Foundations*
      1.   *Babur and Turkish (Timurid) roots*
         a) _____

         b) _____

         c) _____

         d) _____

      2.   *Akbar created a prosperous empire*
         a) _____

         b) _____

         c) _____

         d) _____

         e) _____

         f) _____

      3.   *Foreign trade and the view of Europeans*
         a) _____

         b) _____

         c) _____

   B.   *Hindus and Muslims*
      1.   *Akbar moved toward religious tolerance*
         a) _____

         b) _____

         c) _____

      2.   *Akbar strove for social harmony*
         a) _____

b) _____

c) _____

d) _____

e) _____

f) _____

3.   *Akbar created a new religion*
   a) _____

   b) _____

   c) _____

4.   *Art was influenced by Hindu traditions*
   a) _____

   b) _____

   c) _____

5.   *Patterns of Islamic conversion in India*
   a) _____

   b) _____

   c) _____

   d) _____

   e) _____

   f) _____

   g) _____

   h) _____

6. *Sikhism*
   a) _____

   b) _____

   c) _____

   d) _____

C. *Central Decay and Regional Challenges, 1707–1761*
   1. *Rulers after Aurangzeb (1707) let the empire fall*
      a) _____

      b) _____

      c) _____

      d) _____

      e) _____

   2. *India decentralized into small prosperous states*
      a) _____

      b) _____

      c) _____

      d) _____

      e) _____

   3. *European involvement in India*
      a) _____

      b) _____

      c) _____

V.   *Trade Empires in the Indian Ocean, 1600–1729*

    A.   *Why did the land empires decline while sea empires grew?*

        1.   **Decline**

            a)   _____

            b)   _____

            c)   _____

            d)   _____

        2.   **Growth**

            a)   _____

            b)   _____

            c)   _____

            d)   _____

    B.   *Muslims in the East Indies*

        1.   *There are competing theories for the spread of Islam in Southeast Asia*

            a)   _____

            b)   _____

            c)   _____

        2.   *Islam in the Philippines (Sulu Empire) and the Acheh Sultanate*

            a)   _____

            b)   _____

            c)   _____

            d)   _____

        3.   *A gradual adoption of Muslim practices*

            a)   _____

            b)   _____

c) _____

d) _____

C.   *Muslims in East Africa*
    1.   *East African ports Muslim, but not linked politically or by trade*
        a) _____

        b) _____

        c) _____

        d) _____

    2.   *The Portuguese role*
        a) _____

        b) _____

        c) _____

    3.   *The Omani's maritime empire*
        a) _____

        b) _____

        c) _____

D.   *The Coming of the Dutch*
    1.   *The Dutch drove out the Portuguese*
        a) _____

        b) _____

        c) _____

    2.   *The Dutch had firm control of trade*
        a) _____

        b) _____

        c) _____

3.   ***The Dutch became a colonial power***
      a)   _____

      b)   _____

      c)   _____

VI.   ***Conclusion***
    A.   ***There was a major shift in the world economic and political alignment***
          1.   _____

          2.   _____

          3.   _____

    B.   ***More trade was done by European ships***
          1.   _____

          2.   _____

          3.   _____

    C.   ***The large land-based empires did not realize that they were in decline***
          1.   _____

          2.   _____

          3.   _____

IDENTIFICATIONS

Define each term and explain why it is significant, including any important dates.

	Identification	**Significance**
Ottoman Empire		
Suleiman the Magnificent		

	Identification	Significance
Janissary		
devshirme		
Tulip Period		
Safavid Empire		
Ismail		
Shi'ite Islam		
Hidden Imam		
Istanbul		
Isfahan		
Shah Abas I		
Mughal Empire		

	Identification	Significance
Akbar		
mansabs		
Rajputs		
Sikhism		
Acheh Sultanate		
Oman		
Swahili		
Batavia		

MULTIPLE-CHOICE QUESTIONS

Read the entire question, including *all* the possible answers. Then choose the *one* answer that best fits the question.

1.   Which was the most long-lived of the post-Mongol Muslim empires?
    a.   The Delhi Sultanate
    b.   The Ottoman Empire
    c.   The Safavid Empire
    d.   The Umayyad caliphate
    e.   The Mughal Empire

2. How did the Ottomans' capture of Christian territories in the Balkans late in the fourteenth century enhance Ottoman military strength?

    a. It gave them the strategic and wealthy city of Constantinople.
    b. It gave them crossbow technology.
    c. It gave them gunpowder.
    d. It gave them Christian prisoners of war to use as military slaves.
    e. It gave them spies to use against Europe.

3. When the Ottoman sultan needed money to support the Janissaries in the sixteenth century, he raised it by

    a. reducing the number of landholding cavalry so that he could keep their share of the taxes.
    b. increasing the taxes on peasants.
    c. raiding neighboring lands and thus also spreading Islam.
    d. firing the grand vizier, who was the best-paid official in the empire and was suspected of treason.
    e. increasing tax on trade.

4. Why were the Ottoman sultan's male relatives kept confined to the palace after the mid-seventeenth century?

    a. The plague was raging, and the sultan feared that if he should die there would be no one to take his place.
    b. The sultan worried about their morality if they were exposed to strange women.
    c. This way the sultan could keep them from meddling in politics or from planning coups.
    d. This was the best way to ensure that they would not be kidnapped by the rival Safavid Empire.
    e. The Ottoman royal family gradually became recluses.

5. Which of the following best describes European impact on Ottoman territory?

    a. The Europeans stopped short of colonial settlement and direct political administration.
    b. The Europeans made extensive inroads into the Ottoman heartland.
    c. The Europeans had no impact whatsoever on Ottoman territory.
    d. The Europeans controlled strategic ports comparable to Malacca and Hormuz.
    e. The Europeans paid very high tariffs to the Ottomans because of old trade agreements.

6. Which of the following statements about the Safavid Empire is *not* true?

    a. Its founder, Ismail, unlike later shahs, was mostly a secular man, unconcerned with religion.
    b. The Iranian population was originally Sunni.
    c. Iran underwent a series of brutal persecutions in the process of accepting Islam.
    d. Scholars from Lebanon and Bahrain helped in Iran's religious education.
    e. Many considered its founder Ismail God incarnate.

7. Religious disapproval of homosexuality

    a. was minimal.
    b. resulted in complete heterosexuality in Muslim communities.
    c. obliged homosexuals to hide their sexual orientation.
    d. did not inhibit artistic references to beardless boys or attachments to members of the same sex.
    e. was designed to promote higher fertility rates, as was the encouragement that men take four wives.

8. The Portuguese left the Safavid island of Hormuz in 1622 because

    a.   there was no money to be made in trading with the backward Safavid Empire.
    b.   the Dutch defeated and expelled them.
    c.   the English brought Iranian soldiers to Hormuz so that the Safavids could expel them.
    d.   they moved their headquarters to Malacca, which was more convenient.
    e.   the Chinese expelled them.

9. What single factor distinguished the Mughal Empire from the Ottoman and Safavid Empires?

    a.   India had never been unified under one government before.
    b.   India had never been exposed to Islam before.
    c.   India was a much more sophisticated society than those of the Ottoman and Safavid Empires.
    d.   India was more active in trade than either the Ottomans or Safavids.
    e.   The majority of Indian society was non-Muslim.

10. Akbar's religious attitude can best be described as

    a.   tolerant and inquisitive.
    b.   tolerant but disinterested.
    c.   intolerant and hostile.
    d.   intolerant and disinterested.
    e.   undeveloped and secular.

11. Why was "the army of the pure" formed?

    a.   To fight for universal religious freedom
    b.   To expel foreigners from Muslim lands
    c.   To defend Sikhs' beliefs
    d.   To defend Islam against the Marathas
    e.   To fight in the Crusades against the Europeans

12. Which of the following statements is *not* true about the decline of Mughal India?

    a.   The decline of the central government and the rise of regional states benefited from the removal of the sultan's heavy hand.
    b.   Linguistic and religious communities gained more freedom when the power of central government declined.
    c.   The disintegration of central power favored the intrusion of European powers.
    d.   The decline of the Mughal Empire allowed yet another Muslim sultanate to reunify India.
    e.   The land grant system was a major element of decline.

13. Which of the following statements about the Netherlands in the seventeenth century is *not* true?

    a.   It was able to control the spice trade completely.
    b.   It was one of the least autocratic countries in Europe.
    c.   It allowed the Dutch East Asia Company to deploy almost unlimited power in maintaining its trade monopoly.
    d.   The Dutch fought a series of wars against kingdoms in Southeast Asia.
    e.   The Dutch took Malacca from the Portuguese in 1641.

14. Which of the following did *not* contribute to the success of the European maritime empires?

    a.   Improvements in ship design
    b.   Improved accuracy in navigation
    c.   The use of cannon
    d.   The development of joint-stock companies
    e.   The complex system of Western philosophy, Protestantism, and Progressivism, applied to the method of conquest

15. Why did women lose the right to be leaders in the Acheh Sultanate?

   a. They were poor rulers.
   b. They tended to not have children, and so no heirs were produced.
   c. They were too easily corruptible.
   d. Scholars in Mecca and Medina said that Islam did not approve of female rulers.
   e. Women tended to marry and turn their thrones over to their husbands anyway.

SHORT-ANSWER QUESTIONS

Answer each question in one short paragraph, giving the definition, dates, and significance.

1. How did the Ottoman, Safavid, and Mughal Empires view naval defense or offense?

2. Describe the land-grant system. What was its use? Which Muslim empires tried it, and how successful was it?

3. How does Islam unite its followers regardless of region, ethnicity, or language?

4. Discuss the role and position of women in the Ottoman, Safavid, and Mughal Empires. Compare women's role and position in these empires with their role and position in Christian Europe at similar stages of development.

5. Why was Islam better able to facilitate the growth of merchant communities than Hinduism or Christianity? How did it do so?

6. How was Islam transmitted to kingdoms in Southeast Asia, and to what degree was it understood?

ESSAY QUESTIONS

Make an outline of each question, listing the major points you want to discuss. Then write your practice essay, following your outline carefully and making sure that you do not skip any of your major points. At this time you will want to add the relevant dates and details that will make your essay persuasive and accurate.

1. Compare the rise and decline of the three Muslim empires discussed in this chapter: the Ottoman, the Safavid, and the Mughal.

2. Compare and contrast the role of Islam in the Ottoman, Safavid, and Mughal Empires.

3. Compare and contrast the cities of Istanbul and Isfahan. How did they reflect the greater empires of which they were the capitals?

4. Describe the factors that encouraged the development of the Indian Ocean trade and eventually allowed Europeans to gain control of this trade.

COMPARISON CHARTS

Using information gathered from the text, fill in the blank areas of each chart with the relevant data pertaining to the regions and categories listed. (Not all blank areas will necessarily be used.)

Chart 20.1

THREE EMPIRES

	Reasons for Rise to Power	Strengths	Weaknesses	Relations with Europe
Ottoman				
Safavid				
Mughal				

Chart 20.2

A TALE OF TWO CITIES

	Terrain/Geography	City Layout	Architecture	Housing Styles	Ethnic and Occupational Makeup
Istanbul					
Isfahan					

DIVERSITY AND DOMINANCE

After reading "Diversity and Dominance: Islamic Law and Ottoman Rule" in your text, answer the following additional questions.

What do you think of Ebu's-su'ud the Mufti's assertion that it was reasonable to break treaties with "infidels" if it was considered beneficial to all Muslims? How about his contention that it was acceptable, and indeed holy war, to fight the Safavids?

Do you think that these fatwas were religiously or politically motivated? Even though war against the Safavids was acceptable, why was in not acceptable to enslave Safavid children?

INTERNET ASSIGNMENT

Keywords: **"Taj Mahal"**

                    "Iranian Mosques"

                    "Suleymaniye Mosque" or "Sultanahmet Mosque"

Use the above keywords to find web sites about these fantastic structures that have come to symbolize their cultures. What was the use of each? Though the Mughal, Safavid, and Ottoman Empires were home to distinct cultures, they were all Muslim and all shared certain aspects of religion and aesthetics. Can you find and explain some of the similarities in their architectural styles? What kinds of different ornamentation were used and why? For help in locating Internet material, you might also want to consult the *History WIRED* image library on *The Earth and Its Peoples* web site (refer to the preface of this study guide for information on how to locate the text home page).

INTERNET EXPLORATION

Persians are famous for their beautiful gardens. Use the keywords "Persian Gardens" to explore some of these classic gardens. One site you might enjoy can be located at http://www.iranian.com/History/Oct98/Garden/index.html. What outstanding feature do you observe in the great majority of these gardens? Why is it such a dominant feature? How difficult were these gardens to build and maintain? What does this tell us about their creators?

MAP EXERCISES

On Outline Map 20.1, label these empires:

Ottoman Empire, 1520

Ottoman Empire, 1566

Safavid Empire, 1600

Mughal Empire, 1530

Mughal Empire, 1656

On Outline Map 20.2, mark the colonial possessions of the following:

British

Portuguese

French

Dutch

Spanish

Outline Map 20.1

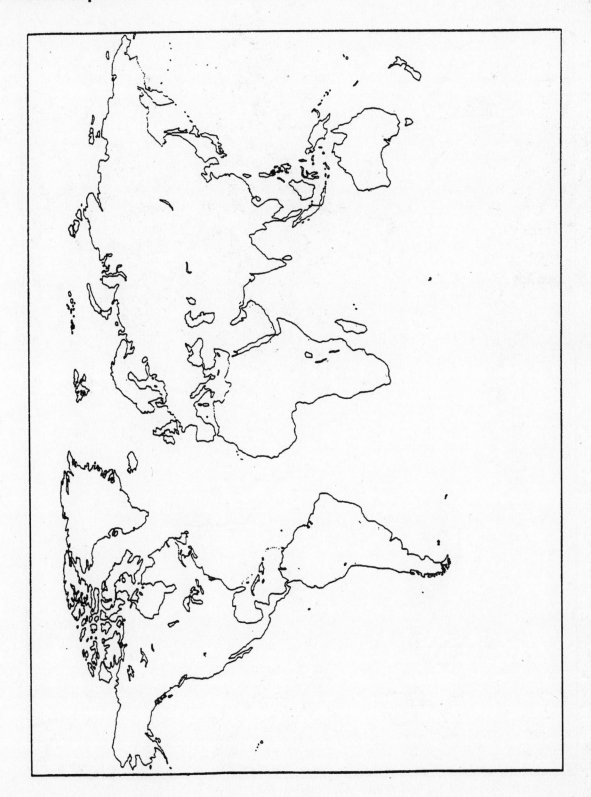

Outline Map 20.2

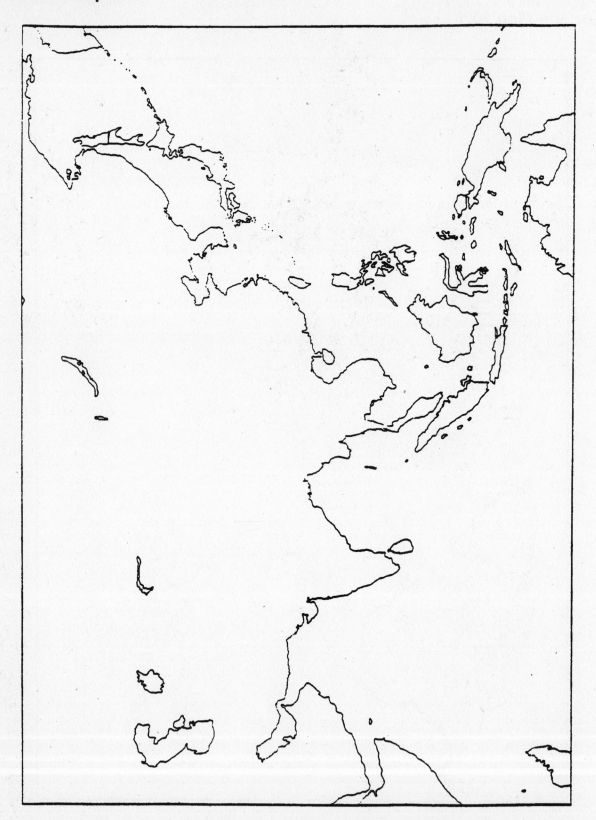

ANSWERS TO MULTIPLE-CHOICE QUESTIONS

1. b   p.526
2. d   p.530
3. a   p.534
4. c   p.534
5. a   p.536
6. a   p.537
7. d   p.540
8. c   p.541
9. e   p.541
10. a   p.543
11. c   p.543
12. d   p.544
13. a   p.548
14. e   p.544
15. d   p.545

CHAPTER 21

Northern Eurasia, 1500–1800

LEARNING OBJECTIVES

After reading Chapter 21 and completing this study chapter, you should be able to explain:

- The similarities and differences between Russia and Qing China and their complex relationship.

- How the two great land empires of Russia and Qing China tried to face the challenges of a changing world.

- How East Asians interacted with European institutions such as the East India Company and the Jesuits.

- How Japan began its transformation to a centralized power on a path much different from Chinese patterns.

CHAPTER OUTLINE

In the outline below, include important themes, concepts, and details in the blank spaces provided. If you find fewer points than you have space for, leave lines blank. If you find more points, add as many lines as necessary.

I.   *Introduction*
   A.   *Weakness of the Ming and Li Zicheng*
      1.   _____

      2.   _____

      3.   _____

      4.   _____

      5.   _____

   B.   *The Ming and Wu Sangui strike back*
      1.   _____

      2.   _____

      3.   _____

C. *The Manchu takeover*
1. _____

2. _____

3. _____

II. *Japanese Reunification*
A. *Civil War and the Invasion of Korea, 1500–1603*
1. *The rise of the daimyo*
a) _____

b) _____

c) _____

d) _____

e) _____

2. *Hideyoshi's invasion of Korea*
a) _____

b) _____

c) _____

3. *Yi Korea and defense against the Japanese invasion*
a) _____

b) _____

c) _____

d) _____

e) _____

B. *The Tokugawa Shogunate, to 1800*
1. *The new shogunate and the daimyo*
a) _____

b) _____

c) _____

2. *Economic integration*

   a) _____

   b) _____

   c) _____

   d) _____

   e) _____

3. *Technical and artistic achievement and merchants*

   a) _____

   b) _____

   c) _____

   d) _____

C. *Japan and the Europeans*

1. *Trade and "gunpowder revolution"*

   a) _____

   b) _____

   c) _____

   d) _____

   e) _____

2. *Catholic missionaries in Asia*

   a) _____

   b) _____

   c) _____

d) _____

e) _____

3.   *Government suspicion of Christianity and persecutions*
   a) _____

   b) _____

   c) _____

   d) _____

   e) _____

4.   *The closing of Japan*
   a) _____

   b) _____

   c) _____

   d) _____

   e) _____

D.   *Elite Decline and Social Crisis*
   1.   *Eighteenth-century population growth and economic decline*
      a) _____

      b) _____

      c) _____

      d) _____

   2.   *Protecting the samurai from decline*
      a) _____

      b) _____

      c) _____

d) _____

e) _____

3. *The Forty-seven Ronin incident*
   a) _____

   b) _____

   c) _____

III. *The Later Ming and Early Qing Empires*
   A. *The Ming Empire, 1500–1644*
      1. *Ming cultural achievements and porcelain*
         a) _____

         b) _____

         c) _____

         d) _____

         e) _____

         f) _____

      2. *Natural disasters and climatic change*
         a) _____

         b) _____

         c) _____

         d) _____

         e) _____

      3. *Economy and money*
         a) _____

         b) _____

      c) _____

  4. *Cities and factories*
      a) _____

      b) _____

      c) _____

  5. *Agricultural decline*
      a) _____

      b) _____

      c) _____

      d) _____

B. *Ming Collapse and the Rise of the Qing*
  1. *Mongols, Manchus, and Pirates*
      a) _____

      b) _____

      c) _____

      d) _____

      e) _____

  2. *Manchu takeover*
      a) _____

      b) _____

      c) _____

C. *Trading Companies and Missionaries*
  1. *The Chinese were reluctant to trade with the Europeans*
      a) _____

      b) _____

      c) _____

      d) _____

  2. ***The Dutch***
      a) _____

      b) _____

      c) _____

  3. ***Catholic missionaries, especially Matteo Ricci***
      a) _____

      b) _____

      c) _____

      d) _____

      e) _____

      f) _____

D. ***Emperor Kangxi, (r.1662–1722)***
  1. ***Fostering recovery***
      a) _____

      b) _____

      c) _____

  2. ***His rise to power and success***
      a) _____

      b) _____

      c) _____

      d) _____

3. *Struggles with the Mongols and Russians*
    a) _____

    b) _____

    c) _____

4. *Manchu success due to use of ideas and technologies from different regions*
    a) _____

    b) _____

    c) _____

    d) _____

    e) _____

    f) _____

5. *Jesuit influence and compromise in China*
    a) _____

    b) _____

    c) _____

    d) _____

E. *Chinese Influences on Europe*
    1. *Anatomy and variolation*
        a) _____

        b) _____

        c) _____

    2. *Chinese things*
        a) _____

        b) _____

c) _____

3. *"Philosopher kings"*
   a) _____

   b) _____

   c) _____

F. ***Tea and Diplomacy***
   1. ***Qing regulation of trade***
      a) _____

      b) _____

      c) _____

   2. ***The British, trade, and tea***
      a) _____

      b) _____

      c) _____

      d) _____

   3. ***The "canton system" and the British trade deficit***
      a) _____

      b) _____

      c) _____

      d) _____

      e) _____

   4. ***The Macarthey mission***
      a) _____

      b) _____

c) _____

d) _____

e) _____

f) _____

5. *European frustration*
   a) _____

   b) _____

   c) _____

G. *Population and Social Stress*
   1. *Population growth in the late 1700s*
      a) _____

      b) _____

      c) _____

      d) _____

   2. *Environmental decline and localized misery*
      a) _____

      b) _____

      c) _____

      d) _____

      e) _____

   3. *The Qing Empire outgrew state control*
      a) _____

      b) _____

      c) _____

d) _____

e) _____

IV. *The Russian Empire*
    A.   *The Drive Across Northern Asia*
        1.   *Muscovy was the foundation for a new state*
           a) _____

           b) _____

           c) _____

           d) _____

           e) _____

        2.   *A new empire*
           a) _____

           b) _____

           c) _____

        3.   *Siberia*
           a) _____

           b) _____

           c) _____

           d) _____

           e) _____

           f) _____

        4.   *Conflicts with China at the Amur River*
           a) _____

           b) _____

c) _____

B. *Russian Society and Politics to 1725*
1. *Ethnicity and the Cossacks*
a) _____

b) _____

c) _____

d) _____

e) _____

f) _____

2. *The first Romanov Tsar*
a) _____

b) _____

c) _____

3. *How the empire affected the peasants*
a) _____

b) _____

c) _____

4. *The development of serfdom*
a) _____

b) _____

c) _____

d) _____

C. **Peter the Great**

   1. **The quest for a warm-water port and Russian protection of Orthodox Christians**

     a) _____

     b) _____

     c) _____

     d) _____

   2. **Peter went to Europe to study success**

     a) _____

     b) _____

     c) _____

     d) _____

   3. **Russia became a major power, and the building of St. Petersburg**

     a) _____

     b) _____

     c) _____

     d) _____

     e) _____

   4. **Westernization**

     a) _____

     b) _____

     c) _____

     d) _____

     e) _____

     f) _____

D.   ***Consolidation of the Empire***
    1.   ***Expansion into Northwest of North America***
        a)   _____

        b)   _____

        c)   _____

        d)   _____

        e)   _____

    2.   ***Catherine the Great (r. 1762–1796)***
        a)   _____

        b)   _____

        c)   _____

        d)   _____

        e)   _____

V.   ***Comparative Perspectives***
    A.   ***Political Comparisons***
        1.   ***China and Russia***
            a)   _____

            b)   _____

            c)   _____

            d)   _____

        2.   ***Japan doesn't fit the mold***
            a)   _____

            b)   _____

            c)   _____

        3.   ***Military status and naval power***
            a)   _____

b) _____

c) _____

d) _____

e) _____

B. *Cultural, Social, and Economic Comparisons*
1. *Result of expansion in China and Russia*
   a) _____

   b) _____

   c) _____

   d) _____

   e) _____

   f) _____

2. *Repressive hierarchies in China and Russia*
   a) _____

   b) _____

   c) _____

   d) _____

   e) _____

3. *Merchants in China and Japan*
   a) _____

   b) _____

   c) _____

   d) _____

VI. *Conclusion*

    A.   **Similarities between Russia and Qing China**

        1. _____

        2. _____

        3. _____

    B.   **Differences between Russia and Qing China**

        1. _____

        2. _____

        3. _____

    C.   **Peter the Great's legacy**

        1. _____

        2. _____

        3. _____

    D.   **Japan took a different path**

        1. _____

        2. _____

        3. _____

IDENTIFICATIONS

Define each term and explain why it is significant, including any important dates.

	Identification	Significance
Manchu		
Samurai		
daimyo		
pirates		
Tokugawa Shogunate		
Ming Empire		
Qing Empire		
Kangxi		
Amur River		
Macartney Mission		
Siberia		

Identification   **Significance**

Muscovy

Ural Mountains

Amur River

Tsar

Cossacks

Serfs

Peter the Great

variolation

tea

"Forty-seven Ronin" incident of 1702

MULTIPLE-CHOICE QUESTIONS

Read the entire question, including *all* the possible answers. Then choose the *one* answer that best fits the question.

1. Under what circumstances did the Tokugawa government regulate the price of rice, the rate of interest, and the activities of moneylenders?

    a.   When the well-being of the peasants was threatened.
    b.   When the well-being of the merchants was threatened.
    c.   When the well-being of the nobles was threatened.
    d.   When the well-being of the samurai was threatened.
    e.   When the well-being of the fledgling Catholic Church was threatened.

2. How did the Japanese respond to Catholicism?

    a.   The shogunal court was hostile, but certain regional lords were receptive.
    b.   The shogunal court was receptive, but certain regional lords were hostile.
    c.   Both the shogunal court and the regional lords were hostile.
    d.   Both the shogunal court and the regional lords were receptive.
    e.   Only the downtrodden peasants found it appealing.

3. Japan's decentralized government system limited its ability to regulate merchant activities

    a.   and so also stunted the economy.
    b.   and actually stimulated the growth of commercial activities.
    c.   and so most merchants remained quite poor.
    d.   and so hurt the merchants and samurai.
    e.   and actually opened the door to widespread Dutch trade.

4. What is the significance of the "Forty-seven Ronin" incident?

    a.   It was the ideological and social crisis of the Tokugawa government.
    b.   It was a socially relevant subject for a play by Chikamatsu.
    c.   It revealed the prevalence of seppuku in Japanese society.
    d.   It symbolized in microcosm the downfall of the Tokugawa shogunate.
    e.   It proved that samurai values were outmoded.

5. The success of Kangxi's rule was due at least in part to

    a.   the smooth transition between the Ming and the Qing dynasties.
    b.   the lack of threat from outside invaders.
    c.   its ability to incorporate ideas and technologies from different regions of Asia.
    d.   European technology enhancing Qing agriculture, trade, and industry.
    e.   Kangxi's rule was unsuccessful.

6. Which of the Jesuit compromises with Chinese culture most upset the pope?

    a.   Their adoption of improper dress
    b.   Their memorization of Confucian texts and use of this ideology to explain Christianity
    c.   Their use of Chinese during Mass
    d.   Their open admiration of Chinese culture
    e.   Their acceptance of ancestor worship as compatible with Christianity

7. Voltaire viewed the Qing emperors as

    a.   model philosopher-kings.
    b.   bloody tyrants.
    c.   foolish children.
    d.   religious demagogues.
    e.   worrisome competitors.

8.　What caused the Qing Empire to limit strictly the access of foreign merchants to China's commercial cities?

   a.　A combination of xenophobia and religious concerns
   b.　A combination of tax protectionism and piracy
   c.　A combination of piracy and xenophobia
   d.　A combination of religious concerns and fear of invasion
   e.　A combination of tax protectionism and inflation control

9.　The Russian word "tsar" means

   a.　khan.
   b.　crown.
   c.　caesar.
   d.　throne.
   e.　representative of God.

10.　The Russians under Peter the Great were determined to

   a.　drive all the Turks from Russia.
   b.　make an alliance with the Jesuits.
   c.　convert to Roman Catholicism.
   d.　secure a warm-water port.
   e.　sever ties with western Europe.

11.　The negotiations for the Treaty of Nerchinsk

   a.　were unsuccessful.
   b.　demonstrated China's power.
   c.　demonstrated the Mongols' power.
   d.　demonstrated that Russia was an important and powerful neighbor to China.
   e.　demonstrated that land empires were in decline.

12.　Which of the following about St. Petersburg is *not* true?

   a.　It was intended as a demonstration of Russian traditional culture.
   b.　It was built on land captured from Sweden.
   c.　It became the capital city in 1712.
   d.　It was intended as a demonstration of Russian sophistication.
   e.　It was Peter's window on the West.

13.　From the Chinese perspective, European contacts were

   a.　uninteresting.
   b.　useful, but not essential.
   c.　very important to its economy.
   d.　essential to solve its technological problems.
   e.　useful only in its competition with Russia for the Amur River region.

14.　Peter the Great banned Jesuits from Russia because

   a.　they supported the Chinese politically.
   b.　they opposed his Westernization plan.
   c.　they wouldn't speak Russian.
   d.　they wouldn't shave their beards.
   e.　he thought them subversive and backward.

SHORT-ANSWER QUESTIONS

Answer each question in one short paragraph, giving the definition, dates, and significance.

1. How did climatic changes affect rural life in Ming seventeenth- and eighteenth-century China?

2. Why was the Ming government unable to respond to the challenge of the seventeenth-century crisis?

3. What were the costs of the Japanese invasion of Korea during the late sixteenth century?

4. Describe the technological exchange between the Qing dynasty and Europeans.

5. How did the shoguns control the regional lords?

6. How did serfdom rise in Russia?

ESSAY QUESTIONS

Make an outline of each question, listing the major points you want to discuss. Then write your practice essay, following your outline carefully and making sure that you do not skip any of your major points. At this time you will want to add the relevant dates and details that will make your essay persuasive and accurate.

1. Discuss the relationship between Russia and Qing China, and how they in turn related to the rest of the world.

2. How did Peter the Great try to modernize Russia, and what role was St. Petersburg to play?

3. Discuss the theory that the fall of the Ming dynasty and the rise of the Qing dynasty were not related only to conditions in China, but also to larger global trends.

4. Discuss the relationship between the Chinese and the Jesuits. How did they influence each other?

5. What role did the East India Companies play in the interrelations between Britain, India, and China?

6. Compare and contrast the Chinese and Japanese response to European influence.

COMPARISON CHARTS

Using information gathered from the text, fill in the blank areas of each chart with the relevant data pertaining to the regions and categories listed. (Not all blank areas will necessarily be used.)

Chart 21.1

TWO GREAT EURASIAN LAND EMPIRES

	Dates/Ethnicity of Rulers	Government Aims	View of Christianity	Relationship with Europe	Methods of Control
Russia					
Quing Dynasty					

Chart 21.2

TWO DIFFERENT PATHS: CHINA AND JAPAN

	Government System	Views Toward Different Cultures	View of Christianity	Relationship with Europe	Methods of Control	Impact
China						
Japan						

DIVERSITY AND DOMINANCE

After reading "Diversity and Dominance: Gendered Violence: The Yangzhou Massacre" in your text, answer the following additional questions.

Why does the writer of this account find it necessary to reassure the reader that he has not made any of it up? Why do later people (in the author's view) need to read his account?

INTERNET ASSIGNMENT

Keywords: **"St. Petersburg History" or "Peter I of Russia"**

                    "Jesuits in China"

Both Russia and China were confronted with the prospect of modernization when faced with rapid Western industrialization. Though both empires were quite similar, they reacted to modernization and Westernization very differently. Use the above keywords to locate Internet materials on Peter I of Russia and the Jesuits in China. How did Peter I modernize Russia? How did the Jesuits attempt to modernize China? How did China react? Why was Russia so much more successful? Why was modernization so much slower in China?

INTERNET EXPLORATION

During the Edo period, Japanese travel went along official government highways, the most famous of which was the Tokaido Road, immortalized in the prints of Ando Hiroshige. Visit http://www.us-japan.org/EdoMatsu and travel with samurai, merchants, and pilgrims along the Tokaido Road, or just visit many of the fascinating sites in old Edo (Tokyo) by clicking on the map. For a look at some artifacts from the period, click on the Home icon and then the Ukioye icon. You might also use the keywords "Ando Hiroshige" to find other interesting sites.

MAP EXERCISE

On Outline Map 21.1, mark the following:

>   Qing homeland
>
>   Qing Empire by 1644
>
>   Qing Empire in 1659
>
>   Territory acquired from Russia in 1659
>
>   Qing Empire by 1783
>
>   Tributary areas

Shade in manufacturing centers.

On Outline Map 21.2, mark the following:

>   Russia in 1533
>
>   Russia in 1598
>
>   Russia in 1721
>
>   Russia in 1796

Outline Map 21.1

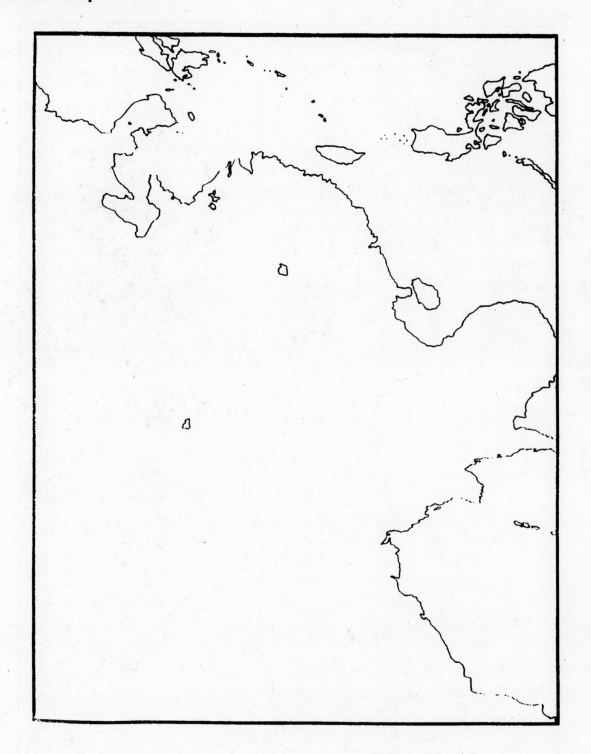

Outline Map 21.2

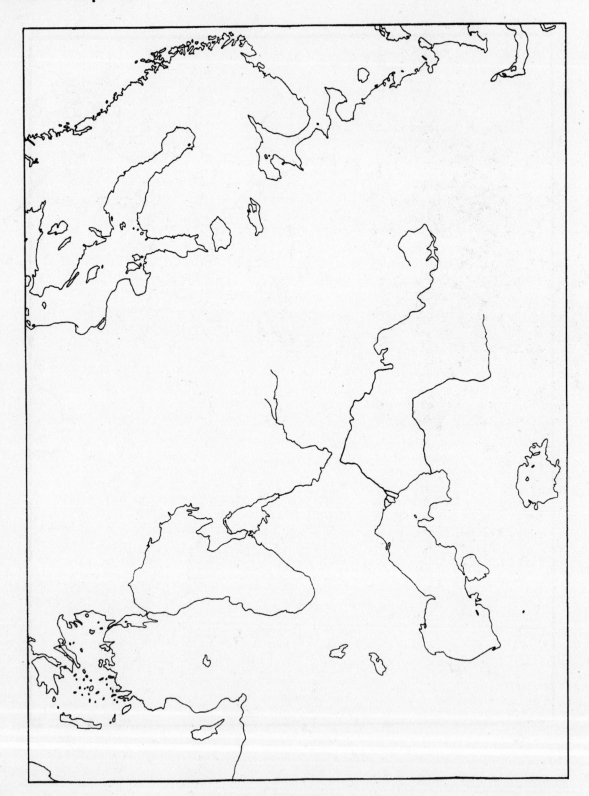

ANSWERS TO MULTIPLE-CHOICE QUESTIONS

1. d   p. 552
2. a   p. 553, 554
3. b   p. 556
4. a   p. 556
5. c   p. 562
6. e   p. 562
7. a   p. 563
8. b   p. 564
9. c   p. 567
10. d   p. 567, 570
11. d   p. 567
12. a   p. 570
13. b   p. 573
14. e   p. 573

Revolutionary Changes in the Atlantic World, 1750–1850

LEARNING OBJECTIVES

After reading Chapter 22 and completing this study chapter, you should be able to explain:

- How the new wealth generated by the Industrial Revolution, along with increases in trade and colonialism, coincided with the new intellectual trends of the Enlightenment to cause a questioning of tradition, which in some cases resulted in revolution.

- How local concerns and conditions affected each revolution, and how the outcome of revolution changed the lives of common people.

- How conservatives reacted to revolution, and what methods they used to try to stem the tide of change.

- In what ways these revolutions began to transform Western political culture and eventually influenced revolutionaries the world over.

CHAPTER OUTLINE

In the outline below, include important themes, concepts, and details in the blank spaces provided. If you find fewer points than you have space for, leave lines blank. If you find more points, add as many lines as necessary.

I.   *Introduction*
   A.   *A meeting of revolutionaries in Haiti*
      1. _____

      2. _____

      3. _____

      4. _____

   B.   *Toussaint L'Ouverture and the Haitian slave rebellion*
      1. _____

      2. _____

      3. _____

4. _____

C. *The legacy of the revolutionary era in the Western world*
   1. _____

   2. _____

   3. _____

   4. _____

II. *Prelude to Revolution: The Eighteenth-Century Crisis*
  A. *Colonial Wars and Fiscal Crises*
    1. *Spain lost colonial power to the Dutch and the British*
      a) _____

      b) _____

      c) _____

    2. *The British and French competed for colonial holdings*
      a) _____

      b) _____

      c) _____

      d) _____

      e) _____

    3. *The cost of making war went up higher and faster than taxes did*
      a) _____

      b) _____

      c) _____

  B. *The Enlightenment and the Old Order*
    1. *The Enlightenment and the application of scientific ideas to human nature*
      a) _____

b)   _____

c)   _____

d)   _____

e)   _____

2.   *The Enlightenment's influence on politics*
   a)   _____

   b)   _____

   c)   _____

   d)   _____

   e)   _____

3.   *Government and the Enlightenment*
   a)   _____

   b)   _____

   c)   _____

4.   *The relationship between the intellectuals of the Enlightenment*
   a)   _____

   b)   _____

   c)   _____

5.   *Women, the middle class, and the Enlightenment*
   a)   _____

   b)   _____

   c)   _____

   d)   _____

e) _____

f) _____

6.   *The Americas, Ben Franklin, and European debates*
   a) _____

   b) _____

   c) _____

   d) _____

   e) _____

   f) _____

   g) _____

C.   *Folk Cultures and Popular Protest*
   1.   *Many peoples resisted the supposedly beneficial changes and reforms; they saw them as threatening to their traditional systems*
      a) _____

      b) _____

      c) _____

      d) _____

   2.   *Attempts were made to restrict many popular cultural traditions deemed "corrupt"*
      a) _____

      b) _____

      c) _____

   3.   *The relationship between popular protest and revolution*
      a) _____

      b) _____

c) _____

III. *The American Revolution, 1775–1800*
   A. *Frontiers and Taxes*
      1. *The British tried to restrict settlement west of the Appalachians and impose more taxes on the American colonists to defray war debts*
         a) _____

         b) _____

         c) _____

         d) _____

         e) _____

         f) _____

      2. *Problems arose between the Amerindians and the British when the British took over French holdings in the Great Lakes region*
         a) _____

         b) _____

         c) _____

         d) _____

         e) _____

      3. *Pontiac, the British response, and colonial dissatisfaction*
         a) _____

         b) _____

         c) _____

      4. *Britain's campaign to raise money from the colonists and boycotts*
         a) _____

         b) _____

c) _____

d) _____

e) _____

f) _____

5. *The Stamp Act of 1765, the Boston Massacre, and a tea party*
   a) _____

   b) _____

   c) _____

   d) _____

   e) _____

   f) _____

6. *Marshal law in Massachusetts*
   a) _____

   b) _____

   c) _____

B. *The Course of Revolution, 1775–1783*
   1. *The Colonists began to take over government institutions and intimidate the Loyalists*
      a) _____

      b) _____

      c) _____

   2. **Common Sense** *and the Declaration of Independence*
      a) _____

      b) _____

c) _____

3. *Britain brought in military forces; the two parties were not able to compromise*
   a) _____

   b) _____

   c) _____

   d) _____

4. *Amerindian involvement*
   a) _____

   b) _____

   c) _____

   d) _____

   e) _____

   f) _____

5. *French involvement*
   a) _____

   b) _____

   c) _____

   d) _____

6. *The end of the war*
   a) _____

   b) _____

   c) _____

   d) _____

C. *The Construction of Republican Institutions, to 1800*
1. *State constitutions and the Confederation government*

a) _____

b) _____

c) _____

d) _____

e) _____

2. *The Constitutional Convention, 1787*

a) _____

b) _____

c) _____

d) _____

e) _____

3. *Who gained full rights? What about free blacks, women, and slaves?*

a) _____

b) _____

c) _____

d) _____

e) _____

f) _____

IV. *The French Revolution, 1789–1815*
A. *French Society and Fiscal Crisis*
1. *The first and second estates*

a) _____

b) _____

c) _____

2. ***The third estate (the "bourgeoisie")***
   a) _____

   b) _____

   c) _____

   d) _____

   e) _____

   f) _____

3. ***The plight of the poor***
   a) _____

   b) _____

   c) _____

   d) _____

   e) _____

   f) _____

4. ***War expenses, new taxes, and debt***
   a) _____

   b) _____

   c) _____

   d) _____

   e) _____

   f) _____

B. *Protest Turns to Revolution, 1789–1792*
  1. *Louis XVI had to call the Estates General into session*
      a) _____

      b) _____

      c) _____

      d) _____

  2. *The creation of the National Assembly*
      a) _____

      b) _____

      c) _____

      d) _____

      e) _____

  3. *Louis brought in the military for protection, but the people acted, resulting in the storming of the Bastille*
      a) _____

      b) _____

      c) _____

      d) _____

      e) _____

      f) _____

  4. *More rights and the* **Declaration of the Rights of Man**
      a) _____

      b) _____

      c) _____

d) _____

e) _____

5. *Women in the revolution*
    a) _____

    b) _____

    c) _____

    d) _____

6. *Radical changes for French society and the European response*
    a) _____

    b) _____

    c) _____

    d) _____

C. *The Terror, 1793–1794*
    1. *The Assembly suspended the King*
        a) _____

        b) _____

        c) _____

        d) _____

    2. *France became a republic*
        a) _____

        b) _____

        c) _____

        d) _____

3. *Robespierre and the Jacobins*
   a) _____

   b) _____

   c) _____

   d) _____

   e) _____

4. *The Committee of Public Safety and loss of rights by women*
   a) _____

   b) _____

   c) _____

   d) _____

5. *The Reign of Terror and the execution of Robespierre*
   a) _____

   b) _____

   c) _____

   d) _____

D. *Reaction and Dictatorship, 1795–1815*
   1. *Dismantling the more radical elements of the revolution*
      a) _____

      b) _____

      c) _____

      d) _____

   2. *Napoleon gave order to an exhausted France*
      a) _____

b) _____

c) _____

d) _____

e) _____

3. *Napoleon made alliances*
a) _____

b) _____

c) _____

d) _____

4. *Individuals lost rights*
a) _____

b) _____

c) _____

d) _____

5. *Napoleon built an empire*
a) _____

b) _____

c) _____

d) _____

6. *Waterloo and defeat*
a) _____

b) _____

c) _____

d) _____

V.   *Revolution Spreads, Conservatives Respond, 1789–1850*
   A.   *The Haitian Revolution, 1789–1804*
      1.   *The wealth of the colony paid for by a brutal slave system*
         a) _____

         b) _____

         c) _____

      2.   *Delegations sent to France*
         a) _____

         b) _____

         c) _____

      3.   *A power vacuum developed in Haiti and the two classes began to fight*
         a) _____

         b) _____

         c) _____

         d) _____

      4.   *Slave rebellion*
         a) _____

         b) _____

         c) _____

         d) _____

         e) _____

      5.   *Napoleon tried to re-establish colonial power and slavery*
         a) _____

         b) _____

       c) _____

       d) _____

    6.   *The role of women in Haiti*
       a) _____

       b) _____

       c) _____

B.   *The Congress of Vienna and Conservative Retrenchment, 1815–1820*
    1.   *Britain, Russia, Austria, and Prussia met to create a European peace settlement that would safeguard the political order of all of Europe*
       a) _____

       b) _____

       c) _____

    2.   *Tried to turn back the clock in France*
       a) _____

       b) _____

       c) _____

    3.   *Also wanted to stem the tide of "subversive" ideas*
       a) _____

       b) _____

       c) _____

C.   *Nationalism, Reform, and Revolution, 1821–1850*
    1.   *Popular support for self-determination*
       a) _____

       b) _____

       c) _____

d) _____

2. *Constitutional monarchy in France*
    a) _____

    b) _____

    c) _____

3. *Domestic reforms made in the United States and Britain, but the governments were fearful of what had happened in France*
    a) _____

    b) _____

    c) _____

    d) _____

    e) _____

4. *Democratic reform movements and backlash*
    a) _____

    b) _____

    c) _____

    d) _____

    e) _____

5. *The reformers tried to reform in Austria and Prussia, but brought about little change*
    a) _____

    b) _____

    c) _____

6. *Revolutions of 1848*
    a) _____

b) _____

c) _____

d) _____

VI. *Conclusion*
    A. *Royal needs for funds clashed with new ideas of reform and revolution*
        1. _____

        2. _____

        3. _____

    B. *The three Revolutions had different characters*
        1. _____

        2. _____

        3. _____

    C. *Conservative retrenchment*
        1. _____

        2. _____

        3. _____

IDENTIFICATIONS

Define each term and explain why it is significant, including any important dates.

	Identification	Significance
Enlightenment		
Benjamin Franklin		
George Washington		

	Identification	Significance
Joseph Brant		
Declaration of Independence		
Constitutional Convention		
Jacobins		
Maximilien Robespierre		
Napoleon Bonaparte		
gens de couleur		
François Dominique		
James Madison		
the three estates		
bourgeoisie		

	Identification	Significance
Estates General		
National Assembly		
Declaration of the Rights of Man		
Toussaint L'Ouverture		
Committee of Public Safety		
Reign of Terror		
the Directory		
Congress of Vienna		
Revolutions of 1848		

MULTIPLE-CHOICE QUESTIONS

Read the entire question, including *all* the possible answers. Then choose the *one* answer that best fits the question.

1. The revolutionary cycle was precipitated in large measure by

   a. the cost of wars to gain new colonial holdings.
   b. the Protestant Reformation.
   c. the cost of opening up new farmlands.
   d. the Scientific Revolution.
   e. the discovery of gold in the New World.

2. What did the complex and diverse movement called the Enlightenment do?

   a. It applied the methods and questions of the Scientific Revolution of the seventeenth century to the study of human society.
   b. It blended the Greco-Roman beliefs rediscovered during the Renaissance with Catholicism.
   c. It applied the technical advances of the Scientific Revolution of the seventeenth century to the fledgling Industrial Revolution of the eighteenth century.
   d. It challenged the prevailing economic notions of the medieval period, resulting in a series of economic and business reforms.
   e. It paved the way for the European conquest of Asia.

3. Which of the following was *not* an objective shared by the majority of European reformers, whether monarchs or intellectuals?

   a. The selection of bureaucrats by merit
   b. The development of national bureaucracies staffed by civil servants based on merit
   c. The creation of national legal systems
   d. The modernization of national tax systems
   e. The reform of and eventual independence for imperial colonies

4. Censorship tended to

   a. enhance the reputation of censored intellectuals and books.
   b. inhibit the spread of new information and ideas.
   c. enhance the power of the monarchs.
   d. eliminate opposition to government policies.
   e. strengthen the position of the Catholic Church.

5. Benjamin Franklin's career demonstrated that

   a. the British colonies in America had grown away from Europe intellectually.
   b. the British colonists had more in common with the Spanish colonists than they did with Europeans.
   c. Europeans did not view the people of the Western Hemisphere as their intellectual equals.
   d. he was against many Enlightenment ideals.
   e. people in the Western Hemisphere shared in the debates of Europe.

6. The Spanish colonial slogan "Long live the King. Death to bad government" meant that

   a. although common people disliked traditional authority, they feared going so far as to voice their opposition to the king himself.
   b. the common people supported their king but were upset at attempts to modify the traditional system to which they were accustomed.
   c. the common people disliked having a female ruler and disliked her policies and that they were relieved to have a male monarch again.
   d. the common people wanted to overthrow the government and were being sarcastic when they said "Long live the King."
   e. the people in the colonies were agitating for independence.

7. Spontaneous popular uprisings and protests greeted nearly every attempt at government reform, but they gained revolutionary potential only when

    a. the peasants had a strong charismatic leader to rally them to revolution.
    b. the common people could obtain weapons.
    c. they coincided with ideological divisions and conflicts within the governing class itself.
    d. the country was too busy with foreign wars or the colonies to notice them.
    e. they were successful.

8. Which of the following had *not* occurred by the end of the revolutions of the eighteenth century?

    a. The authority of the monarchs had been swept away or limited by constitutions.
    b. Religion had lost its dominant place in intellectual life.
    c. The old landed elite had been overthrown throughout Europe and America.
    d. The ideal of a social order determined by birth was gone.
    e. There was a new capitalist vision that emphasized completion and social mobility.

9. Which of the following approaches was *not* used by the colonists to communicate their dissatisfaction with the various reform measures attempted by George III?

    a. Intimidation of royal officials
    b. Boycotts of British goods
    c. Migrations to the Caribbean colonies
    d. Purchase of American-made products
    e. Use of fiery political language against British officials

10. Conditions favorable to revolution in France were created by the

    a. grinding poverty of the French common people.
    b. discontent of intellectuals with censorship.
    c. narrow self-interest and greed of the rich.
    d. death of Louis XV.
    e. failure of the wheat crops and the resulting bread shortages.

11. The Committee of Public Safety was formed to

    a. inspect factories for conditions dangerous to workers.
    b. design safer transportation systems.
    c. train people to protect the French royal family.
    d. seek out and punish domestic enemies of the French Revolution.
    e. stop the spread of malaria in the French colonies.

12. Why was Napoleon Bonaparte so successful?

    a. He made the trains run on time.
    b. He promised order to a society exhausted by the Revolution.
    c. He was handsome and charismatic.
    d. He was a brilliant diplomat.
    e. He promised to restore pre-Revolutionary France.

13. The *gens de couleur* sent representatives to France to request

    a. more home rule and economic freedom.
    b. an end to slavery in Saint Domingue.
    c. an end to race discrimination and the achievement of political equality with whites.
    d. independence.
    e. the right to emigrate to Africa.

SHORT-ANSWER QUESTIONS

Answer each question in one short paragraph, giving the definition, dates, and significance.

1. In what ways did the intellectual ferment of the Enlightenment influence the middle class of Europe and of the Western Hemisphere? What were the results of this influence?

2. How did the policies of European monarchs intellectually and politically undermine the institution of colonialism?

3. How were attempts to ban or curtail such popular traditions as harvest festivals, religious holidays, country fairs, cockfighting, and bearbaiting received by the common people? Why was the government interested in controlling participation in these events?

4. How did European settlers' pushing beyond the Appalachian Mountains affect British-Amerindian relations and British-colonist relations?

5. How did the new United States' Constitution affect the rights of women and African-Americans?

6. Why were there so many poor people in prerevolutionary France? How did they live?

ESSAY QUESTIONS

Make an outline of each question, listing the major points you want to discuss. Then write your practice essay, following your outline carefully and making sure that you do not skip any of your major points. At this time you will want to add the relevant dates and details that will make your essay persuasive and accurate.

1. Describe the Netherlands' relationship with Spain. How did that relationship affect colonial holdings?

2. Why was the American Revolution fought, what were some of the conditions that precipitated it, and how did society in the former colonies change as a result?

3. Describe French society before the French Revolution. How was society changed by the Revolution? Was the outcome of the Revolution all that the revolutionaries had hoped for? What legacy did it leave to the world? Give specific examples.

4. Compare and contrast the role and status of women and women's impact on at least three revolutions in the eighteenth and nineteenth centuries. How did the outcome of these revolutions affect women's lives?

5. Trace the unfolding of events in one of the following: the American Revolution, the French Revolution, or the Revolution in Saint Domingue. Did the common people play a role (if so, what role), or were they just carried along on the tide of change? After discussing this point, evaluate the outcome of the Revolution from their perspective. What gains were made, and what losses suffered?

COMPARISON CHARTS

Using information gathered from the text, fill in the blank areas of each chart with the relevant data pertaining to the regions and categories listed. (Not all blank areas will necessarily be used.)

Chart 22.1

THREE REVOLUTIONS

	Dates	Instigators/ Supporters	Original Goals	Methods	Dramatic Moments/ Turning Points	Role of the Wealthy Aristocracy/ Rulers	Role of Religion or Priests	Role of Middle Class	Role of Peasants	Role and Status of Women	Gains/ Losses
American Revolution											
French Revolution											
Revolution of Saint Domingue											

Chart 22.2

THE REVOLUTIONS OF 1848

	Demands	Government Response	Revolutionary Methods	Government Methods	Role of Women	Gains/Losses
France						
Britain						
Austrian Empire						
Prussia and the German States						

DIVERSITY AND DOMINANCE

After reading "Diversity and Dominance: Robespierre and Wollstonecraft Defend and Explain the Terror" in your text, answer the following additional questions.

What similarities do you see between the French Revolution and the Women's Movement? Do you think that Mary Wollstonecraft felt a kinship with the downtrodden of Paris? Is this why she apologized for their behavior? Do you think that women in the Women's Movement might also have resorted to violence had they not achieved their goals?

INTERNET ASSIGNMENT

Keywords: **"Molly Pitcher"**

                      "Marie Antoinette"

Use the above keywords to find web sites about Molly Pitcher and Marie Antoinette. On the surface these female symbols of two revolutions are quite different. In reality they have many similarities—both were named Mary, both were of Germanic descent, both fought alongside their husbands in revolutionary wars; however, their fates were quite different. What made the lives of these two women so different? What accounts for our very different perceptions of them? Marie Antoinette is often held up as a villain of the French Revolution, but was she really as bad as we think she was?

INTERNET EXPLORATION

In the late eighteenth century the United States was a new country, and it is in this era that we built our national monument and residence for the president: the White House. Most of us cannot get away to visit in person, but http://www.whitehouse.gov/history/whtour/ provides a nice virtual tour of this important state symbol, and more can be found by using "tour White House" as a keyword. How has the White House changed over the years? What makes the White House unique among monuments world wide? What would it be like to live there in Jefferson's time? Roosevelt's? Today? The above site also has tours of the various branches of American government.

MAP EXERCISES

On Outline Map 22.1, plot the following points:

 Lexington

 Boston

 Bunker Hill

 Yorktown

 Valley Forge

 Saratoga

Shade in Saint Domingue.

On Outline Map 22.2, shade in the following:

 French Empire

 Dependent states

 Napoleon's allies

 Regions at war with Napoleon

Outline Map 22.1

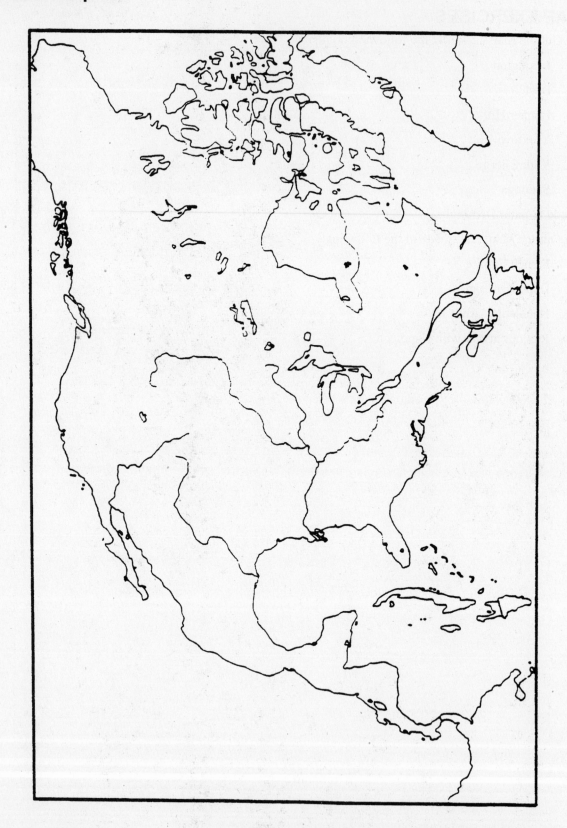

Outline Map 22.2

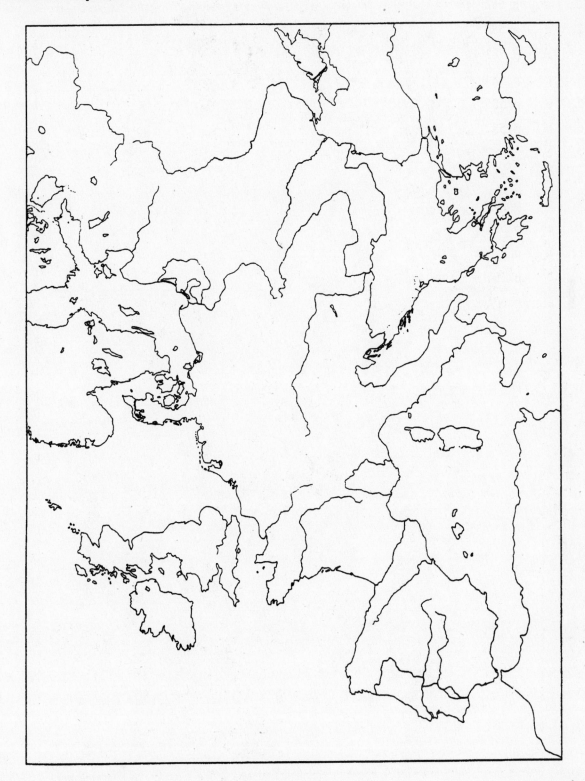

ANSWERS TO MULTIPLE-CHOICE QUESTIONS

1.   a   p. 582
2.   a   p. 582
3.   e   p. 583
4.   a   p. 584
5.   e   p. 585
6.   b   p. 587
7.   c   p. 587
8.   c   p. 587
9.   c   p. 588
10. c   p. 593
11. d   p. 596
12. b   p. 597
13. c   p. 601

CHAPTER 23

The Early Industrial Revolution, 1760–1851

LEARNING OBJECTIVES

After reading Chapter 23 and completing this study chapter, you should be able to explain:

- Why the Industrial Revolution began in Great Britain, and how it transformed the face of Europe, America, and then the world.

- What impact the Industrial Revolution had on the environments and societies that experienced it.

- How the Industrial Revolution and accompanying change influenced politics and economics both at home and abroad.

- What happened in countries in Africa and Asia where the process of industrialization began later than in the West.

CHAPTER OUTLINE

In the outline below, include important themes, concepts, and details in the blank spaces provided. If you find fewer points than you have space for, leave lines blank. If you find more points, add as many lines as necessary.

I. *Introduction*
    A. *The Lunar Society*
        1. _____

        2. _____

        3. _____

    B. *Change for the better*
        1. _____

        2. _____

        3. _____

    C. *Social effects*
        1. _____

        2. _____

3. _____

D. *The effects of the Industrial Revolution were uneven*
1. _____

2. _____

3. _____

II. **Causes of the Industrial Revolution**
A. *Population Growth*
1. *Dramatic population rises in Europe—especially in England and Wales*
a) _____

b) _____

c) _____

2. *Dependable food supplies and job opportunities = high birthrate*
a) _____

b) _____

c) _____

3. *Immigration*
a) _____

b) _____

c) _____

B. *The Agricultural Revolution*
1. *Higher agricultural production aided the Industrial Revolution*
a) _____

b) _____

c) _____

2. *Wealthy landowners "enclosed" the land*
a) _____

b) _____

c) _____

3. *The effects of "enclosure"*
   a) _____

   b) _____

   c) _____

   d) _____

   e) _____

C. *Trade and Inventiveness*
   1. *Most of Europe increased production in traditional ways*
      a) _____

      b) _____

      c) _____

      d) _____

   2. *Trade increased—both locally and internationally*
      a) _____

      b) _____

      c) _____

   3. *Technology and innovation fascinated people*
      a) _____

      b) _____

      c) _____

D. *Britain and Continental Europe*
   1. *Why the Industrial Revolution started in Britain: attitude and society*
      a) _____

b) _____

c) _____

d) _____

e) _____

2. *British water transport, commercial development, and economics*
   a) _____

   b) _____

   c) _____

   d) _____

   e) _____

3. *Everyone else joined the Industrial Revolution*
   a) _____

   b) _____

   c) _____

   d) _____

   e) _____

   f) _____

   g) _____

III. *The Technological Revolution*
   A. *Mass Production: Pottery*
      1. *Before mass production*
         a) _____

         b) _____

c) _____

d) _____

2. *Josiah Wedgwood and the division of labor*

a) _____

b) _____

c) _____

d) _____

e) _____

f) _____

3. *Like minds applied technology to manufacture*

a) _____

b) _____

c) _____

B. *Mechanization: The Cotton Industry*

1. *The demand for cotton fueled innovation*

a) _____

b) _____

c) _____

2. *The spinning jenny and the cotton mill*

a) _____

b) _____

c) _____

d) _____

3. *The mule and the power loom*
   a) _____

   b) _____

   c) _____

   d) _____

   e) _____

4. *Cotton changed the United States*
   a) _____

   b) _____

   c) _____

C. *The Iron Industry*
   1. *Iron was used for weaponry and domestic tools in Eurasia and Africa for thousands of years.*
      a) _____

      b) _____

      c) _____

   2. *Cyclical impact of deforestation*
      a) _____

      b) _____

      c) _____

   3. *Consequences of Abraham Darby's breakthrough*
      a) _____

      b) _____

      c) _____

4. **Changes in manufacturing of guns and tools**
    a) _____

    b) _____

    c) _____

D. **The Steam Engine**
    1. **Newcomen developed the first steam engine**
        a) _____

        b) _____

        c) _____

    2. **James Watt's steam engine**
        a) _____

        b) _____

        c) _____

        d) _____

        e) _____

    3. **Steamboats and steamships**
        a) _____

        b) _____

        c) _____

        d) _____

        e) _____

        f) _____

E. *Railroads*
    1. *Further improvements in the steam engine*
        a) _____

        b) _____

        c) _____

    2. *The Rocket and the railroad mania*
        a) _____

        b) _____

        c) _____

        d) _____

    3. *U.S. railroads*
        a) _____

        b) _____

        c) _____

    4. *The rest of Europe*
        a) _____

        b) _____

        c) _____

F. *Communication over Wires*
    1. *The first practical systems and Samuel Morse*
        a) _____

        b) _____

        c) _____

    2. *Use of the telegraph spreads*
        a) _____

        b) _____

c) _____

IV. *The Impact of the Early Industrial Revolution*
   A.   *The New Industrial Cities*
      1.   *The growth of cities*
         a) _____

         b) _____

         c) _____

         d) _____

         e) _____

      2.   *The lifestyle of the poor*
         a) _____

         b) _____

         c) _____

         d) _____

         e) _____

      3.   *Railroads and diseases*
         a) _____

         b) _____

         c) _____

   B.   *Rural Environments*
      1.   *Changes—especially deforestation—in Europe and the United States*
         a) _____

         b) _____

         c) _____

         d) _____

e) _____

f) _____

g) _____

2. *Industrialization helped Europe's environment*
    a) _____

    b) _____

    c) _____

3. *The transportation revolution: roads, canals, and railroads*
    a) _____

    b) _____

    c) _____

    d) _____

    e) _____

    f) _____

C. *Working Conditions*
    1. *Most industrial work was unskilled, repetitive, and dangerous*
        a) _____

        b) _____

        c) _____

    2. *Industrial work changed family relations and changed women's work*
        a) _____

        b) _____

        c) _____

        d) _____

3. *Child labor*
   a) _____

   b) _____

   c) _____

   d) _____

4. *American industry*
   a) _____

   b) _____

   c) _____

   d) _____

5. *Slavery as part of the Industrial Revolution*
   a) _____

   b) _____

   c) _____

   d) _____

D. *Changes in Society*
   1. *Industrialization increased division between the rich and the poor*
      a) _____

      b) _____

      c) _____

   2. *Wage cuts and wage fluctuations*
      a) _____

      b) _____

      c) _____

d) _____

e) _____

3. *Business cycles and uneven improvement in living conditions*
  a) _____

  b) _____

  c) _____

  d) _____

  e) _____

4. *The real beneficiaries of the Industrial Revolution were the middle class*
  a) _____

  b) _____

  c) _____

  d) _____

  e) _____

  f) _____

V. *New Economic and Political Ideas*
  A. *Laissez Faire and Its Critics*
    1. *Adam Smith*
      a) _____

      b) _____

      c) _____

    2. *Thomas Malthus and David Ricardo*
      a) _____

      b) _____

c) _____

3. *Laissez-faire capitalism*
   a) _____

   b) _____

   c) _____

   d) _____

4. *Jeremy Bentham and Friedrich List and the anti-laissez-faire movement*
   a) _____

   b) _____

   c) _____

   d) _____

B. *Positivists and Utopian Socialists*
   1. *Positivism and the Count of Saint-Simon*
      a) _____

      b) _____

      c) _____

   2. *Utopian socialism and Charles Fourier*
      a) _____

      b) _____

      c) _____

   3. *Robert Owen's "utopia"*
      a) _____

      b) _____

      c) _____

C.   *Protests and Reforms*
     1.   *The coping strategies of the workers*
        a)   _____

        b)   _____

        c)   _____

     2.   *Early labor organizations*
        a)   _____

        b)   _____

        c)   _____

     3.   *Government reforms*
        a)   _____

        b)   _____

        c)   _____

     4.   *The repeal of the corn laws*
        a)   _____

        b)   _____

        c)   _____

VI.   *Industrialization and the Nonindustrial World*
    A.   *China*
     1.   *The Nemesis*
        a)   _____

        b)   _____

        c)   _____

        d)   _____

     2.   *Under attack*
        a)   _____

b) _____

c) _____

B. *Egypt*
1. *Muhammad Ali wanted autonomy and economic success*
    a) _____

    b) _____

    c) _____

    d) _____

2. *The British felt threatened and forced Egypt to eliminate import duties*
    a) _____

    b) _____

    c) _____

3. *Egypt became essentially an economic dependency of Britain*
    a) _____

    b) _____

    c) _____

C. *India*
1. *Britain ruined India's textile industry*
    a) _____

    b) _____

    c) _____

2. *Britain introduced railroads and telegraphs to India*
    a) _____

    b) _____

    c) _____

        3. *The beginning of Indian industry*
            a) _____

            b) _____

            c) _____

VII. *Conclusion*
    A. *New technologies increased humans' power over nature*
        1. _____

        2. _____

        3. _____

    B. *Increased disparity between the rich and the poor*
        1. _____

        2. _____

        3. _____

    C. *Industrialization was a global process*
        1. _____

        2. _____

        3. _____

IDENTIFICATIONS

Define each term and explain why it is significant, including any important dates.

	Identification	Significance
Industrial Revolution		
agricultural revolution		

	Identification	Significance

mass production

Josiah Wedgwood

division of labor

mechanization

Richard Arkwright

cotton

Crystal Palace

mule

iron

steam engine

James Watt

	Identification	Significance
railroads		
electric telegraph		
business cycle		
interchangeable parts		
child labor		
laissez faire		
positivism		
utopian socialism		

MULTIPLE-CHOICE QUESTIONS

Read the entire question, including *all* the possible answers. Then choose the *one* answer that best fits the question.

1. Why did the Industrial Revolution start in Great Britain?
    a. Britain had more innovative people than France or China.
    b. The British put innovations into practice more quickly than other people.
    c. The British were known for their high-quality products.
    d. Britain had unlimited resources.
    e. Britain had the largest empire.

2. Which of the following was *not* one of the five revolutionary innovations that were involved in industrialization?

    a. Mass production through the division of labor
    b. New machines and mechanization
    c. The invention of the time clock
    d. A great increase in the supply of iron
    e. The steam engine and resulting changes

3. Which technological invention allowed the British to undersell high-quality handmade Indian cloth?

    a. The mule
    b. The jenny
    c. The cotton mill
    d. The steam engine
    e. The pyrometer

4. In what two ways did Watt's steam engine differ from previous devices?

    a. It was inexpensive and there was plenty of coal.
    b. It could be used anywhere and there was plenty of coal.
    c. It was inexpensive and could be used anywhere.
    d. It could not be broken by Luddites and was inexpensive.
    e. It used water to create power, and no previous machine had done that.

5. Which of the following diseases was brought about by industrialization?

    a. Tuberculosis
    b. Smallpox
    c. Dysentery
    d. Cholera
    e. Rickets

6. Which of the following statements about Europe's industrialization is true?

    a. In some ways industrialization relieved pressure on the environment.
    b. Industrialization always made the environment worse.
    c. Britain increased its dependence on wood, hay, and wool.
    d. The British used coke exclusively for all industry, especially for smelting iron and baking bread.
    e. Iron was too valuable to be used for anything except steam engines.

7. How much of Ireland's population died in the Potato Famine of 1847–1848?

    a. 5 percent
    b. 10 percent
    c. 25 percent
    d. 40 percent
    e. 50 percent

8. How much of Ireland's population emigrated to England and America due to the Potato Famine of 1847–1848?

    a. 5 percent
    b. 10 percent
    c. 25 percent
    d. 40 percent
    e. 50 percent

9.   Which of the following is *not* true about women in the Industrial Revolution?

    a.   Women generally worked in textiles, just as they had traditionally.
    b.   Women were paid from one-third to one-half of the wages paid to men.
    c.   Other than motherhood, factory work became the main occupation of women.
    d.   Women did work that required less strength than work done by men.
    e.   Women often were domestic workers.

10.   Ordinary people began to benefit from the Industrial Revolution

    a.   immediately.
    b.   by the early 1800s.
    c.   by the 1850s.
    d.   eventually by the 1900s.
    e.   never.

11.   Who were the real beneficiaries of the Industrial Revolution?

    a.   The middle class
    b.   The factory workers
    c.   Women
    d.   Monarchs
    e.   The poor

12.   Which of the following was *not* part of the "cult of domesticity"?

    a.   Middle-class women became solely responsible for the home.
    b.   Middle-class women managed the servants.
    c.   Middle-class women educated the children.
    d.   Middle-class women ran the family's social life.
    e.   Middle-class women ran the family business.

13.   What did Malthus and Ricardo recommend that they felt would solve the plight of the worker?

    a.   Low-cost government loans for home ownership
    b.   The adoption of the minimum wage
    c.   The adoption of the ten-hour work day
    d.   Universal health care
    e.   Sexual abstinence for the workers to prevent pregnancy

SHORT-ANSWER QUESTIONS

Answer each question in one short paragraph, giving the definition, dates, and significance.

1.   Discuss how Josiah Wedgwood's factory can be seen as a microcosm of the Industrial Revolution.

2.   How were rural environments in Britain and western Europe affected by industrialization?

3.   Why were citizens of the United States more wasteful of their forest resources than their European counterparts?

4.   What role did slavery play in the Industrial Revolution in the United States?

5.   Define the "cult of domesticity" and explain its impact.

6.   In what ways did workers respond to harsh working conditions in the factories?

7.   In which regions of the world was industrialization not successful and why?

ESSAY QUESTIONS

Make an outline of each question, listing the major points you want to discuss. Then write your practice essay, following your outline carefully and making sure that you do not skip any of your major points. At this time you will want to add the relevant dates and details that will make your essay persuasive and accurate.

1. List and then discuss the various advantages possessed by Britain during the Industrial Revolution.

2. Many historians have asserted that the steam engine was the single most important invention of the Industrial Revolution. Give their reasons and discuss the impact of this invention.

3. Many groups benefited from the Industrial Revolution—for instance, the entrepreneurs and industrialists. Which groups did not? What was the social cost of the Industrial Revolution?

4. Discuss the revolutions in transportation and communication brought about by the Industrial Revolution.

5. Discuss the various philosophies for and against laissez-faire capitalism (such as those of Smith, Malthus, Ricardo, Bentham, List, Saint-Simon, Fourier, and Owen).

COMPARISON CHARTS

Using information gathered from the text, fill in the blank areas of each chart with the relevant data pertaining to the regions and categories listed. (Not all blank areas will necessarily be used.)

Chart 23.1

FIVE REVOLUTIONARY INNOVATIONS

	Mass Production: Pottery	Mechanization: The Cotton Industry	The Iron Industry	The Steam Engine	Communication over Wires	Social Impact
China						
United States						
Britain						
Belgium/ France						

Chart 23.2

GLOBAL INDUSTRIALIZATION

	Starting Date	Industry	Government Support	Environmental Impacts	Successes	Failures
Britain						
Belgium/ France						
China						
Egypt						
India						
United States						

DIVERSITY AND DOMINANCE

After reading "Diversity and Dominance: Adam Smith and the Division of Labor" in your text, please answer the following additional questions.

Do you think that pin makers would find Smith's treatise inspiring? Or do you think that he is writing more for factory owners? Did most of the technology of the Industrial Revolution benefit the workers?

INTERNET ASSIGNMENT

Keywords: **"Industrial Revolution"**

                       "Romantic Era"

The Industrial Revolution was an era of machines, production, and efficiency. Using the above keywords, explore the images and ideology of the Industrial Era. Now use the last keyword to examine another intellectual and artistic trend occurring during the Industrial Revolution: Romanticism. How are the two related? For additional web materials, you might want to consult the image library at *History WIRED* on *The Earth and Its Peoples* web site (refer to the preface of this study guide for information on how to locate the text home page).

INTERNET EXPLORATION

Railroads have played a vital role in the development of our nation. Use the keywords "Railroad, history" or look at http://cprr.org/Museum/Exhibits.html for several images of the early development of railroads. What effects did the railroads have on the development on the West and towns? What kinds of peoples built the railroads? What kinds of technology were used to build the railroads?

MAP EXERCISE

On Outline Map 23.1, label the following:

        London

        Sheffield

        Birmingham

        Liverpool

        Manchester

        Leeds

        Bristol

Trace the railroad routes in the United Kingdom and Europe.

Outline Map 23.1

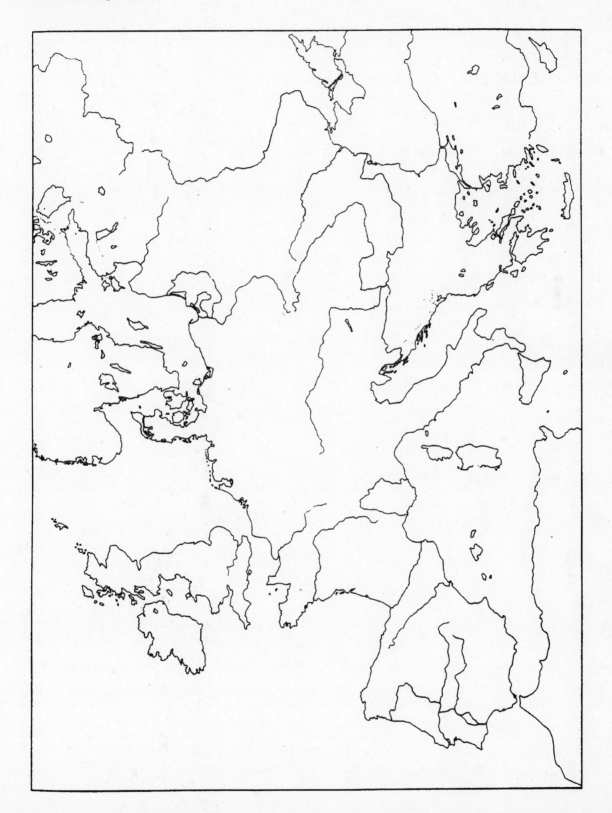

ANSWERS TO MULTIPLE-CHOICE QUESTIONS

1. b   p. 611
2. c   p. 614
3. a   p. 615
4. b   p. 619
5. e   p. 623, 624
6. a   p. 624
7. c   p. 626
8. c   p. 626
9. e   p. 625
10. c   p. 626
11. a   p. 626
12. e   p. 626
13. e   p. 627

CHAPTER 24

Nation Building and Economic Transformation in the Americas, 1800–1890

LEARNING OBJECTIVES

After reading Chapter 24 and completing this study chapter, you should be able to explain:

- How the independence movements of North and South America began, what groups were involved, and how the colonizers responded.

- How these new nations developed their own distinct institutions, and how the land, powerful individuals, economics, and their neighbors influenced their development.

- What role non-northern European peoples—such as former African slaves, Amerindians, southern Europeans, and Asian immigrants—played in the development and success of nations.

- What kinds of reforms Americans called for, and what was involved in promoting sometimes difficult movements, such as the abolition of slavery, the protection of native lands, and the women's movement.

- What changes people made in the environment, what benefits they derived from those changes, and what price they paid for them.

CHAPTER OUTLINE

In the outline below, include important themes, concepts, and details in the blank spaces provided. If you find fewer points than you have space for, leave lines blank. If you find more points, add as many lines as necessary.

I. *Introduction*
   A. *The French under Napoleon III seized power in Mexico*
      1. _____

      2. _____

      3. _____

   B. *Maximilian deposed*
      1. _____

      2. _____

      3. _____

 C. *Spanish and Portuguese colonies in the Americas gain independence*

   1. _____

   2. _____

   3. _____

 D. *Problems with which new nation-states must grapple*

   1. _____

   2. _____

   3. _____

   4. _____

II. *Independence in Latin America, 1800–1830*

 A. *Roots of Revolution, to 1810*

   1. *Great works of the Enlightenment and Napoleon III's decision to invade Portugal*

    a) _____

    b) _____

    c) _____

   2. *The Junta Central*

    a) _____

    b) _____

    c) _____

   3. *The growth of American nationalism*

    a) _____

    b) _____

    c) _____

B. *Spanish South America, 1810–1825*

   1. *Independence declared in Caracas Venezuela in 1811*

      a) _____

      b) _____

      c) _____

   2. *Simón Bolívar*

      a) _____

      b) _____

      c) _____

      d) _____

      e) _____

      f) _____

   3. *Gran Colombia*

      a) _____

      b) _____

      c) _____

   4. *Buenos Aires and Río de la Plata*

      a) _____

      b) _____

      c) _____

      d) _____

      e) _____

      f) _____

C. *Mexico, 1810–1823*
 1. *Spain's richest colony*
  a) _____

  b) _____

  c) _____

 2. *Revolution against Spanish control*
  a) _____

  b) _____

  c) _____

 3. *Miguel Hidalgo y Costilla*
  a) _____

  b) _____

  c) _____

  d) _____

 4. *José María Morelos and Col. Agustín de Iturbide*
  a) _____

  b) _____

  c) _____

  d) _____

D. *Brazil, to 1831*
 1. *King John VI must return to Portugal*
  a) _____

  b) _____

  c) _____

2. ***Brazilians began to reevaluate Brazil's relationship with Portugal***
   a) _____

   b) _____

   c) _____

3. ***Pedro I***
   a) _____

   b) _____

   c) _____

   d) _____

   e) _____

   f) _____

III. ***The Problem of Order, 1825–1890***
   A. ***Constitutional Experiments***
      1. ***Constitutionalism***
         a) _____

         b) _____

         c) _____

      2. ***The British North Americans and the Spanish and Portuguese South Americans have different experience in self-government***
         a) _____

         b) _____

         c) _____

      3. ***Canada***
         a) _____

         b) _____

c) _____

d) _____

e) _____

f) _____

4.   *Latin American nations struggle*
    a) _____

    b) _____

    c) _____

5.   *The political role of the Catholic Church*
    a) _____

    b) _____

    c) _____

6.   *Limiting the power of the military*
    a) _____

    b) _____

    c) _____

B.   *Personalist Leaders*
    1.   *Many used newly earned revolutionary status to gain power*
        a) _____

        b) _____

        c) _____

        d) _____

        e) _____

2. *Personalist politics were more influential in Latin America*
   a) _____

   b) _____

   c) _____

   d) _____

3. *Marginalized groups and populist leaders*
   a) _____

   b) _____

   c) _____

4. *José Antonio Páez (Venezuela)*
   a) _____

   b) _____

   c) _____

   d) _____

   e) _____

5. *Andrew Jackson (United States)*
   a) _____

   b) _____

   c) _____

   d) _____

   e) _____

   f) _____

6. *Personalist leaders in Latin America*

    a) _____

    b) _____

    c) _____

C. *The Threat of Regionalism*
1. *Newly independent states were weak and many suffered overthrow*

    a) _____

    b) _____

    c) _____

    d) _____

2. *Mexico, Central America, and "Gran Colombia"*

    a) _____

    b) _____

    c) _____

    d) _____

3. *Argentina*

    a) _____

    b) _____

    c) _____

    d) _____

4. *The United States*

    a) _____

    b) _____

    c) _____

d) _____

e) _____

f) _____

D.   *Foreign Interventions and Regional Wars*
1.   *Wars helped establish regional powers*
a) _____

b) _____

c) _____

2.   *The War of 1812*
a) _____

b) _____

c) _____

3.   *British and French threat to Latin America*
a) _____

b) _____

c) _____

d) _____

e) _____

4.   *The United States expanded territory through warfare with Mexico*
a) _____

b) _____

c) _____

d) _____

e) _____

5.   **France and Mexico**
   a) _____

   b) _____

   c) _____

6.   **Chile asserted dominance and Uruguay and Paraguay get caught in the middle of regional conflict**
   a) _____

   b) _____

   c) _____

   d) _____

   e) _____

E.   **Native Peoples and the Nation-State**
   1.   **Colonial government tried to control settlement into Amerindian lands**
      a) _____

      b) _____

      c) _____

   2.   **The Amerindian threat through 1812**
      a) _____

      b) _____

      c) _____

      d) _____

      e) _____

   3.   **U.S. invasion of Amerindian lands and the loss of Native American culture**
      a) _____

b) _____

c) _____

d) _____

e) _____

f) _____

g) _____

h) _____

4. *Indigenous peoples of Argentina and Chile*
   a) _____

   b) _____

   c) _____

   d) _____

   e) _____

5. *The Maya in Mexico*
   a) _____

   b) _____

   c) _____

   d) _____

   e) _____

IV. *The Challenge of Social and Economic Change*
   A. *The Abolition of Slavery*
      1. *The struggle for abolition in the United States*
         a) _____

         b) _____

c) _____

d) _____

e) _____

2. *Women and free African-Americans were disenfranchised and yet played important roles*

a) _____

b) _____

c) _____

d) _____

e) _____

3. *Abraham Lincoln and the Civil War*

a) _____

b) _____

c) _____

d) _____

4. *Brazil*

a) _____

b) _____

c) _____

d) _____

e) _____

5. *Abolition in the Caribbean and the British role*

a) _____

b) _____

c) _____

d) _____

e) _____

f) _____

6. *Cuba and Puerto Rico*

a) _____

b) _____

c) _____

d) _____

e) _____

B. *Immigration*

1. *Early immigration was mostly non-European*

a) _____

b) _____

c) _____

2. *European immigration increased dramatically during the nineteenth century*

a) _____

b) _____

c) _____

d) _____

3. *Asian immigration and hostility*

a) _____

b) _____

        c) _____

        d) _____

        e) _____

        f) _____

    4.   ***Some Europeans faced discrimination too***

        a) _____

        b) _____

        c) _____

        d) _____

        e) _____

        f) _____

    5.   ***Assimilation seen as the only solution***

        a) _____

        b) _____

        c) _____

C. ***American Cultures***

    1.   ***Coping mechanisms of immigrants***

        a) _____

        b) _____

        c) _____

    2.   ***Acculturation***

        a) _____

        b) _____

c) _____

3. *Immigrants influence new countries: language, food, music, and unions*
   a) _____

   b) _____

   c) _____

D. *Women's Rights and the Struggle for Social Justice*
   1. *Women were active in social causes and fought for more rights*
      a) _____

      b) _____

      c) _____

      d) _____

      e) _____

      f) _____

   2. *Poor women entered the work force in large numbers*
      a) _____

      b) _____

      c) _____

   3. *Racial discrimination persisted despite abolition and attempts at racial integration*
      a) _____

      b) _____

      c) _____

   4. *Latin America*
      a) _____

      b) _____

c) _____

d) _____

e) _____

E. *Development and Underdevelopment*
   1. **Industrial Revolution products and diversification**
      a) _____

      b) _____

      c) _____

   2. **The mining boom**
      a) _____

      b) _____

      c) _____

   3. **Economic integration and foreign capital**
      a) _____

      b) _____

      c) _____

      d) _____

      e) _____

      f) _____

   4. **Two distinct economic tracks developed: developed and underdeveloped**
      a) _____

      b) _____

      c) _____

d) _____

e) _____

5. *The United States' development*
   a) _____

   b) _____

   c) _____

   d) _____

   e) _____

6. *Canada*
   a) _____

   b) _____

   c) _____

7. *Latin America*
   a) _____

   b) _____

   c) _____

   d) _____

   e) _____

   f) _____

F. *Altered Environments*
   1. *Unwise forestry and agricultural practices*
      a) _____

      b) _____

      c) _____

      d) _____

  2. *Rapid urbanization and the demand for building materials put heavy pressure on the environment*

      a) _____

      b) _____

      c) _____

      d) _____

      e) _____

  3. *Mining*

      a) _____

      b) _____

      c) _____

  4. *Beginning conservation movements*

      a) _____

      b) _____

      c) _____

V. *Conclusion*

  A. *Independence did not always lead to internal stability*

    1. _____

    2. _____

    3. _____

  B. *The effects of industrialization*

    1. _____

    2. _____

3. _____

C. *Improvements and challenges*
    1. _____

    2. _____

    3. _____

IDENTIFICATIONS

Define each term and explain why it is significant, including any important dates.

	Identification	Significance

Napoleon III

Simón Bolívar

Miguel Hidalgo y Costilla

José María Morelos

Confederation of 1867

personalist leaders

Andrew Jackson

José Antonio Páez

	Identification	Significance
Benito Juárez		
Tecumseh		
Caste War		
abolitionists		
acculturation		
Indian Removal Act		
Frederick Douglass		
Abraham Lincoln		
Chinese Exclusion Act		
Women's Rights Convention		
development		

Identification   Significance

underdevelopment

MULTIPLE-CHOICE QUESTIONS

Read the entire question, including *all* the possible answers. Then choose the *one* answer that best fits the question.

1. What spurred the Spanish and Portuguese colonies in the Americas to declare independence?

   a. Numerous slave revolts throughout South America weakened colonists' confidence in the Crowns' ability to administer their distant colonies.

   b. The colonies developed a sense of distinct identity, separate from Europeans.

   c. The treaties signed with the native peoples for land had run out, but the colonists did not want to give up their homes, and so they declared independence.

   d. Christian belief and colonialism were incompatible.

   e. Napoleon invaded Spain and Portugal, which caused a crisis in legitimacy.

2. What kinds of troops did José de San Martín find most effective in his battles for South American independence?

   a. Members of the aristocracy

   b. Deserters from the Spanish army

   c. Mercenary soldiers

   d. Former slaves and gauchos

   e. Priests

3. Which of the following was Spain's richest and most populous colony in the early nineteenth century?

   a. Mexico

   b. Argentina

   c. San Domingue

   d. Peru

   e. Río de la Plata

4. The arrival of the Portuguese royal family in Brazil in 1808

   a. caused a peasant uprising.

   b. helped to maintain the loyalty of the colonial elite.

   c. galvanized the Catholic Church's nationalism.

   d. depressed the local economy.

   e. spurred and independence movement.

5. In reaction to the arbitrary tyrannical authority of colonial rulers, revolutionary leaders in the Americas

   a. espoused constitutionalism.

   b. advocated immediate military action against the government.

   c. instigated social unrest and anarchy.

   d. requested better representation in the colonial government.

   e. turned to assassination of government officials.

6. How many constitutions, combined, were ratified and then rejected by Venezuela and Chile from 1811 to 1833?

    a. Two
    b. Nine
    c. Sixteen
    d. Twenty-seven
    e. Fifty-three

7. Why did power often end up in the hands of the Latin American military?

    a. Military leaders were needed to put down frequent slave insurrections and revolts by native peoples.
    b. Since Latin American countries were always at war with each other, they needed strong military governments to defend themselves.
    c. The military leaders had more experience running governments.
    d. Few citizens were willing to support civilian politicians against the military.
    e. A strong military was necessary to keep the former colonizing country from taking over again.

8. What factor made personalist politics more influential in Latin America than in the United States?

    a. Latin American leaders were more charismatic than North American leaders.
    b. Latin America developed stable political institutions much more slowly than did North America.
    c. North Americans had a stronger belief in democracy.
    d. North Americans did not think that their individual politicians were strong enough to challenge political institutions.
    e. Spain was still feudal and England was not.

9. Which of the following did nearly all of the first American republics' constitutions have in common?

    a. They granted women the right to vote.
    b. They abolished private property.
    c. They were adamantly against the abolition of slavery.
    d. They excluded large numbers of poor citizens from full political participation.
    e. They granted enormous power to the church.

10. Which of the following about Andrew Jackson is *not* true?

    a. He defeated British forces in 1815 at the Battle of New Orleans.
    b. He seized Florida from the Spanish in 1818.
    c. He was always careful to follow the instructions of the civil authorities.
    d. He was popular among frontier residents because of his courage and individuality.
    e. He had an untidy personal life, and often dueled.

11. The most far-reaching effect of the U.S. Civil War, besides the abolition of slavery, was

    a. the transfer of political power from the plantation South to the industrial North.
    b. the passage of laws that guaranteed equality to all men.
    c. a complete restructuring of the U.S. economic system.
    d. the apprenticeship of former slaves to new industrial northern employers.
    e. the assassination of Abraham Lincoln.

12. What three American countries achieved income levels similar to Europe by 1900?

    a. Mexico, Canada, and the United States
    b. Canada, the United States, and Brazil
    c. Brazil, Argentina, and Uruguay
    d. The United States, Argentina, and Canada
    e. Jamaica, Haiti, and the United States

13. Which one of the following did *not* improve the profitability of the cattle industry?

    a. Barbed wire
    b. Tariffs
    c. Refrigeration
    d. Lower freight costs
    e. Telegraphs

14. Which of the following did *not* foster rapid economic growth in the United States?

    a. Foreign investment in high technology
    b. Rapid population growth due to immigration
    c. Widespread land ownership
    d. High levels of individual wealth
    e. High literacy rates

15. Georgia cotton farmers abandoned crop rotation after 1870

    a. but this was a bad idea because it caused soil exhaustion.
    b. because the government encouraged them to clear new land.
    c. because chemical fertilizers were developed, making crop rotation unnecessary.
    d. because the bottom fell out of the market.
    e. because they switched to tobacco, which is better for the soil.

SHORT-ANSWER QUESTIONS

Answer each question in one short paragraph, giving the definition, dates, and significance.

1. Simón Bolívar was an influential figure in Latin American independence. Discuss the success rates of his methods.

2. Discuss the impact that the notion of popular sovereignty had on the Western Hemisphere. What institutions did people want to put in place, and how successful were their efforts?

3. What was the character of the relationship between the Catholic Church and the newly formed Latin American governments?

4. How did the movements of white settlers across the American continent affect the Amerindians? How did the different local governments respond?

5. How did new technologies transform the lives of the Plains Indians? Be sure to discuss the changing role of women.

6. Discuss one reform movement in the Americas. What were the goals of the reformers, and how successful were they in achieving these goals?

7. Discuss the nineteenth-century American encouragement of assimilation. What were the advantages and disadvantages of this policy?

8. Discuss the beginning and impact of the women's movement in America. What were its goals, who participated, and how successful was the movement?

ESSAY QUESTIONS

Make an outline of each question, listing the major points you want to discuss. Then write your practice essay, following your outline carefully and making sure that you do not skip any of your major points. At this time you will want to add the relevant dates and details that will make your essay persuasive and accurate.

1.   Trace the rise of three political leaders, choosing them from both North and Latin America. Compare and contrast their careers.

2.   Who were the abolitionists in the Americas and what were their goals? How did slaves help in their own emancipation? How did the abolition of slavery affect the Americas?

3.   Discuss the internal struggles faced by the developing countries of Latin America. Why were things so difficult?

4.   Discuss European and non-European immigration to the Americas. Why did these immigrants come, and how were they received by people already living in the United States?

5.   How was the American environment changed during the nineteenth and early twentieth centuries? What benefits did people gain from manipulating the environment? What problems did such manipulation cause?

COMPARISON CHARTS

Using information gathered from the text, fill in the blank areas of each chart with the relevant data pertaining to the regions and categories listed. (Not all blank areas will necessarily be used.)

Chart 24.1

LATIN AMERICAN INDEPENDENCE

	Imperial Country and Date of Independence	Individuals and Social Classes Supporting Revolution	Individuals and Social Classes Opposing Revolution	Methods	Challenges to the Old Order	New Government Systems	Religion	Legacy
Venezuela, Colombia, and Ecuador								
Argentina, Uruguay, Paraguay, and Bolivia								
Chile and Peru								
Mexico								

Chart 24.2

UNEQUAL PROTECTION: CONSTITUTION AND CHALLENGES

	Native Peoples	Women	Non-Property Owners	Slaves/Former Slaves	Regional Interests	Secessionist Movements and Revolutions
United States						
Canada						
Brazil						
Mexico						
Argentina						

DIVERSITY AND DOMINANCE

After reading "Diversity and Dominance: The Afro-Brazilian Experience, 1828" in your text, answer the following additional questions.

The introduction to this article mentions that Reverend Robert Walsh's account "reflects racial attitudes of the time." Can you see an additional explanation for his comparison of slaves to animals?

How does Walsh feel about the semi-free and free Blacks? On what did Walsh believe the character of Africans in America depended? What conclusion does he therefore reach?

INTERNET ASSIGNMENT

Keywords: **"Native American Removal Act"**

                "Oregon Trail, Images"

Both the westward migrations of Native Americans, and the migration of peoples on the Oregon Trail were westward migrations of Americans, but they were quite different. Use the above keywords to find written and visual sources about these topics. You might also want to consult the *History WIRED* image library on *The Earth and Its Peoples* web site (refer to the preface of this study guide for information on how to locate the text home page). What inspired and precipitated each movement? What was the result of each? How were they connected ideologically?

INTERNET EXPLORATION

The Underground Railroad brought together blacks and whites in the noble cause of human freedom, but despite its high ideals, it was a difficult and dangerous task. Take a virtual trip from the slave states of the south to Canada by using the keywords "Underground Railroad" or visiting one or both of these sites: www.nps.gov/undergroundrr/contents.htm and www.nationalgeographic.com/railroad to see what travelers on the Underground Railroad experienced.

MAP EXERCISES

On Outline Map 24.1, shade in the following:

> Mexico in 1821
>
> Gran Colombia
>
> United Provinces of Central America
>
> Empire of Brazil
>
> United Provinces of Río de la Plata

On Outline Map 24.2, indicate these changes by using different colors for shading:

> The Dominion of Canada in 1873
>
> The growth of the United States from 1783 to 1853

Outline Map 24.1

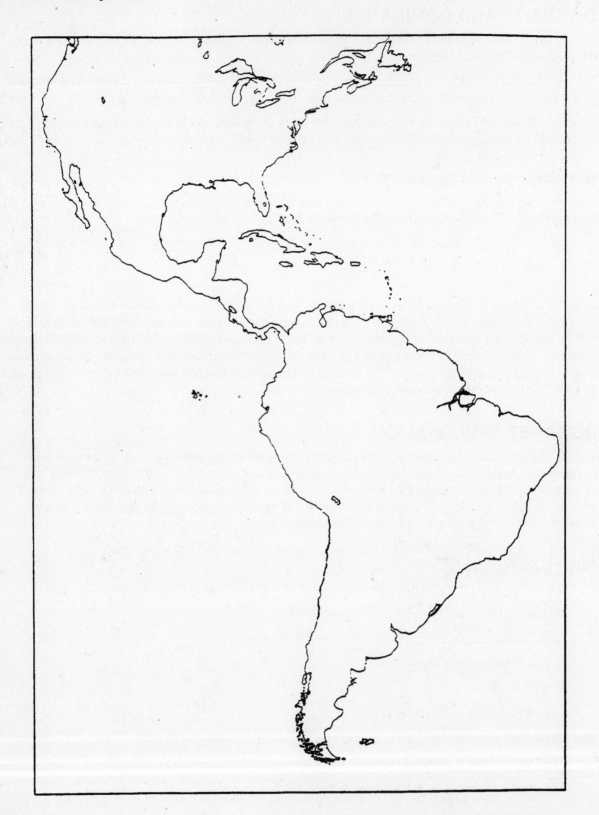

Outline Map 24.2

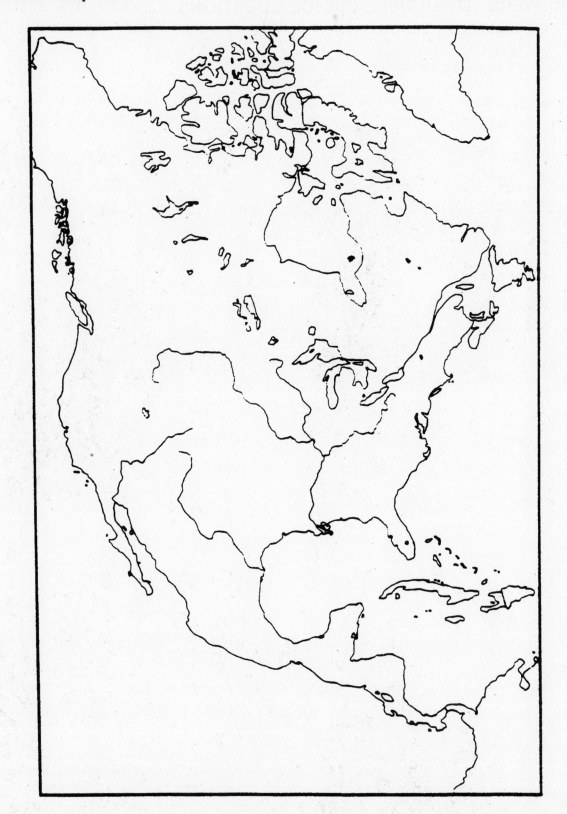

ANSWERS TO MULTIPLE-CHOICE QUESTIONS

1. e   p. 634
2. d   p. 637
3. a   p. 637
4. b   p. 638
5. a   p. 639
6. b   p. 639
7. d   p. 642
8. b   p. 643
9. d   p. 643
10. c   p. 643
11. a   p. 646
12. d   p. 656
13. b   p. 656
14. a   p. 657
15. a   p. 660

CHAPTER 25

Africa, India, and the New British Empire, 1750-1870

LEARNING OBJECTIVES

After reading Chapter 25 and completing this study chapter, you should be able to explain:

- How new or revitalized states arose in Africa, what challenges they faced, and how they confronted those challenges.

- How the end of the exportation of African slaves outside Africa changed the types of goods traded, the types of workers used on plantations and where they came from, and how it influenced the increase in slavery in Africa.

- How colonizers, especially Great Britain, influenced their colonies, what different styles of control they chose to use, how they were received by native peoples, and in what ways colonial rule facilitated the rise of nationalism in some countries, particularly India.

- How the colonies of Australia and New Zealand were established, and how they differed in conception and execution from Britain's other colonies.

CHAPTER OUTLINE

In the outline below, include important themes, concepts, and details in the blank spaces provided. If you find fewer points than you have space for, leave lines blank. If you find more points, add as many lines as necessary.

I. *Introduction*
   A. *Tippu Sultan tried to use the French against the British to drive the British East India Company out of India*
      1. _____

      2. _____

      3. _____

      4. _____

      5. _____

      6. _____

B. *Battle between Britain and France*
   1. _____

   2. _____

   3. _____

C. *Tippu suffered defeat*
   1. _____

   2. _____

   3. _____

II. *Changes and Exchanges in Africa*
  A. *New Africa States*
    1. *Shaka and the Zulu Kingdom*
      a) _____

      b) _____

      c) _____

      d) _____

      e) _____

      f) _____

    2. *Islamic reform movements created new states*
      a) _____

      b) _____

      c) _____

    3. *Sokoto Caliphate*
      a) _____

      b) _____

      c) _____

4. *Education and the spread of Islam*
    a) _____

    b) _____

    c) _____

    d) _____

B. *Modernization in Egypt and Ethiopia*
   1. *Muhammad Ali's plan to strengthen Egypt*
    a) _____

    b) _____

    c) _____

    d) _____

    e) _____

    f) _____

   2. *Ismail, cotton, and debt in Egypt*
    a) _____

    b) _____

    c) _____

    d) _____

   3. *Ethiopia*
    a) _____

    b) _____

    c) _____

    d) _____

e) _____

C. *European Penetration*
   1. *The French in Algeria*
      a) _____

      b) _____

      c) _____

      d) _____

      e) _____

   2. *Explorers search for the origins and courses of Africa's great rivers*
      a) _____

      b) _____

      c) _____

      d) _____

   3. *David Livingstone (1813–1873)*
      a) _____

      b) _____

      c) _____

      d) _____

D. *Abolition and Legitimate Trade*
   1. *The growth of trade and Europe's role*
      a) _____

      b) _____

      c) _____

   2. *The abolition of the slave trade and the role of the British*
      a) _____

b) _____

c) _____

d) _____

e) _____

f) _____

3. *There was resistance to ending the slave trade*
   a) _____

   b) _____

   c) _____

4. *"Legitimate" trade and the Niger Delta slavery*
   a) _____

   b) _____

   c) _____

   d) _____

   e) _____

5. *African slavery and Jaja*
   a) _____

   b) _____

   c) _____

   d) _____

6. *The spread of Western cultural influences*
   a) _____

   b) _____

c) _____

d) _____

e) _____

f) _____

   E.   *Secondary Empires in Eastern Africa*
      1.   *The slave trade moved to Eastern Africa and the trade empires*
         a) _____

         b) _____

         c) _____

         d) _____

         e) _____

         f) _____

      2.   *Tippu Tip and Zanzibari traders*
         a) _____

         b) _____

         c) _____

         d) _____

      3.   *Egypt's expansion*
         a) _____

         b) _____

         c) _____

III. *India Under British Rule*
   A.   *Company Men*
      1.   *The weakening of Mughal power*
         a) _____

b) _____

c) _____

2. *The success of the East India Companies was due to the "Company Men"*
   a) _____

   b) _____

   c) _____

3. *The British in Bengal*
   a) _____

   b) _____

   c) _____

4. *The British in Southern India and Bombay*
   a) _____

   b) _____

   c) _____

   d) _____

B. *Raj and Rebellion, 1818–1857*
   1. *The beginnings of the East India Company*
      a) _____

      b) _____

      c) _____

   2. *The British wanted to create an India in their own image*
      a) _____

      b) _____

      c) _____

d) _____

e) _____

f) _____

3.   *The bolstering of "traditions"*
   a) _____

   b) _____

   c) _____

   d) _____

4.   *The transformation of the economy was a double-edged sword*
   a) _____

   b) _____

   c) _____

   d) _____

5.   *Discontent and the "Sepoy Rebellion"*
   a) _____

   b) _____

   c) _____

   d) _____

   e) _____

   f) _____

C.   *Political Reform and Industrial Impact*
   1.   *The impact of the Sepoy Rebellion on British rule*
      a) _____

      b) _____

c) _____

d) _____

e) _____

2. *The Indian Civil Service*
    a) _____

    b) _____

    c) _____

    d) _____

    e) _____

3. *Technology and agricultural products*
    a) _____

    b) _____

    c) _____

    d) _____

4. *Transportation and communication—especially railroads*
    a) _____

    b) _____

    c) _____

    d) _____

    e) _____

5. *Cholera*
    a) _____

    b) _____

c) _____

d) _____

D. *Rising Indian Nationalism*
   1. *Brahmo Samaj: an Indian attempt at reform*
      a) _____

      b) _____

      c) _____

      d) _____

   2. *The use of Western secular values to reform India*
      a) _____

      b) _____

      c) _____

      d) _____

   3. *The middle class and nationalism*
      a) _____

      b) _____

      c) _____

IV. *Britain's Eastern Empire*
   A. *Colonies and Commerce*
      1. *The end of competition from the French*
         a) _____

         b) _____

         c) _____

      2. *The British took over Dutch possessions*
         a) _____

b) _____

c) _____

d) _____

e) _____

3. *Cape Colony and Afrikaners*
   a) _____

   b) _____

   c) _____

   d) _____

4. *The British in Southeast Asia*
   a) _____

   b) _____

   c) _____

   d) _____

   e) _____

B. *Imperial Policies and Shipping*
   1. *A reluctant empire?*
      a) _____

      b) _____

      c) _____

   2. *Free trade and expanding trade networks*
      a) _____

      b) _____

      c) _____

d) _____

3. *Manufactured goods go to the colonies and the beneficial aspects of trade*
   a) _____

   b) _____

   c) _____

   d) _____

4. *Great improvements in shipbuilding*
   a) _____

   b) _____

   c) _____

   d) _____

   e) _____

C. *Colonization of Australia and New Zealand*
   1. *Captain Cook and Australia and New Zealand*
      a) _____

      b) _____

      c) _____

      d) _____

      e) _____

   2. *British patterns in Australia*
      a) _____

      b) _____

      c) _____

3. **British settlers in New Zealand**
    a) _____

    b) _____

    c) _____

    d) _____

D. *New Labor Migrations*
    1. **Many non-European immigrants worked on sugar plantations where they replaced slave labor**
        a) _____

        b) _____

        c) _____

    2. **Indian, Chinese, and African labor trade**
        a) _____

        b) _____

        c) _____

    3. **These laborers went to places which had not known slavery and cheap transport**
        a) _____

        b) _____

        c) _____

    4. **Indentured servants**
        a) _____

        b) _____

        c) _____

        d) _____

        e) _____

f) _____

V.   *Conclusion*
    A.   *A theory of European dominance*
       1.   _____

       2.   _____

       3.   _____

    B.   *British commercial expansion: positives and negatives*
       1.   _____

       2.   _____

       3.   _____

    C.   *The importance of local cultures and Asian and African power*
       1.   _____

       2.   _____

       3.   _____

       4.   _____

IDENTIFICATIONS

Define each term and explain why it is significant, including any important dates.

	Identification	**Significance**

Zulu

Sokoto Caliphate

modernization

	Identification	Significance

Muhammad Ali

"legitimate" trade

palm oil

recaptives

nawab

Company Men

sepoy

British Raj

Sepoy Rebellion

durbar

Indian Civil Service

	Identification	Significance
Indian National Congress		

Cape Colony

clipper ship

Captain James Cook

contract of indenture

MULTIPLE-CHOICE QUESTIONS

Read the entire question, including *all* the possible answers. Then choose the *one* answer that best fits the question.

1. What made possible the seclusion of women in their homes in the Sokoto Caliphate?
    a. The government tax relief given to families for following strict Muslim practices
    b. An increase in the slavery used for agricultural production
    c. A popular movement led by the women themselves for closer compliance with the Quran
    d. More wealth generated by increased trade
    e. Occupation of the caliphate by the British

2. What led to Egypt's partial occupation by the French and the British?
    a. Muhammad Ali's aggressive modernization
    b. The collapse of the market for Egyptian cotton, which made it impossible for Egypt to pay its debts
    c. Debt incurred in the building of the Suez Canal
    d. Egypt's invasion of Algeria
    e. Ismail's failed alliance with India to end European colonization

3. Which of the following was *not* a goal of independent African explorers?

    a. Finding the source of Africa's mighty rivers
    b. Tracing the course of Africa's rivers and streams
    c. Scouting out locations for possible Christian missions
    d. Assessing the continent's possible mineral wealth
    e. Stirring up political discord so that their imperial sponsors could move in and take advantage of the resulting unrest

4. To which group can be best attributed the pillage and havoc that took place in the once peaceful center of Africa in the late nineteenth century?

    a. Tippu Tip and his followers
    b. Zanzibari traders
    c. Europeans who both supplied the weapons and consumed the cloves
    d. The slave traders of the sixteenth through nineteenth centuries
    e. The peasants during widespread uprisings and protests over the renewed slave trade

5. When Mughal power weakened in the eighteenth century, which foreign nation was the first to intrude?

    a. Great Britain
    b. Iran
    c. United States
    d. Japan
    e. France

6. Britain used "traditions" in India to

    a. impress foreign ambassadors.
    b. help institute reforms.
    c. help make British citizens abroad feel less homesick.
    d. exalt the position of British citizens and their followers.
    e. help ordinary Indian people.

7. What change occurred in India's economic situation under British imperial control?

    a. India changed from being the world's largest exporter of cotton textiles in the eighteenth century to being predominantly an exporter of raw cotton to Britain in the nineteenth century.
    b. India changed from being a war-torn country under Mughal control to one in which infant mortality, starvation, disease, and poverty were virtually eradicated by the twentieth century.
    c. India changed from being a country of ethnic harmony to one in which ethnic strife was rampant.
    d. British control actually had little effect on India's economy.
    e. India changed from being a country with frequent religion-inspired divisiveness to a modern nation in which law, democracy, and equality were paramount.

8. Which of the following was *not* a cause for discontent among the sepoys?

    a. The active recruitment of Sikhs as sepoys
    b. The active recruitment of Gurkhas as sepoys
    c. The use of new ammunition greased with forbidden animal fats
    d. The requirement that they wear shoes, which is against Hindu custom
    e. The requirement that sepoys serve overseas

9. The key reason blocking qualified Indians' entry into the upper administration of their country was

    a. lack of education.
    b. the resentment they felt, which discouraged them from pursuing a career in government.
    c. lack of initiative and foresight on the part of Indian parents.
    d. the racist contempt that most British officials felt for the people they ruled.
    e. the exams were held in England, and Indians were not allowed to travel there.

10. The British-built railroad system in India was the

    a. largest in the world.
    b. the fifth largest in the world.
    c. the eighth largest in the world.
    d. the twenty-first largest in the world.
    e. the smallest in the world.

11. The first Indian National Congress was convened in 1885

    a. to request that the British quit interfering with Indian traditions.
    b. to demand an end to the caste system.
    c. to lobby the British government for more opportunities for Indians in the civil service.
    d. to demand independence.
    e. to request that more Indians be allowed in the military.

12. Why did the Dutch authorize the British to take over Dutch possessions overseas?

    a. As a reward for helping out in the War of Austrian Succession
    b. To keep these possessions out of the hands of the French
    c. As part of war reparations for their defeat in the Franco-Prussian War
    d. So that the two East India Companies could merge, thus increasing profits for both nations
    e. The Dutch did not authorize this; the British took these possessions by force

13. What event of 1851 hastened the end of Australia's use as a penal colony?

    a. The Great Queensland Prison Revolt
    b. A petition circulated by the prisoners demanding freedom and promising good behavior
    c. The discovery of gold
    d. A parliamentary vote against the inhumanity of the penal colony system
    e. An uprising of the Aborigines

SHORT-ANSWER QUESTIONS

Answer each question in one short paragraph, giving the definition, dates, and significance.

1. What conditions made it possible for the British to defeat the Mughal Empire?

2. Discuss the career of Shaka Zulu. Why was his movement necessary and what techniques did he use? Was he successful?

3. Discuss Muhammad Ali's use of Western technology. Did it benefit Egypt? Why or why not?

4. Discuss the increase of slavery in Africa in the nineteenth century. What motivated this increase, and what were its results?

5. Discuss Britain's attempt at social reform in India.

6. Why did the British governors of South Africa prohibit any expansion of the white-settler frontier, and how did the Afrikaners respond?

ESSAY QUESTIONS

Make an outline of each question, listing the major points you want to discuss. Then write your practice essay, following your outline carefully and making sure that you do not skip any of your major points. At this time you will want to add the relevant dates and details that will make your essay persuasive and accurate.

1. Discuss British participation in the establishment and enforcement of the ban on the export of new slaves from Africa. What motivated the British, what methods did they use to carry out their agenda, and how successful were they?

2. What inspired the establishment of free African states in West Africa? How were they run, and what challenges did they face?

3. Discuss the underlying goal of the new British Empire. What challenges did the British face, and how successful were they in attaining their goals?

4. Discuss the reciprocal relationship between any three colonies and their colonizer(s). How did each operate, and what benefits were gained from the systems?

5. Describe the new labor migrations of the nineteenth century. Why did individuals choose to migrate, why did certain governments encourage immigration, from where and to where did people migrate, and what were the results of these migrations?

COMPARISON CHARTS

Using information gathered from the text, fill in the blank areas of each chart with the relevant data pertaining to the regions and categories listed. (Not all blank areas will necessarily be used.)

Chart 25.1

EUROPEAN PRESSURE IN THREE REGIONS

	Imperial Nation	Private Enterprise	Native Elite	European Elite	Pressures	Products	Slavery	Methods of Control	Losers	Beneficiaries
West Africa										
India										
Southeast Asia, Australia, and the Pacific										

Chart 25.2

THE SUN NEVER SETS

	West Africa, East Africa, and South Africa	India	Southeast Asia	Caribbean	Australia and New Zealand	Canada
British Imports						
British Exports						

DIVERSITY AND DOMINANCE

After reading "Diversity and Dominance: Ceremonials of Imperial Domination" in your text, answer the following additional questions.

What role do you think the viceroy fulfilled for the British Empire? With all of the ceremonies and state occasions attended by the viceroy of India, when did he have time to get any work done?

INTERNET ASSIGNMENT

Keywords: **"British Raj, India"**

                "Ethiopia, Menelik II"

The late nineteenth century was a time of growing imperialism by Europeans. It was during this time that many formerly independent nations in Asia and Africa came under colonial control. Use the above keywords to compare British India with Ethiopia, one of the few regions in Africa to escape New Imperialism. How did the two nations differ in style of government, goods produced, relationship with Europe, and standard of living? How did British rule affect the people, particularly economically and technologically? Be sure you look for images of the people, both ruler and ruled.

INTERNET EXPLORATION

Whaling was a very important industry in the nineteenth century, and a difficult if romantic lifestyle. Use the keywords "history of whaling" to locate interesting sites on history and conservation. Imagine yourself as a member of the crew: what was your daily life like? How often did you get to visit home? What was your life expectancy?

MAP EXERCISES

On Outline Map 25.1, shade in the major African kingdoms and European colonies of the late nineteenth century:

> Sokoto Caliphate
>
> Tippu Tip's Sphere
>
> Bornu
>
> Ethiopia, 1880
>
> Ethiopia, 1900

In addition, trace the routes of the following:

> The Great Trek

On Outline Map 25.2, outline the extent of the Mughal Empire in 1707. Then shade in the regions to reflect the changes in control by the following:

> Muslims in 1765
>
> Muslims in 1805
>
> Hindus in 1805
>
> British East India Company in 1805

On Outline Map 25.3, shade in the regions dominated by Europeans during the sixteenth through nineteenth centuries.

Outline Map 25.1

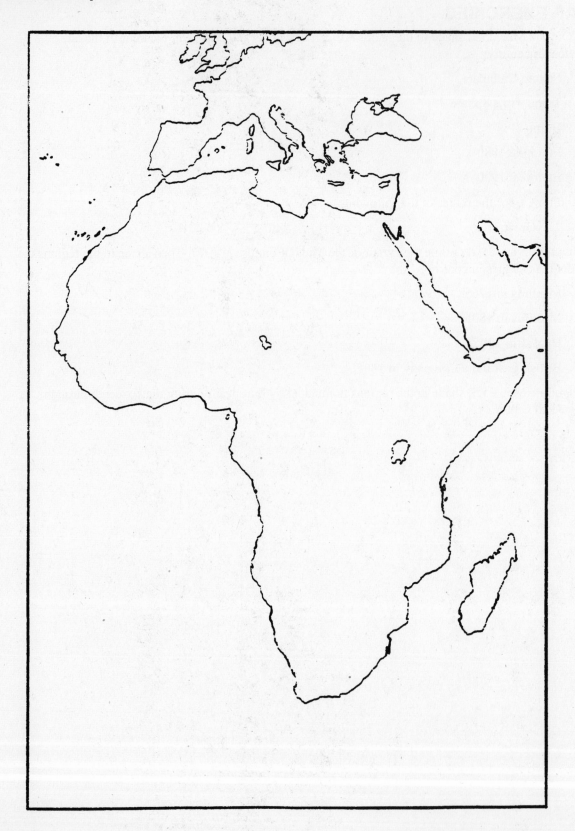

Outline Map 25.2

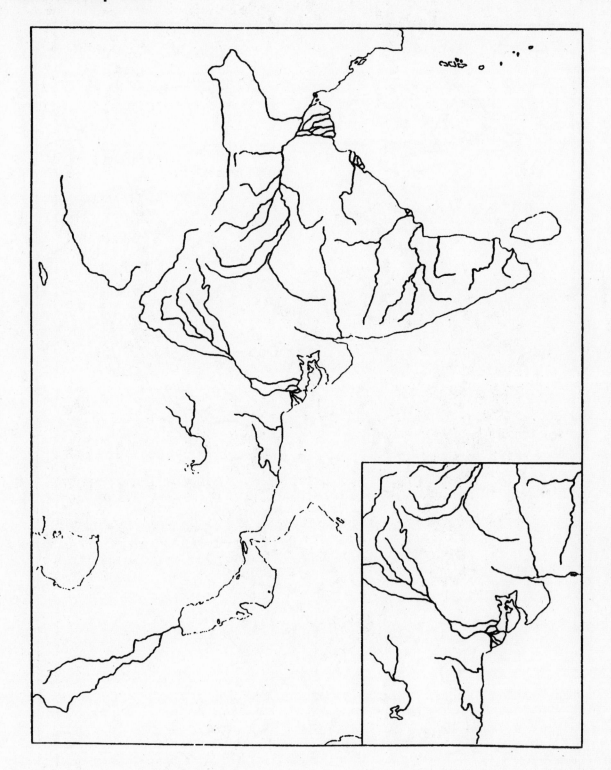

Outline Map 25.3

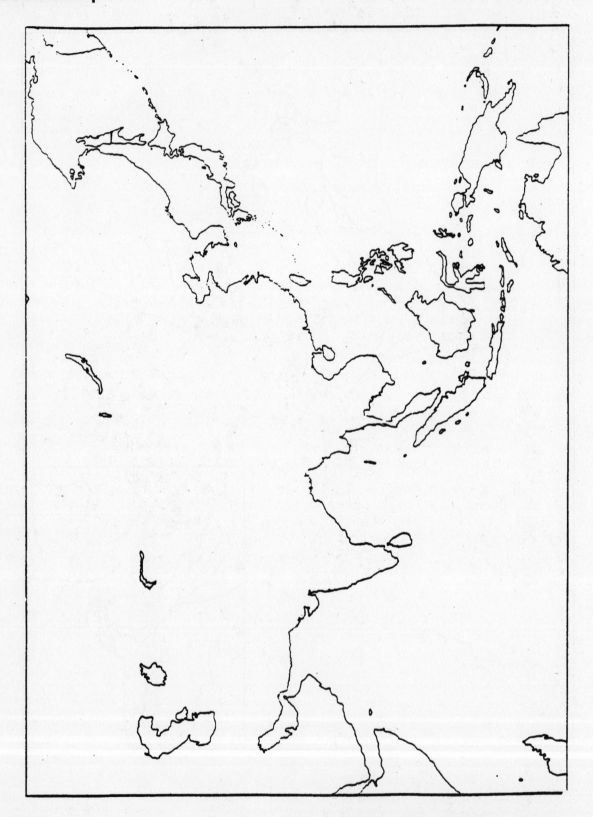

ANSWERS TO MULTIPLE-CHOICE QUESTIONS

1. b   p. 667, 668
2. b   p. 668
3. e   p. 670
4. c   p. 672
5. b   p. 673
6. d   p. 675
7. a   p. 675
8. d   p. 675
9. d   p. 677
10. b   p. 677
11. c   p. 681
12. b   p. 681
13. c   p. 684

CHAPTER 26

Land Empires in the Age of Imperialism, 1800-1870

LEARNING OBJECTIVES

After reading Chapter 26 and completing this study chapter, you should be able to explain:

- How the land-based empires of Eurasia struggled to develop, and what domestic factors were involved in their development.

- How European economic and political aims interfered with the development of the Ottoman regions and China.

- How Europe and Russia interacted during Russia's development.

- How the role of women changed in the Ottoman, Russian, and Qing Empires.

CHAPTER OUTLINE

In the outline below, include important themes, concepts, and details in the blank spaces provided. If you find fewer points than you have space for, leave lines blank. If you find more points, add as many lines as necessary.

I.   *Introduction*
  A.   *Heshen and corruption in the Qing*
    1. _____

    2. _____

    3. _____

  B.   *Corruption, bankruptcy, and internal problems*
    1. _____

    2. _____

    3. _____

  C.   *The Qing's problems were similar to those of other land-based empires*
    1. _____

    2. _____

3. _____

II. **The Ottoman Empire**
   A. **Egypt and the Napoleonic Example, 1798–1840**
      1. **French invasion of Egypt**
         a) _____

         b) _____

         c) _____

      2. **Muhammad Ali**
         a) _____

         b) _____

         c) _____

         d) _____

         e) _____

      3. **Ibrahim invades Syria and European reaction**
         a) _____

         b) _____

         c) _____

         d) _____

         e) _____

   B. **Ottoman Reform and the European Model, 1807–1853**
      1. **Attempts to reform the military, provincial government, and the tax system**
         a) _____

         b) _____

         c) _____

2. *Violent opposition from the Janissaries*
    a) _____

    b) _____

    c) _____

3. *Serbian independence*
    a) _____

    b) _____

    c) _____

    d) _____

    e) _____

4. *Many nobles and the ulama were against the reforms*
    a) _____

    b) _____

    c) _____

    d) _____

    e) _____

5. *Greek independence*
    a) _____

    b) _____

    c) _____

    d) _____

    e) _____

6. *Dissolution of the Janissaries and more reforms*
    a) _____

b) _____

c) _____

7. *Tanzimat (reorganization)*
   a) _____

   b) _____

   c) _____

   d) _____

   e) _____

8. *Education and communication*
   a) _____

   b) _____

   c) _____

   d) _____

9. *The social impact of improvements in military technology*
   a) _____

   b) _____

   c) _____

   d) _____

10. *Secularization of culture and the legal code*
   a) _____

   b) _____

   c) _____

   d) _____

e) _____

11. *Women*
    a) _____

    b) _____

    c) _____

    d) _____

    e) _____

C. *The Crimean War and Its Aftermath, 1853–1877*
    1. *Conflict between Russians and Ottomans and their allies*
       a) _____

       b) _____

       c) _____

       d) _____

       e) _____

    2. *Effects of the Crimean War and "The Eastern Question"*
       a) _____

       b) _____

       c) _____

       d) _____

       e) _____

       f) _____

       g) _____

3.   *The Crimean War was the first modern war*

    a) _____

    b) _____

    c) _____

4.   *New guns and the disappearance of cavalries*

    a) _____

    b) _____

    c) _____

    d) _____

    e) _____

    f) _____

5.   *Monetary reform and chronic insolvency*

    a) _____

    b) _____

    c) _____

    d) _____

    e) _____

6.   *Cities and their role*

    a) _____

    b) _____

    c) _____

    d) _____

    e) _____

7. *Calls for a constitution*
    a) _____

    b) _____

    c) _____

8. *Young Ottomans*
    a) _____

    b) _____

    c) _____

III. *The Russian Empire*
    A. *Russia and Europe*
        1. *Urbanization and railroads*
            a) _____

            b) _____

            c) _____

            d) _____

            e) _____

        2. *Russia wanted to industrialize, but feared political reform*
            a) _____

            b) _____

            c) _____

            d) _____

            e) _____

        3. *Similarities between Russia and Europe, Slavophiles, and Pan-Slavism*
            a) _____

            b) _____

c) _____

d) _____

e) _____

B. *Russia and Asia*
    1. *Russian drive to the east, and its effects*
        a) _____

        b) _____

        c) _____

    2. *Russian drive to the south, and its effects*
        a) _____

        b) _____

        c) _____

    3. *Britain's concerns about a strong Russia in Central Asia*
        a) _____

        b) _____

        c) _____

C. *Cultural Trends*
    1. *Russia had a head start in Westernization*
        a) _____

        b) _____

        c) _____

        d) _____

    2. *Limited success of the reforms and opposition to them*
        a) _____

        b) _____

c) _____

d) _____

e) _____

3. ***The Decembrist Revolt***

a) _____

b) _____

c) _____

4. ***Alexander II's reforms***

a) _____

b) _____

c) _____

d) _____

5. ***Education***

a) _____

b) _____

c) _____

d) _____

6. ***Russia belonged to two different spheres of development***

a) _____

b) _____

c) _____

IV. ***The Qing Empire***

  A. ***Economic and Social Disorder, 1800–1839***

  1. ***Economic success and population growth***

  a) _____

    b) _____

    c) _____

    d) _____

  2. *Discontent grew*

    a) _____

    b) _____

    c) _____

    d) _____

  3. *The White Lotus Rebellion*

    a) _____

    b) _____

    c) _____

B. *The Opium War and Its Aftermath, 1839–1850*

  1. *The trade deficit and opium*

    a) _____

    b) _____

    c) _____

    d) _____

    e) _____

    f) _____

  2. *The war: British superior military vs. Chinese outdated military*

    a) _____

    b) _____

    c) _____

d) _____

e) _____

f) _____

g) _____

3. *The Treaty of Nanking*
   a) _____

   b) _____

   c) _____

   d) _____

   e) _____

4. *New privileges for Europeans, colonization of parts of the Qing land, and Chinese resentment*
   a) _____

   b) _____

   c) _____

   d) _____

   e) _____

   f) _____

C. *The Taiping Rebellion, 1850–1864*
   1.   *The founding of the Taiping movement and Hong Xiuquan*

      a) _____

      b) _____

      c) _____

      d) _____

      e) _____

      f) _____

   2.   *The rebellion appealed to the Hakka and then brought in other disgruntled groups*

      a) _____

      b) _____

      c) _____

      d) _____

      e) _____

      f) _____

   3.   *The Qing fought back*

      a) _____

      b) _____

      c) _____

      d) _____

      e) _____

   4.   *France and Britain enter the skirmish and a second opium war (the Arrow War)*

      a) _____

      b) _____

c) _____

d) _____

e) _____

f) _____

5. *The legacy of the Taiping Rebellion*

a) _____

b) _____

c) _____

d) _____

e) _____

D. *Decentralization at the End of the Qing Empire, 1864–1875*

1. *Extreme financial distress and actions by France and Britain*

a) _____

b) _____

c) _____

d) _____

2. *Zeng Guofan's reforms*

a) _____

b) _____

c) _____

d) _____

e) _____

f) _____

3. ***Decentralization and reformers***

a) _____

b) _____

c) _____

d) _____

e) _____

V. ***Conclusion***

A. ***The challenge of Europe***

1. _____

2. _____

3. _____

4. _____

B. ***Policies of the Ottomans, Qing, and Russia***

1. _____

2. _____

3. _____

4. _____

C. ***Legacy***

1. _____

2. _____

3. _____

4. _____

IDENTIFICATIONS

Define each term and explain why it is significant, including any important dates.

	Identification	Significance
Muhammad Ali		
Janissaries		
Serbia		
Tanzimat		
Crimean War		
percussion cap		
breech-loading rifle		
extraterritoriality		
Young Ottomans		
Slavophile		

	Identification	Significance

Pan-Slavism

Decembrist Revolt

Opium War

opium

Bannermen

Treaty of Nanjing/Nanking

treaty ports

most-favored-nation status

Zeng Guofan

Taiping Rebellion

MULTIPLE-CHOICE QUESTIONS

Read the entire question, including *all* the possible answers. Then choose the *one* answer that best fits the question.

1. Which of the following was *not* done by the leaders of the Ottoman Empire in their reform program?

    a.   They made the military more effective.
    b.   They strengthened the power of the religious elite.
    c.   They standardized the tax system.
    d.   They brought the empire under more centralized control.
    e.   They gave women more economic rights, especially over their dowry money.

2. Traumatic episodes such as the execution of Selim III taught the Ottomans that reform

    a.   was hopeless.
    b.   needed to be carried out more gradually and sympathetically.
    c.   needed to be carried out systematically and forcefully.
    d.   needed to be carried out only with the complete agreement of all parties concerned.
    e.   could only be carried out with the help of Europeans.

3. Under the new Ottoman reforms, which of the following remained in the sphere of religious law?

    a.   The Janissaries
    b.   Foreign policy
    c.   Education
    d.   Marriage, inheritance, and divorce
    e.   The economy

4. The wearing of beards in the Ottoman military was regarded by Mahmud II's officials as

    a.   a sign of traditional Turkish dress and retained to encourage nationalism.
    b.   too close to the styles worn by the rebellious Greeks and so deemed treasonous.
    c.   a sign of virility and so encouraged among officers.
    d.   old-fashioned, and a symbolic barrier to modernization.
    e.   a fire hazard, and so they ordered that beards be removed.

5. Which language did the Russians consider to be the language of European culture?

    a.   Russian
    b.   English
    c.   French
    d.   Italian
    e.   Latin

6. What is Pan-Slavism?

    a.   A militant political doctrine advocating the political unity of all Slavic peoples everywhere
    b.   A militant political doctrine similar to Nazism
    c.   An art movement based on the Slavic languages
    d.   A movement within Russia only, advocating rule by Slavic peoples
    e.   A post–Cold War reaction to the Warsaw Pact

7. What do historians mean when they say that Russia belonged to two different spheres of development?

    a. It was culturally similar to the Ottoman East, but technically similar to Europe.

    b. It was technically similar to the Ottoman East, but socially similar to China.

    c. It was partially controlled by two different outside forces: Britain and France.

    d. It was a recognized force in European politics, but in other ways it was like the Ottoman Empire.

    e. Militarily the Russian were quite advanced, but socially they lagged behind the West.

8. Why did people begin to migrate across China during the early Qing period?

    a. They were migrating to the Ottoman Empire.

    b. They were moving to the cities to work in factories.

    c. They were looking for less crowded conditions.

    d. They were fleeing the Mongols.

    e. They were moving to new farmland opened by the government.

9. The White Lotus Rebellion had what as its goal?

    a. The introduction of Buddhism to China

    b. The introduction of Buddhism to Japan

    c. The spread of Buddhism outside of China and into Mongolia and Russia

    d. The restoration of the Ming Dynasty and the coming of the Buddha

    e. The unification of China

10. What was the only product successfully used by the British to correct the trade imbalance between them and the Qing Empire?

    a. Cotton cloth

    b. Opium

    c. Silver

    d. Porcelain

    e. Tobacco

11. China's civil war during the nineteenth century was called the Taiping Rebellion because

    a. it started in Taiping China.

    b. the Taiping founder thought he was Christ's younger brother.

    c. the members of the Taiping movement were mostly Hakka people.

    d. the members of the Taiping movement promised to bring a "Heavenly Kingdom of Great Peace" to China: *taiping* means "great peace."

    e. the founder's name was Taiping.

12. Why did Russia enjoy a comparative advantage over the Ottoman Empire and Qing China in its relationship with Europe?

    a. It was less appealing to rapacious European merchants and strategists.

    b. It was militarily stronger.

    c. It had enormous oil reserves.

    d. It easily withstood Europe's inroads and demands.

    e. It was more isolated.

SHORT-ANSWER QUESTIONS

Answer each question in one short paragraph, giving the definition, dates, and significance.

1.   Why did economic development lag during the rule of the Qing dynasty?

2.   Why was the Ottoman Empire able to begin reforms earlier than China? What was the result?

3.   How did opium use affect Chinese society?

4.   Compare and contrast the weaponry of the Qing and British forces.

5.   How did the treaty system affect China culturally? How did it affect the British? Give specific examples.

ESSAY QUESTIONS

Make an outline of each question, listing the major points you want to discuss. Then write your practice essay, following your outline carefully and making sure that you do not skip any of your major points. At this time you will want to add the relevant dates and details that will make your essay persuasive and accurate.

1.   What internal and external challenges faced land-based empires in the nineteenth century? How did the empires deal with those challenges and how successful were they in meeting them?

2.   Discuss European influence in the Ottoman Empire. Why were the Europeans interested in the Ottoman Empire? What benefits were to be gained by both parties? What is the legacy of this relationship?

3.   Discuss the philosophy and tactics of the Taiping movement. What were the effects of this and other rebellions on China?

4.   Discuss Russia's growth and relationship with Europe during the nineteenth century. What countries influenced Russia, and how did Russia interact with them?

COMPARISON CHARTS

Using information gathered from the text, fill in the blank areas of each chart with the relevant data pertaining to the regions and categories listed. (Not all blank areas will necessarily be used.)

Chart 26.1

THE SUCCESS AND CHALLENGES OF THREE EMPIRES

	Dates	Government Systems	Economic Systems	Traditional Systems	Reforms	Methods	Successes	Failures
Ottoman Empire								
Qing Empire								
Russia								

Chart 26.2

THE CHANGING ROLE OF WOMEN IN MODERNIZING EURASIA

	Property Rights	Domestic Control	Earning Power	Professions Available	Education	Voting Rights	Marriage	Children
Ottoman Empire								
Qing China								

DIVERSITY AND DOMINANCE

After reading "Diversity and Dominance: The French Occupation of Egypt" in your text, answer the following additional questions.

Do you find it incongruous that Napoleon, who came from a Catholic country, made use of so much Muslim symbolism, and even mentions Muhammad as God's Prophet and refers to the Quran instead of the Bible?

How would you assess Napoleon's advice to the soldiers on their behavior? What did you think about his reference to Rome?

INTERNET ASSIGNMENT

Keywords: **"Emperor Napoleon I"**

                   "Muhammad Ali, Egypt"

                   "Tsar Alexander I"

These three men left their imprints on their respective empires. How did their different personalities affect the path their countries took and the way others responded to them?

INTERNET EXPLORATION

Opium consumption has been blamed for the downfall of many youths in Europe, Asia, and America, as well as being the catalyst for the British defeat of China in 1842. Use the keywords "opium history" or visit the web site http://www.pbs.org/wgbh/pages/frontline/shows/heroin/etc/history.html, to trace the history of this famous, but deadly, drug.

MAP EXERCISES

On Outline Map 26.1, shade in the Ottoman Empire to show its territorial losses in these periods:

   From 1829 to 1877

   From 1878 to 1913

Then trace the boundaries of the Ottoman Empire in 1914.

On Outline Map 26.2, shade in areas controlled by Taiping forces in these years:

   From 1853 to 1857

   From 1857 to 1863

Also, mark the following treaty ports:

   Hong Kong

   Guangzhou (Canton)

   Shanghai

   Fuzhou

   Xiamen (Amoy)

Outline Map 26.1

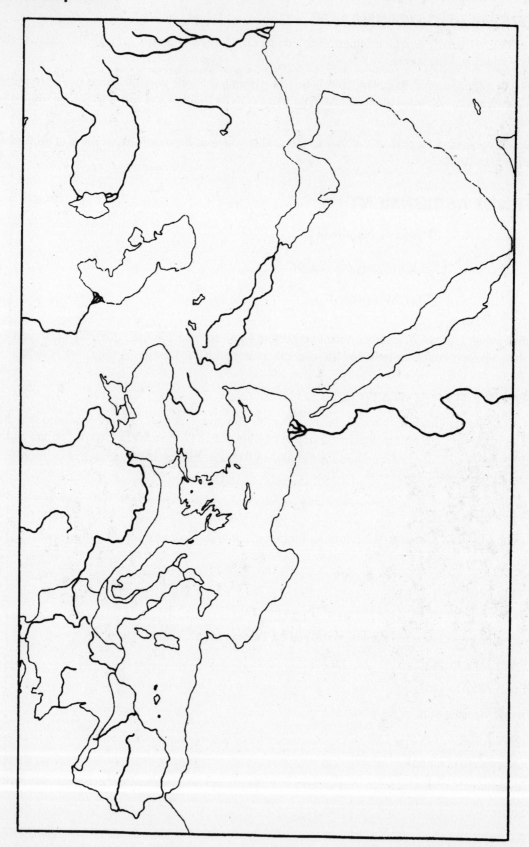

Outline Map 26.2

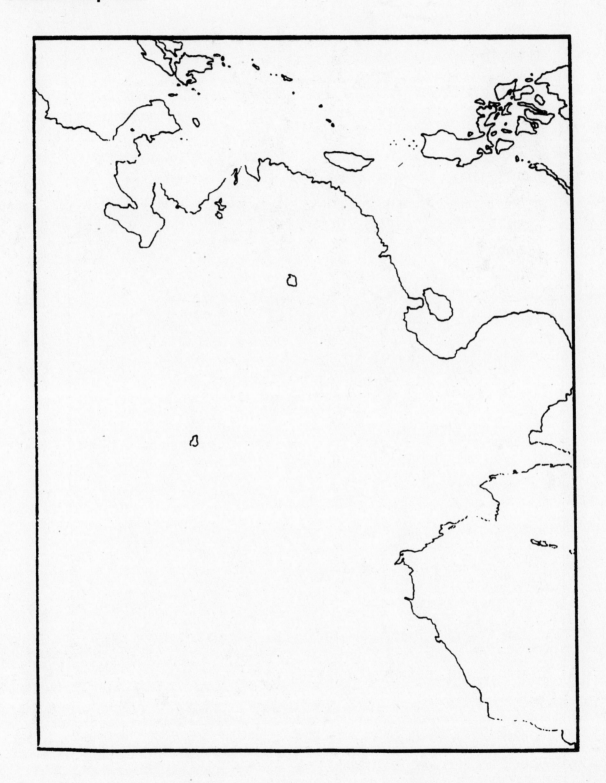

ANSWERS TO MULTIPLE-CHOICE QUESTIONS

1. b p. 693
2. c p. 696
3. d p. 696, 698
4. e p. 697
5. c p. 703
6. a p. 705
7. d p. 707
8. c p. 707
9. d p. 707
10. b p. 708
11. d p. 710
12. a p. 715

CHAPTER 27

The New Power Balance, 1850–1900

LEARNING OBJECTIVES

After reading Chapter 27 and completing this study chapter, you should be able to explain:

- How industry and new technologies transformed the economies, environments, societies, and politics of western Europe, Russia, the United States, and Japan.

- What role Victorian culture played in the development of the Western world, and how it affected the daily life of women, men, and children of all classes.

- How nationalism compelled people to unite with others similar to them, sometimes resulting in unification, as was the case for Germany, and sometimes resulting in splintering, as was the case for the Ottoman Empire.

- How industrialism spurred development in countries outside of Europe, especially the United States and Japan, and the societal changes resulting from industrialization.

- How certain movements and systems—such as socialism, labor unions, the women's movement, and the U.S. national parks system—developed in response to the ills caused by industrialization and nationalism.

CHAPTER OUTLINE

In the outline below, include important themes, concepts, and details in the blank spaces provided. If you find fewer points than you have space for, leave lines blank. If you find more points, add as many lines as necessary.

I.   *Introduction*
    A.   *The unification of Germany, 1871*
        1. _____

        2. _____

        3. _____

        4. _____

        5. _____

    B.   *The "Great Powers"*
        1. _____

2. _____

3. _____

C. *The "New Imperialism"*
   1. _____

   2. _____

   3. _____

II. *New Technologies and the World Economy*
   A. *Railroads*
      1. *The success of railroads*
         a) _____

         b) _____

         c) _____

      2. *The United States and non-industrialized regions*
         a) _____

         b) _____

         c) _____

         d) _____

         e) _____

      3. *Environmental costs*
         a) _____

         b) _____

         c) _____

   B. *Steamships and Telegraph Cables*
      1. *Improvements in ship design and more support for shipping*
         a) _____

         b) _____

c) _____

d) _____

2. *Shipping lines*
    a) _____

    b) _____

    c) _____

3. *Submarine telegraph cables*
    a) _____

    b) _____

    c) _____

C. *The Steel and Chemical Industries*
    1. *The development of steel production*
        a) _____

        b) _____

        c) _____

        d) _____

        e) _____

        f) _____

    2. *Chemical dyes*
        a) _____

        b) _____

        c) _____

    3. *Chemical explosives and the German chemical industry*
        a) _____

b) _____

c) _____

d) _____

e) _____

4. *Impact of industrialization*
   a) _____

   b) _____

   c) _____

   d) _____

D. *Electricity*
   1. *Early development and lighting*
      a) _____

      b) _____

      c) _____

      d) _____

      e) _____

   2. *Other uses of electricity*
      a) _____

      b) _____

      c) _____

E. *World Trade and Finance*
   1. *The cost of shipping dropped and boom and bust cycles*
      a) _____

      b) _____

       c) _____

   2. *Tariffs and Britain's industrial dominance*
       a) _____

       b) _____

       c) _____

   3. *Non-industrial areas were tied to the world economy as never before*
       a) _____

       b) _____

       c) _____

III. *Social Changes*
   A. *Population and Migrations*
      1. *Mass immigrations of Europeans overseas*
       a) _____

       b) _____

       c) _____

      2. *Populations grew as the death rate dropped and food production increased*
       a) _____

       b) _____

       c) _____

      3. *Asian immigration*
       a) _____

       b) _____

       c) _____

   B. *Urbanization and Urban Environments*
      1. *Cities grew in size—both area and population*
       a) _____

b) _____

c) _____

2. *Public transport and tenements*
   a) _____

   b) _____

   c) _____

3. *Improved sanitation and neighborhoods*
   a) _____

   b) _____

   c) _____

   d) _____

   e) _____

   f) _____

4. *The development of zones and the middle class*
   a) _____

   b) _____

   c) _____

5. *Immigrant housing and urban environments*
   a) _____

   b) _____

   c) _____

C. *Middle Class Women's "Separate Sphere"*
   1. *The rules of behavior and the ideology of the Victorian Age*
      a) _____

b) _____

c) _____

d) _____

e) _____

f) _____

2. *Running a middle-class home and new technology*
    a) _____

    b) _____

    c) _____

    d) _____

3. *Child-rearing and legal discrimination*
    a) _____

    b) _____

    c) _____

    d) _____

4. *Careers and education*
    a) _____

    b) _____

    c) _____

    d) _____

    e) _____

    f) _____

    5. *Women and social activism*

        a) _____

        b) _____

        c) _____

D. *Working-Class Women*

    1. *Women and domestic work*

        a) _____

        b) _____

        c) _____

        d) _____

    2. *Women and factory work*

        a) _____

        b) _____

        c) _____

    3. *Married women with children*

        a) _____

        b) _____

        c) _____

        d) _____

        e) _____

IV. *Socialism and Labor Movements*

  A. *Marx and Socialism*

    1. *Theory*

        a) _____

        b) _____

        c) _____

d) _____

2. *Social inequity*
   a) _____

   b) _____

   c) _____

   d) _____

   e) _____

3. *Politics*
   a) _____

   b) _____

   c) _____

   d) _____

B. *Labor Movements*
   1. *Creation*
      a) _____

      b) _____

      c) _____

   2. *Electoral politics*
      a) _____

      b) _____

      c) _____

   3. *Germany*
      a) _____

      b) _____

        c) _____

    4.   *Women in the labor movement*
        a) _____

        b) _____

        c) _____

V.   *Nationalism and the Unification of Germany and Italy*
   A.   *Language and National Identity Before 1871*
      1.   *The problem of language and nationalism*
        a) _____

        b) _____

        c) _____

        d) _____

        e) _____

        f) _____

      2.   *Liberalism*
        a) _____

        b) _____

        c) _____

      3.   *Mass politics*
        a) _____

        b) _____

        c) _____

   B.   *The Unification of Italy, 1860–1870*
      1.   *Conservative approach in the north*
        a) _____

b) _____

c) _____

2. *Radical approach in the south*
    a) _____

    b) _____

    c) _____

C. *The Unification of Germany, 1866–1871*
    1. *Potential plans for unification*
        a) _____

        b) _____

        c) _____

        d) _____

    2. *War with Austria and the early German state*
        a) _____

        b) _____

        c) _____

    3. *War with France and the finished German state*
        a) _____

        b) _____

        c) _____

D. *Nationalism After 1871*
    1. *The political climate of Europe and public opinion*
        a) _____

        b) _____

        c) _____

       d) _____

       e) _____

       f) _____

  2.   *How governments used nationalism*

       a) _____

       b) _____

       c) _____

       d) _____

       e) _____

  3.   *Nationalism and minorities*

       a) _____

       b) _____

       c) _____

VI.   *The Great Powers of Europe, 1871–1900*
    A.   *Germany at the Center of Europe*
      1.   *International relations*

       a) _____

       b) _____

       c) _____

      2.   *Domestic policy*

       a) _____

       b) _____

       c) _____

       d) _____

e) _____

3. *Wilhelm II's "global policy"*
   a) _____

   b) _____

   c) _____

B. *The Liberal Powers: France and Great Britain*
   1. *France in second place*
      a) _____

      b) _____

      c) _____

   2. *French internal divisions*
      a) _____

      b) _____

      c) _____

      d) _____

      e) _____

   3. *British-Irish resentment and economy*
      a) _____

      b) _____

      c) _____

      d) _____

   4. *Preoccupation with empire and "splendid isolation"*
      a) _____

      b) _____

c) _____

d) _____

e) _____

C. *The Conservative Powers: Russia and Austria-Hungary*
1. *Issues facing the Austro-Hungarian Empire*
   a) _____

   b) _____

   c) _____

   d) _____

   e) _____

2. *Russia's ethnic diversity*
   a) _____

   b) _____

   c) _____

   d) _____

   e) _____

3. *Reforms in Russia*
   a) _____

   b) _____

   c) _____

   d) _____

4. *Russian weakness and defeat in the Russo-Japanese War*
   a) _____

   b) _____

c) _____

VII. *Japan Joins the Great Powers, 1865–1905*
   A.   *China, Japan, and the Western Powers, to 1867*
      1.   **Why China weakened**
         a) _____

         b) _____

         c) _____

         d) _____

      2.   **Japan's shogunate**
         a) _____

         b) _____

         c) _____

         d) _____

         e) _____

      3.   **Commodore Matthew C. Perry and crisis in the shogunate**
         a) _____

         b) _____

         c) _____

         d) _____

         e) _____

         f) _____

      4.   **Foreign affairs and expansionism**
         a) _____

         b) _____

c) _____

d) _____

e) _____

B. *The Meiji Restoration and the Modernization of Japan, 1868–1894*
1. *Civil war*
    a) _____

    b) _____

    c) _____

2. *Japan fends against the West*
    a) _____

    b) _____

    c) _____

3. *Cultural borrowing*
    a) _____

    b) _____

    c) _____

    d) _____

    e) _____

4. *Industry*
    a) _____

    b) _____

    c) _____

    d) _____

e) _____

C.   *The Birth of Japanese Imperialism, 1894–1905*
1.   *Motive and methods*
a) _____

b) _____

c) _____

2.   *China was growing weaker*
a) _____

b) _____

c) _____

3.   *The Boxer Uprising, 1900*
a) _____

b) _____

c) _____

4.   *Japan's growing power in Asia*
a) _____

b) _____

c) _____

VIII. *Conclusion*
A.   *A golden age to some*
1.   _____

2.   _____

3.   _____

4.   _____

5.   _____

    B.   *The role of the nation-state*
       1. _____

       2. _____

       3. _____

    C.   *Nationalism*
       1. _____

       2. _____

       3. _____

IDENTIFICATIONS

Define each term and explain why it is significant, including any important dates.

	Identification	Significance
railroads		
submarine telegraph cables		
steel		
electricity		
Thomas Edison		
socialism		

	Identification	Significance
labor unions		
Karl Marx		
anarchist		
nationalism		
liberalism		
Victorian Age		
"separate spheres"		
Giuseppe Garibaldi		
Otto von Bismarck		
Empress Dowager Cixi		

	Identification	Significance

Meiji Restoration

Yamagata Aritomo

MULTIPLE-CHOICE QUESTIONS

Read the entire question, including *all* the possible answers. Then choose the *one* answer that best fits the question.

1. The unification of Germany was accomplished by

   a. victories on the battlefield.
   b. popular participation by German citizens.
   c. an official act of the Prussian king.
   d. default; no one else wanted a land of so few resources.
   e. the conference at Versailles in 1871.

2. What country had the largest rail system in the world in 1865?

   a. The United States
   b. Great Britain
   c. France
   d. Japan
   e. Russia

3. Why were the Germans leaders in the new sciences in the nineteenth century?

   a. Germans were the best-educated Europeans of the time.
   b. Since Germany had few resources, it needed to develop high technology.
   c. The German government actively supported and financed education in the sciences and the development of technology.
   d. Non-military technology could be used to develop better weapons.
   e. Germany was the wealthiest country of Europe.

4. Electricity made streets

   a. more polluted.
   b. cleaner.
   c. more crowded.
   d. more beautiful.
   e. less crowded.

5. What percentage of Britain's population lived in cities in 1914?

   a. 20 percent
   b. 40 percent
   c. 60 percent
   d. 80 percent
   e. 90 percent

6. Which of the following did *not* improve during the late nineteenth century?

   a. Air quality
   b. Water quality
   c. Diet
   d. Health
   e. Fire protection

7. To middle-class Victorians, the home symbolized

   a. a place of education for girls but not boys.
   b. a refuge from the dog-eat-dog world of competition.
   c. a dark, depressing place that people were anxious to leave at adulthood.
   d. a place for socializing, especially for the husband.
   e. a place for socializing, especially for the wife.

8. Did technological advances, such as vacuum cleaners and washing machines, mean less work for women?

   a. Yes
   b. No
   c. Middle-class women did not work at all, because they had servants.
   d. They meant more work due to higher standards of cleanliness.
   e. Yes, because men operated the new machines.

9. Why was teaching considered an appropriate profession for women?

   a. Men did not want to do it.
   b. It was not a physically demanding profession.
   c. It was not an intellectually demanding profession.
   d. It was seen as an extension of women's motherly duties.
   e. Due to the new laws mandating compulsory education, large numbers of teachers were needed.

10. How did instituting laws to protect women from industrial abuse actually harm them?

   a. It resulted in their being replaced by men in all professions but nursing and teaching—two safe professions.
   b. It resulted in the use of children instead, as they were not covered by the laws.
   c. It resulted in women being denied access to better-paid jobs, some of which might be considered dangerous.
   d. It resulted in labor union strikes that hurt their job security.
   e. It eventually resulted in women leaving the workplace altogether.

11. What finally allowed the "friendly societies" to develop into labor unions in Britain?
    a. Abuse and exploitation of the workers
    b. Universal calls for the implementation of company ownership of corporations
    c. The abolition of British anticombination laws
    d. Competition from foreign labor
    e. Workers finally realized that there was a great disparity between their lifestyles and the lifestyles of the factory owners

12. As politicians tried to use popular feelings to bolster their governments, they were greatly aided by
    a. schools.
    b. the press.
    c. churches.
    d. the entrepreneurs.
    e. the workers.

13. How did the Japanese manage to keep their country relatively free of Western imperialism?
    a. By making a preemptive attack on the United States
    b. By becoming a world-class industrial and military power as quickly as possible
    c. By refusing to open Japan to Western trade
    d. By becoming a major importer of Western goods
    e. By forming an alliance with China

SHORT-ANSWER QUESTIONS

Answer each question in one short paragraph, giving the definition, dates, and significance.

1. What kind of services developed in the cities, and what impact did they have on people's daily lives?

2. Discuss the labor movements that arose in response to industrialization: what were their goals and how did they develop?

3. Discuss some of the challenges facing Victorian women, paying special attention to the concerns of women of different classes.

4. How did the education of boys and girls differ? What were the aims in educating children?

5. Discuss Otto von Bismarck's policies and the motivations behind them.

ESSAY QUESTIONS

Make an outline of each question, listing the major points you want to discuss. Then write your practice essay, following your outline carefully and making sure that you do not skip any of your major points. At this time you will want to add the relevant dates and details that will make your essay persuasive and accurate.

1. Discuss the three innovations that transformed the world in the late nineteenth century. How did they affect technology, politics, economics, and people's daily lives?

2. What made the communication and transportation revolutions possible? How did the development of these technologies change the world?

3. What economic factors caused the boom and bust cycles of the nineteenth century in Europe and America?

4.   Define Victorianism and describe how it affected the lives of women, men, and children of all classes.

5.   Discuss the concept of nationalism. What made people have nationalistic feelings for other people? How did nationalism bring nations together and tear them apart? Use specific examples.

6.   Discuss the rise of Japan: what motivations drove its progress, and what were its goals?

COMPARISON CHARTS

Using information gathered from the text, fill in the blank areas of each chart with the relevant data pertaining to the regions and categories listed. (Not all blank areas will necessarily be used.)

Chart 27.1

GENDER AND CLASS IN VICTORIAN ENGLAND AND AMERICA

	Education	Type of Employment	Place of Employment	Professions Open to Them	Exploitation	The Home	Social Responsibilities	Daily Activities	Role of Technology	Marriage	Leisure Time	Child Rearing and Children
Upper- and Middle-Class Men												
Working-Class and Poor Men												
Upper- and Middle-Class Women												
Working-Class and Poor Women												

Chart 27.2

MEETING THE CHALLENGES FROM THE WEST

	Contact Date	How Contact Was Made	Attitude of China or Japan	Results in Technology	Results in Culture	Results in Politics	Benefits to Asians	Detriments to Asians
China								
Japan								

DIVERSITY AND DOMINANCE

After reading "Diversity and Dominance: Marx and Engels on Global Trade and the Bourgeoisie" in your text, answer the following additional questions.

How do Marx and Engels characterize life in the countryside before influence by the bourgeoisie?

How do you think Marx and Engels would recommend that the process of the Western bourgeoisie re-creation of the world in its image could be stopped?

INTERNET ASSIGNMENT

Keywords: **"Steamships" or "Civil War Ironclad Ships"**

                       "The Summer Palace"

The nineteenth century was a time of modernization and industrialization for the Western world, particularly Britain and the United States; however, not everyone was modernizing. China was still firmly an agricultural nation, with little need for, or even understanding of, the significance of industrialization. Use the above keywords to find written and visual web materials. The steamship and Empress Cixi's ivory pleasure boat, located at the Summer Palace, can both been seen as symbols of the cultures of Britain and China in the nineteenth century. Why? What are the purposes of the two kinds of boats? How expensive were they to produce? What value did they gain for their peoples?

INTERNET EXPLORATION

The Bowlers, a modern English family, lived for three months just as people had in Victorian England. To share their experiences visit http://pbs.org/wnet/1900house. Why did they choose to do this? How did they do without "essential" modern conveniences? What did they miss the most from their world? What did they like the best from 1900? Could you do it? For other interesting sites, use the keywords "The 1900 House-Victorian Houses."

MAP EXERCISES

On Outline Map 27.1, shade in the areas gained by Japan from 1894 to 1910.

Outline Map 27.1

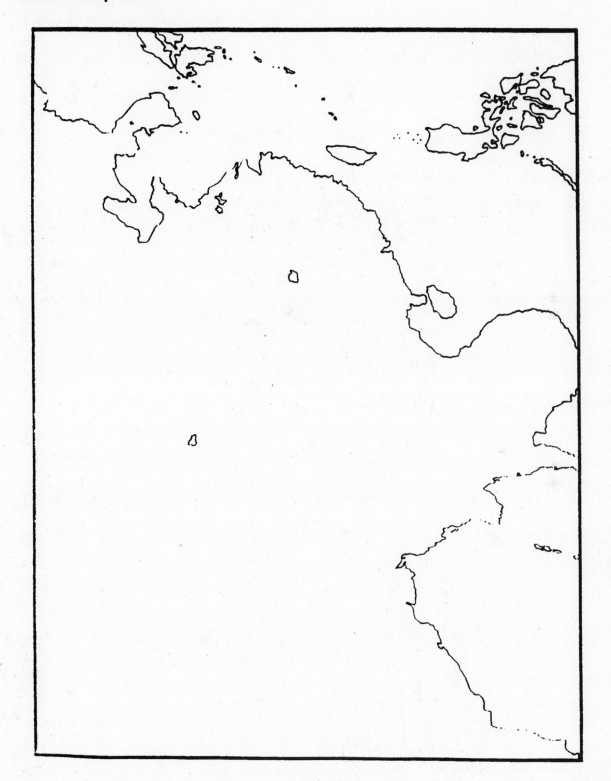

ANSWERS TO MULTIPLE-CHOICE QUESTIONS

1. a   p. 723
2. a   p. 724
3. c   p. 725
4. e   p. 726
5. d   p. 729
6. a   p. 730
7. b   p. 730
8. d   p. 730
9. d   p. 731
10. c   p. 732
11. c   p. 733
12. b   p. 738
13. b   p. 746

CHAPTER 28

The New Imperialism, 1869–1914

LEARNING OBJECTIVES

After reading Chapter 28 and completing this study chapter, you should be able to explain:

- What motives and methods were involved in Western New Imperialism in the late nineteenth and early twentieth centuries, and how European and American actions affected both Westerners and non-Westerners.

- How the Scramble for Africa was inspired, what made it possible, and how it changed the world.

- How colonies dominated by the same European power could have distinct differences based on the type of colonial rule instituted there.

- What the goals and methods of New Imperialism were in Asia and Africa, and how the goals and methods in Latin America differed.

- How tropical environments first influenced people indigenous to the region and then Western imperialists, and how those regions were changed by New Imperialism.

CHAPTER OUTLINE

In the outline below, include important themes, concepts, and details in the blank spaces provided. If you find fewer points than you have space for, leave lines blank. If you find more points, add as many lines as necessary.

I. *Introduction*
    A. *The inauguration of the Suez Canal*
        1. _____

        2. _____

        3. _____

        4. _____

        5. _____

        6. _____

    B. *The Suez Canal was successful*
        1. _____

2. _____

3. _____

C. *But the Suez Canal did not bring an era of harmony; instead it brought European domination*

1. _____

2. _____

3. _____

II. *The New Imperialism: Motives and Methods*
A. *Political Motives*
1. *Establish or increase prestige*
a) _____

b) _____

c) _____

d) _____

2. *Many colonies gained through on-the-spot border skirmishes*
a) _____

b) _____

c) _____

d) _____

B. *Cultural Motives*
1. *Exporting their norms of "civilized" behavior*
a) _____

b) _____

c) _____

2. *Missionaries softened colonialism, but also clashed with local peoples*
a) _____

b) _____

c) _____

d) _____

e) _____

3. *Cultural superiority and progress*
   a) _____

   b) _____

   c) _____

4. *Imperialism gained mass appeal*
   a) _____

   b) _____

   c) _____

C. *Economic Motives*
   1. *Entrepreneurs demanded stable supplies of goods*
      a) _____

      b) _____

      c) _____

   2. *Entrepreneurs sought the help of governments*
      a) _____

      b) _____

      c) _____

   3. *Increased power enabled conquests*
      a) _____

      b) _____

        c) _____

D.   **The Tools of the Imperialists**
    1.   **Steamships**
        a) _____

        b) _____

        c) _____

        d) _____

    2.   **Quinine**
        a) _____

        b) _____

        c) _____

    3.   **The breech-loader, smokeless powder, and repeating rifles**
        a) _____

        b) _____

        c) _____

        d) _____

        e) _____

    4.   **The Battle of Omdurman**
        a) _____

        b) _____

        c) _____

E.   **Colonial Agents and Administration**
    1.   **The system of colonialism and the transformation of Africa and Asia**
        a) _____

        b) _____

c) _____

2. *Different types of colonies and styles*
    a) _____

    b) _____

    c) _____

    d) _____

3. *Europeans in the colonies participated in government*
    a) _____

    b) _____

    c) _____

4. *Cooperation of local elites*
    a) _____

    b) _____

    c) _____

5. *Women and colonialism*
    a) _____

    b) _____

    c) _____

    d) _____

    e) _____

    f) _____

III. *The Scramble for Africa*
   A. *Egypt*
      1. *Modernization*
          a) _____

b) _____

c) _____

2. *Debt and resulting British and French intervention*
   a) _____

   b) _____

   c) _____

   d) _____

3. *British occupation of Egypt and economic development*
   a) _____

   b) _____

   c) _____

   d) _____

   e) _____

   f) _____

B. *Western and Equatorial Africa*
   1. *The French conquest of Sudan*
      a) _____

      b) _____

      c) _____

   2. *Three people conquered the Congo Basin*
      a) _____

      b) _____

      c) _____

3. *The "scramble" for Africa*
    a) _____

    b) _____

    c) _____

    d) _____

4. *"Effective occupation"*
    a) _____

    b) _____

    c) _____

    d) _____

    e) _____

    f) _____

5. *The Rubber Boom and public outcry*
    a) _____

    b) _____

    c) _____

C. *Southern Africa*
    1. *Had been occupied by Europeans for quite a while*
        a) _____

        b) _____

        c) _____

    2. *The new El Dorado*
        a) _____

        b) _____

3. *The Zulu and King Cetshwayo*
   a) _____

   b) _____

   c) _____

   d) _____

4. *The gold rush, diamonds, and Afrikaners*
   a) _____

   b) _____

   c) _____

   d) _____

   e) _____

   f) _____

5. *The Union of South Africa*
   a) _____

   b) _____

   c) _____

D. *Political and Social Consequences*
   1. *People reacted differently to colonial rule—from welcome to pastorialist protest*
      a) _____

      b) _____

      c) _____

      d) _____

      e) _____

      f) _____

2. *People with longtime contact with Europeans also fought back*
   a) _____

   b) _____

   c) _____

3. *Ethiopia*
   a) _____

   b) _____

   c) _____

   d) _____

4. *Most people tried to remain unaffected but this was not possible due to the many changes that occurred under colonialism*
   a) _____

   b) _____

   c) _____

   d) _____

   e) _____

   f) _____

E. *Cultural Responses*
   1. *Missionaries, mission schools, and Western ideals*
      a) _____

      b) _____

      c) _____

      d) _____

      e) _____

2. *"Ethiopian" churches*
   a) _____

   b) _____

   c) _____

3. *The spread of Islam and the role of colonialism*
   a) _____

   b) _____

   c) _____

IV. *Asia and Western Dominance*
   A.   *Central Asia*
      1.   *The Russians able to take over Kazakhstan*
          a) _____

          b) _____

          c) _____

      2.   *The Russians took fabled Silk Road cities*
          a) _____

          b) _____

          c) _____

      3.   *Russian impact*
          a) _____

          b) _____

          c) _____

   B.   *Southeast Asia and Indonesia*
      1.   *The region had experienced contact with outsiders for many years—now they were colonized*
          a) _____

b) _____

c) _____

2. *Good area for agriculture—especially imported cash crops*
   a) _____

   b) _____

   c) _____

3. *Colonialism brought benefits and changes in ethnic/cultural profiles*
   a) _____

   b) _____

   c) _____

   d) _____

   e) _____

4. *Self-awareness and nationalism*
   a) _____

   b) _____

   c) _____

C. *Hawaii and the Philippines, 1878–1902*
   1. *The United States began a program of outside expansion*
      a) _____

      b) _____

      c) _____

   2. *Annexations in the Pacific*
      a) _____

      b) _____

c) _____

d) _____

3. *Annexation of the Philippines and the U.S. occupation*

a) _____

b) _____

c) _____

d) _____

e) _____

4. *Philippine independence*

a) _____

b) _____

c) _____

V. *Imperialism in Latin America*

  A. *Railroads and the Imperialism of Free Trade*

    1. *Needed to open up the interior to develop the potential of Latin America*

a) _____

b) _____

c) _____

    2. *Argentina*

a) _____

b) _____

c) _____

    3. *Countries with political elites vs. countries populated by poor Indians*

a) _____

b) _____

c) _____

B. *American Expansionism and the Spanish-American War, 1898*
   1. *Four reasons why Europe did not try to gain territory in Latin America*
       a) _____

       b) _____

       c) _____

       d) _____

   2. *Cuba*
       a) _____

       b) _____

       c) _____

       d) _____

   3. *The Spanish-American War*
       a) _____

       b) _____

       c) _____

C. *American Intervention in the Caribbean and Central America, 1901–1914*
   1. *The poor nations of Central America and the Caribbean seemed open to intervention*
       a) _____

       b) _____

       c) _____

   2. *United States policy and interference*
       a) _____

       b) _____

       c) _____

3. *Panama and the Panama Canal*
   a) _____

   b) _____

   c) _____

   d) _____

   e) _____

VI. *The World Economy and the Global Environment*
   A. *Expansion of the World Economy*
       1. *The Industrial Revolution expanded the demand for tropical products*
          a) _____

          b) _____

          c) _____

       2. *Traditional methods could not meet demand*
          a) _____

          b) _____

          c) _____

       3. *Transportation: shorter time and less costly*
          a) _____

          b) _____

          c) _____

   B. *Transformation of the Global Environment*
       1. *Cultivation and exploitation of tropical plants*
          a) _____

          b) _____

          c) _____

          d) _____

e) _____

2. *Displacement of forests and traditional agriculture by modern agricultural techniques*
    a) _____

    b) _____

    c) _____

3. *Irrigation systems and railroads*
    a) _____

    b) _____

    c) _____

    d) _____

    e) _____

4. *The search for minerals*
    a) _____

    b) _____

    c) _____

    d) _____

VII. *Conclusion*
    A. *The opening of the Suez Canal was the symbolic beginning of New Imperialism*
        1. _____

        2. _____

        3. _____

   B.   *Rapid conquest: motivations and means*

      1. _____

      2. _____

      3. _____

   C.   *The Panama Canal confirmed the new power of the industrializing nations*

      1. _____

      2. _____

      3. _____

IDENTIFICATIONS

Define each term and explain why it is significant, including any important dates.

	Identification	Significance
Suez Canal		
New Imperialism		
Battle of Omdurman		

Identification   **Significance**

colonialism

"scramble" for Africa

Henry Morton Stanley

King Leopold II (Belgium)

Savorgnan de Brazza

Berlin Conference

Afrikaners

Cecil Rhodes

Asante

Menelik

Emilio Aguinaldo

Identification	Significance

free-trade imperialism

Panama Canal

MULTIPLE-CHOICE QUESTIONS

Read the entire question, including *all* the possible answers. Then choose the *one* answer that best fits the question.

1. The Suez Canal
    a. inaugurated an era of harmony among the peoples of Africa, Asia, and Europe, just as Ismail had intended.
    b. made Egypt powerful and independent.
    c. made an enormous sum of money for France, which had contributed half of the funds and most of the engineers to build the canal.
    d. was never completed, because no foreign country was willing to invest in such a radical project.
    e. provided the British with an excuse for occupying Egypt to protect their interests.
2. How did European nations gain much of their land in West Africa, Southeast Asia, and the Pacific islands?
    a. They fought each other for it.
    b. Most European nations had an "imperialism plan" designed by entrepreneurs and the military that was supposed to increase trade.
    c. Many of these nations asked European nations for help in civil wars and then in gratitude offered them a reward of land.
    d. Most of the lands were gained in the War of Austrian Succession.
    e. Most lands were gained when troops stationed in a region took part in frontier wars; the Crown then felt obligated to assume direct control of these lands.
3. Which of the following statements best characterizes the role of missionary women in the colonies?
    a. They had little or no impact.
    b. They simply promoted the interests of the dominant colonizing power.
    c. They usually supported the cultural norms already present among the native peoples of the colony.
    d. Their influence often softened the harshness of colonial rule.
    e. Their influence usually brought about the end of colonialism in whichever colony they worked.

4.   Which single factor was most responsible for the ability of industrial peoples to overcome non-industrial peoples?

a.   Religion
b.   Politics
c.   Technology
d.   Science
e.   Money

5.   As Asians and Africans acquired old weapons that European armies had discarded,

a.   they became better able to defend themselves.
b.   they gained more bargaining power, for the battles were more costly to Europeans.
c.   they were better armed, but because new weapons technology was far superior, the Europeans still had the upper hand.
d.   the occurrence of civil war in Asia and Africa increased.
e.   nothing changed, because spears and arrows were plenty deadly to European armies.

6.   The impact of colonial rule depended

a.   mostly on the type of colonial rule instituted by the colonizer.
b.   mostly on economic and social conditions in the colony.
c.   on the retention of indigenous rulers by Western powers.
d.   on how peaceful was the original takeover.
e.   on how strong indigenous culture was.

7.   The arrival of white women in Asia and Africa

a.   led to increasing racial segregation.
b.   often brought about a greater degree of equality between whites and nonwhites because of women's civilizing influence.
c.   led to intermarriage between European women and indigenous men.
d.   always resulted in better treatment of indigenous peoples.
e.   rarely had any impact at all.

8.   The British government, wary of costly commitments overseas,

a.   dismantled its colonial empire.
b.   rarely responded to its citizens' requests for assistance.
c.   encouraged European settlers to manage their own affairs.
d.   encouraged its colonies to declare independence.
e.   hired other countries to run its colonial governments.

9.   Which of the following kingdoms was one of the few to successfully resist European takeover?

a.   The kingdom of Asante
b.   Ethiopia
c.   South Africa
d.   Java
e.   Egypt

10.   Which of the following European imperial policies was especially disruptive?

    a.   Changes in local marriage traditions
    b.   Changes in landholding practices
    c.   Changes in local government
    d.   Changes in religious practices
    e.   Changes in the traditional authority systems

11.   European colonialism may have aided the diffusion of Islam in Africa by

    a.   outlawing tribal religions.
    b.   building cities and increasing trade.
    c.   outlawing Islam.
    d.   starting missionary schools, thereby giving Africans a negative view of Christianity.
    e.   their attempts to suppress Islam, therefore triggering a backlash.

12.   Which country in Southeast Asia managed to retain its independence in the face of European colonialism?

    a.   Siam (Thailand)
    b.   Burma
    c.   Singapore
    d.   Malaya
    e.   Indochina

13.   Most of the material wealth of Southeast Asia was

    a.   generally kept in Southeast Asia.
    b.   usually exported to Europe and North America.
    c.   divided equally between the colony and the colonizer.
    d.   generally reinvested in the development of Southeast Asia.
    e.   squandered by incompetent or unscrupulous managers.

14.   The Filipinos were

    a.   happy with Spanish rule.
    b.   happier with American rule.
    c.   happy with any colonial rule.
    d.   not anxious to trade one master for another.
    e.   not ready for independence.

15.   Which of the following was *not* one reason that the British avoided acquiring a large territorial empire in Latin America?

    a.   Latin American governments were hostile to European investment.
    b.   The British were already overextended in Asia and Africa.
    c.   Latin Americans were quite capable of resisting invasions.
    d.   The United States declared, through the Monroe Doctrine, its opposition to European intervention in the Americas.
    e.   They didn't need to construct a traditional empire, because they could get what they wanted with the backing of Latin America's leaders.

SHORT-ANSWER QUESTIONS

Answer each question in one short paragraph, giving the definition, dates, and significance.

1. Discuss the role of indigenous peoples in colonial government. Were they passive receivers of colonial policy, or were they active participants, either supporting or resisting imperialism?

2. Discuss the role of women in New Imperialism. Did their roles differ from the roles of the men?

3. How and why did the British takeover of the Suez Canal occur?

4. Were Christian ideals compatible with colonialism? Explain.

5. Describe the ethnic composition of Southeast Asia. How did it get this way, and how did ethnic diversity affect the region?

ESSAY QUESTIONS

Make an outline of each question, listing the major points you want to discuss. Then write your practice essay, following your outline carefully and making sure that you do not skip any of your major points. At this time you will want to add the relevant dates and details that will make your essay persuasive and accurate.

1. The late nineteenth century was a time of empire building. Identify the countries that did the building and the regions that became a part of these empires. What inspired imperialist nations to expand? What tools did they use? How were their actions received by native peoples? What were some of the long-term results of this imperialism?

2. Discuss the sense of moral duty and cultural superiority felt by Europeans toward non-Western peoples. How was this manifested in European relationships with indigenous peoples? Give specific examples.

3. Discuss the different types of colonial government. What factors influenced which type would be chosen? Did these governments run smoothly? Why or why not?

4. Compare and contrast either three regions of Asia or three regions of Africa. How did their occupiers treat the various regions differently, and why? Use specific examples.

5. Discuss the role of Islam in the face of European colonialism. What made Islam an attractive religion, and how did it help indigenous peoples?

6. Discuss imperialism in Latin America. How was it different from imperialism in Asia and Africa?

COMPARISON CHARTS

Using information gathered from the text, fill in the blank areas of each chart with the relevant data pertaining to the regions and categories listed. (Not all blank areas will necessarily be used.)

Chart 28.1

THE SCRAMBLE FOR AFRICA

	European Nations Involved	Individuals Involved	Dates	Motives	Methods	Technology	Resources	Products	European Cultural Responses	Native Peoples', Cultural Resources
Egypt										
Western and Equatorial Africa										
Southern Africa										

Chart 28.2

WORLD ECONOMY AND TROPICAL ENVIRONMENTS

	Region of Origin	Region Where Transplanted	Country Responsible for Transfer	Date	Use	Technology Involved	Environmental Impact
Cotton							
Tea							
Rubber							
Latex							
Tobacco							
Cinchona							

DIVERSITY AND DOMINANCE

After reading "Diversity and Dominance: Two Africans Recall the Arrival of the Europeans" in your text, answer the following additional questions.

Why did the women hide themselves from the Europeans? Why do you think that the Habe welcomed the Europeans, but the Fulani did not?

Why would the slavers kill Oleka and Katinga's baby? Why are the experiences of these two women so different?

INTERNET ASSIGNMENT

Keywords: **"Panama Canal"**

                    "Telegraph History"

In this age of innovation, some inventions stand out as revolutionary. Use the above keywords to find both written and visual web materials. You might also want to consult the *History WIRED* image library on *The Earth and Its Peoples* web site (refer to the preface of this study guide for information on how to locate the text home page). How did the creation of the Panama Canal and the invention of the telegraph "shrink the world," and therefore change the course of history? How were they viewed by Westerners? How do you suppose local peoples viewed them? What would our world today be like without their invention?

INTERNET EXPLORATION

Today we view tea as the quintessential English drink, but it was not always so. Learn how tea became an important part of British life, society, and culture by using the keywords "tea, history" or by visiting http://www.panix.com/~kendra/tea/afternoon_tea.html. What products accompanied tea? What economic role did tea and its accompaniments play in British history? How did tea and tea parties influence women? Why did Americans become coffee drinkers?

MAP EXERCISES

On Outline Map 28.1, mark the extent of colonial presence in 1878. Then shade in the regions controlled by Europeans by the early twentieth century. Use different colors for different colonizers.

On Outline Map 28.2, shade in the regions controlled by Europeans by the late nineteenth and early twentieth centuries. Use different colors for different colonizers.

Outline Map 28.1

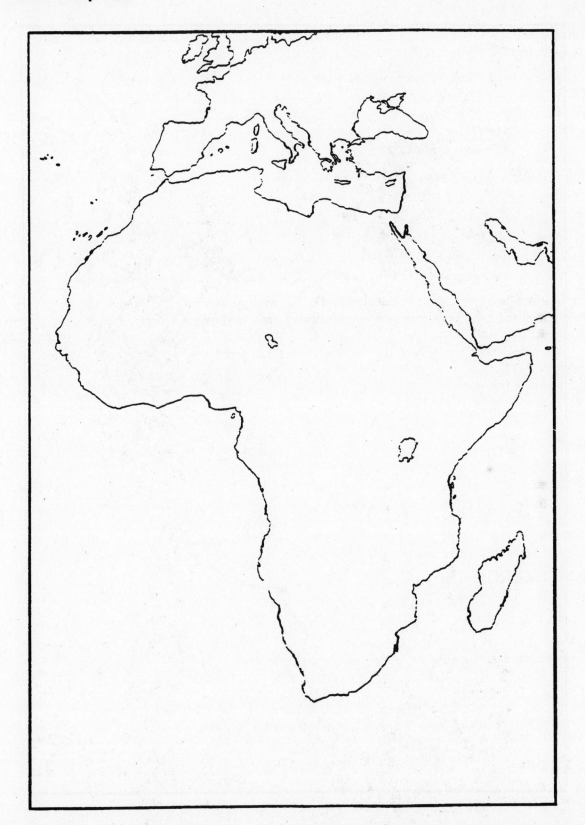

Outline Map 28.2

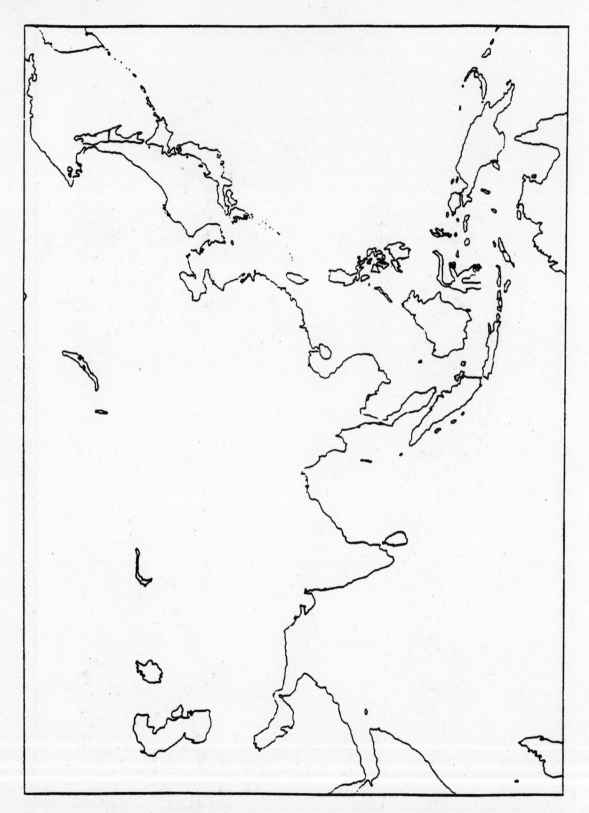

ANSWERS TO MULTIPLE-CHOICE QUESTIONS

1. e p. 749
2. e p. 750
3. d p. 750
4. c p. 752
5. c p. 753
6. b p. 754
7. a p. 754
8. c p. 758
9. b p. 759
10. b p. 759
11. b p. 761
12. a p. 765
13. b p. 765
14. d p. 766
15. a p. 770

CHAPTER 29

The Crisis of the Imperial Order, 1900–1929

LEARNING OBJECTIVES

After reading Chapter 29 and completing this study chapter, you should be able to explain:

• What caused the Great War and how it differed from most of the wars fought in the past.

• How the Great War affected Russia, and the subsequent revolution that resulted in the formation of a new nation, the USSR.

• How the Great War changed the world, and particularly how it affected the Middle East, Africa, and East Asia.

• What changes became apparent in Western society in the aftermath of the Great War, including rising consumerism and environmental transformation.

• How China and Japan changed in the early twentieth century, and how they went from being similar to being quite different.

CHAPTER OUTLINE

In the outline below, include important themes, concepts, and details in the blank spaces provided. If you find fewer points than you have space for, leave lines blank. If you find more points, add as many lines as necessary.

I. *Introduction*
   A. *The assassination of the Archduke Ferdinand and his wife*
      1. _____

      2. _____

      3. _____

   B. *Global war*
      1. _____

      2. _____

      3. _____

II.   *Origins of the Crisis in Europe and the Middle East*
    A.   *The Ottoman Empire and the Balkans*
        1.   *The "Sick man of Europe"*
            a) _____

            b) _____

            c) _____

        2.   *Territorial losses*
            a) _____

            b) _____

            c) _____

            d) _____

            e) _____

        3.   *The Europeans meddle in Ottoman affairs and Ottoman reaction*
            a) _____

            b) _____

            c) _____

        4.   *The new regime (1909)*
            a) _____

            b) _____

            c) _____

            d) _____

    B.   *Nationalism, Alliances, and Military Strategy*
        1.   *Nationalism: unity and division*
            a) _____

            b) _____

c) _____

d) _____

e) _____

f) _____

2. *Nationalism: liberty or vengeance?*
    a) _____

    b) _____

    c) _____

3. *Alliances*
    a) _____

    b) _____

    c) _____

    d) _____

4. *Inflexible military planning and mobilization*
    a) _____

    b) _____

    c) _____

    d) _____

    e) _____

    f) _____

5. *The declaration of war and German plans*
    a) _____

    b) _____

c) _____

d) _____

e) _____

III. *The "Great War" and the Russian Revolutions, 1914–1918*
    A.   *Stalemate, 1914–1917*
        1.   *The character of war changed*
            a) _____

            b) _____

            c) _____

            d) _____

            e) _____

        2.   *The Western Front, machine guns, and trenches*
            a) _____

            b) _____

            c) _____

            d) _____

            e) _____

        3.   *Casualties, 1916, and sea battles*
            a) _____

            b) _____

            c) _____

        4.   *New innovations had little impact*
            a) _____

            b) _____

c) _____

d) _____

B.   *The Home Front and the War Economy*
1.   *Rationing and new people entered the work force*
a) _____

b) _____

c) _____

d) _____

e) _____

2.   *German civilians paid a high price*
a) _____

b) _____

c) _____

d) _____

e) _____

3.   *Hardships in Europe's African colonies*
a) _____

b) _____

c) _____

d) _____

e) _____

f) _____

4.   *United States*
a) _____

b) _____

c) _____

C.   *The Ottoman Empire at War*
  1.   *The Ottomans join the war*
  a) _____

  b) _____

  c) _____

  d) _____

  e) _____

  2.   *The British made alliances to defeat the Ottomans*
  a) _____

  b) _____

  c) _____

  d) _____

  e) _____

  3.   *The Zionist movement and the promise of Israel*
  a) _____

  b) _____

  c) _____

  d) _____

  e) _____

  4.   *Mesopotamia and India*
  a) _____

b) _____

c) _____

D.   *Double Revolution in Russia, 1917*
1.   *Military failures and shortages*
  a) _____

  b) _____

  c) _____

  d) _____

  e) _____

2.   *The food ran out, and a Provisional Government was established*
  a) _____

  b) _____

  c) _____

  d) _____

3.   *The Bolsheviks, the Mensheviks, and Lenin*
  a) _____

  b) _____

  c) _____

  d) _____

  e) _____

4.   *Tug-of-war between Kerensky and Lenin*
  a) _____

  b) _____

  c) _____

   d) _____

5.   *The Bolsheviks win*
   a) _____

   b) _____

   c) _____

E.   *The End of the War in Western Europe, 1917–1918*
   1.   *The Germans' submarines brought an isolationist U.S. into the war, 1917*
      a) _____

      b) _____

      c) _____

   2.   *The soldiers began to mutiny*
      a) _____

      b) _____

      c) _____

      d) _____

      e) _____

   3.   *The Germans pushed to Paris, but victory eluded them*
      a) _____

      b) _____

      c) _____

IV.   *Peace and Dislocation in Europe, 1919–1929*
   A.   *The Impact of the War*
      1.   *Death, destruction, and dislocation*
         a) _____

         b) _____

c) _____

d) _____

e) _____

f) _____

2.   *The great influenza epidemic of 1918–1919*
a) _____

b) _____

c) _____

3.   *Environmental damage*
a) _____

b) _____

c) _____

B.   *The Peace Treaties*
1.   *"Three all-powerful, all-ignorant men, sitting there and carving up continents"*
a) _____

b) _____

c) _____

2.   *Three different agendas—little success*
a) _____

b) _____

c) _____

d) _____

e) _____

f) _____

3. ***Germany signed the Treaty of Versailles***
    a) _____

    b) _____

    c) _____

    d) _____

4. ***The Treaty of Saint-Germain***
    a) _____

    b) _____

    c) _____

    d) _____

    e) _____

C. ***Russian Civil War and the New Economic Policy***
    1. ***War in Russia continued and foreign intervention***
        a) _____

        b) _____

        c) _____

        d) _____

        e) _____

        f) _____

    2. ***Rebuilding an empire***
        a) _____

        b) _____

        c) _____

d) _____

e) _____

3. *A ruined economy*
   a) _____

   b) _____

   c) _____

4. *The New Economic Policy*
   a) _____

   b) _____

   c) _____

   d) _____

   e) _____

   f) _____

5. *Lenin's death and the scramble for power*
   a) _____

   b) _____

   c) _____

D. *An Ephemeral Peace*
   1. *Dreams and expectations following the war*
      a) _____

      b) _____

      c) _____

      d) _____

      e) _____

f) _____

2. *Crisis in Germany*
   a) _____

   b) _____

   c) _____

   d) _____

   e) _____

   f) _____

3. *A few years of peace and prosperity (1924–1929)*
   a) _____

   b) _____

   c) _____

4. *Russia and Germany made a pact, and the League of Nations*
   a) _____

   b) _____

   c) _____

   d) _____

V. *China and Japan: Contrasting Destinies*
   A. *Social and Economic Change*
      1. *Decline in agricultural production, flood in China, and calamities in Japan*
         a) _____

         b) _____

         c) _____

         d) _____

e) _____

f) _____

2. *Chinese social structure*
   a) _____

   b) _____

   c) _____

   d) _____

   e) _____

3. *Japanese growth, electricity, and social tensions*
   a) _____

   b) _____

   c) _____

   d) _____

   e) _____

   f) _____

4. *The zaibatsu and foreign trade*
   a) _____

   b) _____

   c) _____

   d) _____

   e) _____

B. *Revolution and War, 1900–1918*
    1. *Cixi and the Boxers*
        a) _____

        b) _____

        c) _____

    2. *Sun Yat-sen and the military*
        a) _____

        b) _____

        c) _____

        d) _____

        e) _____

        f) _____

    3. *Yuan Shikai and the Guomindang*
        a) _____

        b) _____

        c) _____

    4. *The Japanese tried to further their interests in China and the Pacific*
        a) _____

        b) _____

        c) _____

        d) _____

        e) _____

C. *Chinese Warlords and the Guomindang, 1919–1929*
    1. *The May Fourth (1919) Movement*
        a) _____

b) _____

c) _____

2. *Sun Yat-sen and ties to communism*
    a) _____

    b) _____

    c) _____

3. *Chiang Kai-shek and unsuccessful attempts to modernize*
    a) _____

    b) _____

    c) _____

    d) _____

    e) _____

VI. *The New Middle East*
  A. *The Mandate System*
    1. *The beginning and purpose of the system*
      a) _____

      b) _____

      c) _____

    2. *C and B mandates*
      a) _____

      b) _____

      c) _____

    3. *A mandates*
      a) _____

b) _____

c) _____

B.   **The Rise of Modern Turkey**
1.   **Turkey invaded and then the nationalists repelled invaders and expelled Greek citizens**
a) _____

b) _____

c) _____

d) _____

e) _____

2.   **Mustafa Kemal (Atatürk) embarked on a campaign of modernization**
a) _____

b) _____

c) _____

d) _____

3.   **Kemal also Westernized society**
a) _____

b) _____

c) _____

d) _____

e) _____

C.   **Arab Lands and the Question of Palestine**
1.   **Protests, social changes, and population**
a) _____

b) _____

c) _____

2. *Westernization and European dominance of colonies*
   a) _____

   b) _____

   c) _____

   d) _____

3. *The French in Algeria, Tunisia, and Morocco*
   a) _____

   b) _____

   c) _____

4. *The British in Syria, Iraq, and Egypt*
   a) _____

   b) _____

   c) _____

   d) _____

   e) _____

5. *Palestine*
   a) _____

   b) _____

   c) _____

   d) _____

   e) _____

VII. *Society, Culture, and Technology in the Industrialized World*
    A.   **Class and Gender**
        1.   *Class distinctions were ending, and growth of the middle class*
            a) _____

            b) _____

            c) _____

        2.   *Government sponsored infrastructure and the working class*
            a) _____

            b) _____

            c) _____

        3.   *Women's lives changed rapidly*
            a) _____

            b) _____

            c) _____

            d) _____

        4.   *Women and social movements*
            a) _____

            b) _____

            c) _____

            d) _____

            e) _____

    B.   **Revolution in the Sciences**
        1.   *The new physics: Planck and Einstein*
            a) _____

            b) _____

c) _____

d) _____

2. *The new social sciences: Freud and Durkheim*

a) _____

b) _____

c) _____

d) _____

3. *The very superiority of Western civilization challenged*

a) _____

b) _____

c) _____

C. *The New Technologies of Modernity*
1. *The latest inventions*

a) _____

b) _____

c) _____

2. *Airplanes*

a) _____

b) _____

c) _____

d) _____

e) _____

3. *Electricity*

a) _____

b) _____

c) _____

4. *The radio*
   a) _____

   b) _____

   c) _____

5. *Film*
   a) _____

   b) _____

   c) _____

   d) _____

   e) _____

   f) _____

6. *Health and hygiene*
   a) _____

   b) _____

   c) _____

   d) _____

7. *The cult of cleanliness*
   a) _____

   b) _____

   c) _____

   d) _____

D.   *Technology and the Environment*
    1.   *Skyscrapers*
        a) _____

        b) _____

        c) _____

        d) _____

        e) _____

        f) _____

    2.   *Automobiles in urban areas*
        a) _____

        b) _____

        c) _____

        d) _____

        e) _____

        f) _____

    3.   *Automobiles in rural areas*
        a) _____

        b) _____

        c) _____

        d) _____

        e) _____

VIII. *Conclusion*
    A.   *A major realignment*
        1. _____

2. _____

3. _____

4. _____

    B.   *Only two countries benefited from the war*

       1. _____

       2. _____

       3. _____

    C.   *The destructive power of technology*

       1. _____

       2. _____

       3. _____

IDENTIFICATIONS

Define each term and explain why it is significant, including any important dates.

	Identification	**Significance**
Western Front		
Faisal		
Theodore Herzl		
Balfour Declaration		

	Identification	Significance
nationalism		
Bolsheviks		
Vladimir Lenin		
trenches		
Woodrow Wilson		
League of Nations		
Treaty of Versailles		
New Economic Policy		
Sun Yat-sen		
Yuan Shikai		
Goumindang		

	Identification	Significance
Chiang Kai-shek		
mandate system		
submarines		
Margaret Sanger		
Max Planck		
Albert Einstein		
Wilbur and Orville Wright		
radio		

MULTIPLE-CHOICE QUESTIONS

Read the entire question, including *all* the possible answers. Then choose the *one* answer that best fits the question.

1.   Who was the "sick man of Europe?"
    a.   Otto von Bismarck
    b.   Franz Ferdinand
    c.   Tsar Nicholas II
    d.   Serbia
    e.   The Ottoman Empire

2.   Which of the following statements about nationalism is *not* true?

    a.   It was one of the causes of the Great War.
    b.   It was deeply rooted in European culture.
    c.   It was a powerful unifying force.
    d.   It could be a divisive force.
    e.   It was not really a factor in Europe since the French Revolution.

3.   Why could no country's mobilization be canceled or postponed without creating chaos?

    a.   The country would have lost face.
    b.   The element of surprise would have been lost.
    c.   The trains ran on precise schedules that were inflexible.
    d.   The boats took a long time to load.
    e.   There were so many cars on the road that traffic jams were common.

4.   During the Great War, machine guns and trench warfare

    a.   guaranteed that the war would be over quickly, but with a lot of casualties.
    b.   imposed a stalemate that lasted four years.
    c.   made warfare less personal.
    d.   meant that sea battles were even more decisive to the war's outcome
    e.   were new innovations invented for use in the Great War.

5.   Why did socialists and labor unions actively support the war?

    a.   They saw it as their chance to overthrow the government and institute communism.
    b.   The war effort provided union jobs.
    c.   They saw regulation imposed by the government as preferable to the free enterprise system.
    d.   They were given special recruitment rights to join the military and fight in the war.
    e.   They wanted larger empires to bring greater prosperity to the workers.

6.   Why did nutrition improve among the poor in France and Britain during the war?

    a.   There was more food to eat.
    b.   Great numbers of people joined the military, and the government fed them.
    c.   France and Britain could no longer export food to their colonies because of blockades.
    d.   Food rations were allotted on the basis of need.
    e.   There were improvements in agricultural technology.

7.   Why did the Russians go hungry in the Great War?

    a.   There was no food.
    b.   They ran out of ration cards.
    c.   With so many men in the army, railroads broke down for lack of fuel and parts, affecting distribution.
    d.   The Bolsheviks controlled the food and would not let the people disloyal to them have any.
    e.   All of the food went to the troops on the Western Front.

8.   Which of the following countries never joined the League of Nations?

    a.   Germany
    b.   France
    c.   The United States
    d.   Britain
    e.   Japan

9. Why did the Germans allow Lenin to cross through Germany on his way to Russia?

    a. They had to because of the Hitler-Stalin Pact.
    b. They were hoping that Lenin would get assassinated.
    c. They wanted Lenin in Russia, where they hoped he would cause trouble.
    d. They wanted control of Siberia, which Lenin had promised.
    e. They did not know that he passed through Germany because he was disguised as a Polish prince.

10. By the mid 1930s, 89 percent of which of the following country's households had electric lights?

    a. The United States
    b. England
    c. Japan
    d. India
    e. France

11. What finally got the United States to enter the Great War?

    a. The Germans tried to starve the British into submission using a submarine blockade.
    b. The United States was finally able to build enough ships.
    c. The United States' economy was failing due to a lack of markets because of the war.
    d. Britain and France were about to win.
    e. Germany was about to win.

12. Which of the following was *not* a reason for the Bolshevik victory?

    a. The anti-Bolshevik forces were never really united.
    b. The Bolsheviks held a geographically central position.
    c. The Bolshevik army was more disciplined.
    d. The Europeans fought on the side of the Bolsheviks against the Mensheviks.
    e. The peasants feared that a return of the tsars would bring their landlords back.

13. What caused the peasants and the Communists to be bitter enemies?

    a. The peasants, for the most part, supported the old tsarist system.
    b. The Communists taxed the peasants heavily to pay for the industrialization of the USSR.
    c. The Communists favored the factory workers, and not the peasants, when it came to reform.
    d. The peasants wanted to be collectivized, but the Communists thought that collectivization would not work.
    e. The Communists refused to try to control the economy.

14. What were students protesting during the May Fourth, 1919 Movement?

    a. Japan's Twenty-One Demands on China
    b. The Treaty of Versailles
    c. British inroads into China
    d. Empress Cixi's policies, particularly the Boxer Uprising
    e. Control by regional warlords

15. The Middle East mandate system

    a. was merely a thinly disguised form of colonization.
    b. was beneficial to the Middle East.
    c. was a plan to modernize the Middle East.
    d. was a plan to quickly install democracy in the Middle East.
    e. was applied equally to the entire region.

16.   What was the only nation to grant women the right to vote before the twentieth century?

a.   Turkey
b.   New Zealand
c.   Britain
d.   The United States
e.   Japan

SHORT-ANSWER QUESTIONS

Answer each question in one short paragraph, giving the definition, dates, and significance.

1.   Why was there a stalemate during the Great War? How did it finally end?

2.   How did the war affect women and African-Americans? Did the war change their status or what was expected of them? Did any changes last?

3.   Why did the Empress Cixi encourage the Boxers to rise up?

4.   What goals and plans did the Bolsheviks have, and how did they realize them?

5.   Discuss the League of Nations. What were its successes and failures?

6.   What technology transformed the landscape in the Western world more than any other? Explain this transformation.

7.   Discuss British and French goals and tactics in the Middle East. What was their legacy?

ESSAY QUESTIONS

Make an outline of each question, listing the major points you want to discuss. Then write your practice essay, following your outline carefully and making sure that you do not skip any of your major points. At this time you will want to add the relevant dates and details that will make your essay persuasive and accurate.

1.   Discuss the factors that historians generally believe led up to the Great War.

2.   How was the Great War different from the wars the generals had studied and from the war they expected?

3.   Compare and contrast the personalities of Woodrow Wilson, David Lloyd George, and Georges Clemenceau, and how those personalities affected the negotiations to end the Great War. How did they attempt to create a new world order through the Treaty of Versailles? Were they successful?

4.   Compare Russia before the Great War and the USSR afterward. What remained the same and what changed? What effect did the war have?

5.   Discuss the two sides of progress. How did technology both improve lives and worsen the quality of life? Use specific examples.

6.   Discuss the political and economic developments in China that brought on the fall of the Qing and the rise of Republican China. What factors and events plagued China up through the First World War?

COMPARISON CHARTS

Using information gathered from the text, fill in the blank areas of each chart with the relevant data pertaining to the regions and categories listed. (Not all blank areas will necessarily be used.)

Chart 29.1

THE GREAT WAR

	Russia	Serbia	France	Britain	United States	China	Japan	Germany	Austria-Hungary	Ottoman Empire
Treaties and Alliances										
Territory Desired										
Territory Gained										
Resources Desired										
Resources Gained										
Other Goals										
Technology										
Methods										
Home Front										
Casualties—Military										
Casualties—Civilian										

Chart 29.2

THE BOLSHEVIK REVOLUTION

	Government System	Social System	Economic System	Role of Religion	Role of Women	Technology	Allies	Diplomatic Relations
Russia Before the Revolution								
USSR After the Revolution								

DIVERSITY AND DOMINANCE

After reading "Diversity and Dominance: The Middle East After World War I" in your text, answer the following additional questions.

In light of the events of recent decades, do Balfour and Wilson sound a bit naïve? Do the members of the General Syrian Congress take a more practical view? Would it have been more effective then? Why or why not?

INTERNET ASSIGNMENT

Keywords: **"Aircraft of the Great War"**

"The Gates Flying Circus" or "The Golden Age of Aviation"

Today we think nothing of cross-country, or even transatlantic flights, but early in the twentieth century air travel was new. Use the above keywords to find images of early pilots and their planes and read about their accomplishments. You might also want to consult the *History WIRED* image library on *The Earth and Its Peoples* web site (refer to the preface of this study guide for information on how to locate the text home page). The keywords represent two different uses of airplanes. How were the planes similar, and why? To what use were airplanes put in the First World War? How were flying circuses important to the development of aviation? Do you find mention of any famous aviators in the ranks of barnstormers?

INTERNET EXPLORATION

This site, http://www.csse.monash.edu.au/~pringle/silent/, has everything you want to know about silent films: movie descriptions and reviews, stars, promotional materials, and external links to local film festivals and television schedules. What subjects and themes were important in early-twentieth-century films? How have movie tastes changed over the years? Why have many of these films remained popular? For other interesting sites, use the keywords "silent film history."

MAP EXERCISES

On Outline Map 29.1, shade in the following:

> The Entente Powers and the Allies
>
> The Central Powers
>
> Neutral nations
>
> Farthest German-Austrian advance during the Great War

On Outline Map 29.2, mark the borders of the Ottoman Empire in 1914, then shade in regions controlled by France and Great Britain in 1920.

Outline Map 29.1

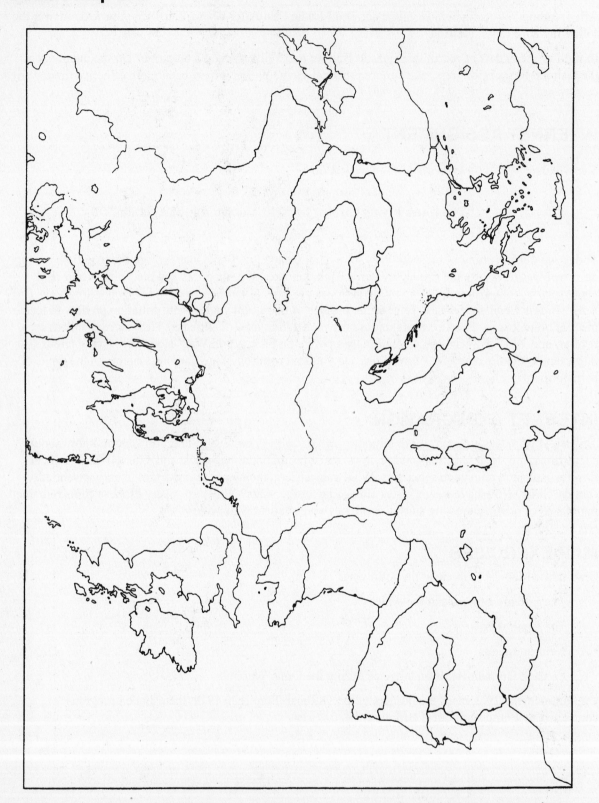

Outline Map 29.2

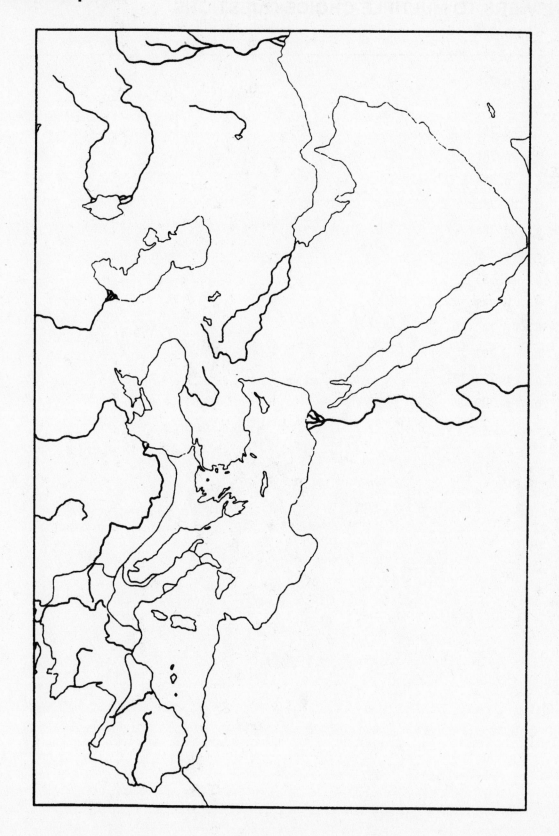

ANSWERS TO MULTIPLE-CHOICE QUESTIONS

1. e   p. 776
2. e   p. 777, 778
3. c   p. 778
4. b   p. 781
5. c   p. 781
6. d   p. 781
7. c   p. 784
8. c   p. 786
9. c   p. 785
10. c   p. 790
11. a   p. 785
12. d   p. 788
13. b   p. 788
14. b   p. 792
15. a   p. 792, 793
16. b   p. 799

CHAPTER 30

The Collapse of the Old Order, 1929–1949

LEARNING OBJECTIVES

After reading Chapter 30 and completing this study chapter, you should be able to explain:

- How the Second World War involved more countries and caused far more death and destruction than any war before it.

- How economic and social problems unsolved by the First World War encouraged the development of fascism in Europe and Asia, eventually resulting in a new war.

- How the termination of the Second World War effectively ended colonialism because the colonial powers were too weakened to hold on to their colonies, concluding nearly five hundred years of European domination.

- How new technology and scientific advancements changed the face of modern warfare.

- How difficult it was to return to a pre–world war society since many groups, such as women, had become more acknowledged as participants in world affairs.

CHAPTER OUTLINE

In the outline below, include important themes, concepts, and details in the blank spaces provided. If you find fewer points than you have space for, leave lines blank. If you find more points, add as many lines as necessary.

I.   *Introduction*
      A.   *The end of an era*
            1. _____

            2. _____

            3. _____

      B.   *"Normalcy" too quickly became Depression*
            1. _____

            2. _____

            3. _____

      C.   *Some countries chose to solve their problems by violent means*
            1. _____

2. _____

3. _____

4. _____

5. _____

II.   **The Stalin Revolution**
    A.   **Five-Year Plans**
        1.   **Stalin's rise to power and his plan for Russia**
           a) _____

           b) _____

           c) _____

        2.   **Rapid industrialization**
           a) _____

           b) _____

           c) _____

           d) _____

        3.   **Environmental impact**
           a) _____

           b) _____

           c) _____

    B.   **Collectivization of Agriculture**
        1.   **The process of collectivization**
           a) _____

           b) _____

           c) _____

d) _____

e) _____

f) _____

2. *Propaganda and protest*
   a) _____

   b) _____

   c) _____

   d) _____

   e) _____

3. *Starvation and the second Five-Year Plan*
   a) _____

   b) _____

   c) _____

   d) _____

C. *Terror and Opportunities*
   1. *The secret police (NKVD) and Stalin's paranoia*
      a) _____

      b) _____

      c) _____

      d) _____

      e) _____

   2. *Purges in the party and arrests among ordinary citizens*
      a) _____

      b) _____

c) _____

d) _____

e) _____

f) _____

3. *The hardships of rapid industrialization paid off*

a) _____

b) _____

c) _____

d) _____

e) _____

f) _____

III. *The Depression*

   A.   *Economic Crisis*

     1.   *The most widespread depression in history*

       a) _____

       b) _____

       c) _____

       d) _____

       e) _____

       f) _____

     2.   *Layoffs of workers and lost production*

       a) _____

       b) _____

c) _____

3. **"Beggar thy neighbor" tariffs**
    a) _____

    b) _____

    c) _____

B. **Depression in Industrial Nations**
    1. **New York banks called in loans to Germany and Austria**
        a) _____

        b) _____

        c) _____

    2. **Government intervention to alleviate economic problems**
        a) _____

        b) _____

        c) _____

    3. **Germany and Japan suffer greatly**
        a) _____

        b) _____

        c) _____

C. **Depression in Nonindustrial Regions**
    1. **India and China**
        a) _____

        b) _____

        c) _____

    2. **Misery for countries dependent on exports**
        a) _____

        b) _____

c) _____

d) _____

e) _____

3. *Latin America*

a) _____

b) _____

c) _____

4. *South Africa*

a) _____

b) _____

c) _____

IV. *The Rise of Fascism*

A. *Mussolini's Italy*

1. *Young men were discontent*

a) _____

b) _____

c) _____

2. *Mussolini's rise to power*

a) _____

b) _____

c) _____

d) _____

e) _____

f) _____

3. *Propaganda*
   a) _____

   b) _____

   c) _____

   d) _____

   e) _____

B. *Hitler's Germany*
   1. *Causes for discontent in Germany in the 1920s and 1930s*
      a) _____

      b) _____

      c) _____

   2. *The rise of Hitler*
      a) _____

      b) _____

      c) _____

      d) _____

      e) _____

   3. *Hitler became chancellor*
      a) _____

      b) _____

      c) _____

      d) _____

      e) _____

4. *Hitler's plan for Germany*
   a) _____

   b) _____

   c) _____

   d) _____

   e) _____

   f) _____

5. *Economic and social policies*
   a) _____

   b) _____

   c) _____

C. *The Road to War, 1933–1939*
   1. *Military buildup allowed by Allies*
      a) _____

      b) _____

      c) _____

   2. *Italy invaded Ethiopia*
      a) _____

      b) _____

      c) _____

   3. *Hitler began annexing German-speaking regions of Europe*
      a) _____

      b) _____

      c) _____

d) _____

e) _____

4. *Why did the Allies allow appeasement?*
    a) _____

    b) _____

    c) _____

5. *Too late to stop it by the time they realized that it was happening*
    a) _____

    b) _____

    c) _____

V. *East Asia, 1931–1945*
    A. *The Manchurian Incident of 1931*
        1. *The Japanese military took over Manchuria*
            a) _____

            b) _____

            c) _____

            d) _____

        2. *Boycotts prompted the Japanese to occupy Shanghai and declare Manchurian "independence"*
            a) _____

            b) _____

            c) _____

        3. *Japan resigned from the League of Nations and prepared for war*
            a) _____

            b) _____

            c) _____

d) _____

B. *The Chinese Communists and the Long March*
   1. *The rise of the Communists and Mao Zedong*
       a) _____

       b) _____

       c) _____

       d) _____

       e) _____

       f) _____

   2. *The Communists in Jiangxi*
       a) _____

       b) _____

       c) _____

       d) _____

   3. *Mao's support of women*
       a) _____

       b) _____

       c) _____

       d) _____

       e) _____

   4. *Guerilla warfare and the Long March*
       a) _____

       b) _____

c) _____

d) _____

C. *The Sino-Japanese War, 1937–1945*
  1. *The Japanese attacked China and were condemned by the League of Nations*
    a) _____

    b) _____

    c) _____

    d) _____

    e) _____

    f) _____

  2. *Chinese fought hard and suffered many losses; there was no victory for Japan either*
    a) _____

    b) _____

    c) _____

    d) _____

    e) _____

    f) _____

  3. *Japanese atrocities*
    a) _____

    b) _____

    c) _____

  4. *Chinese plans against the Communists and Chiang Kai-shek*
    a) _____

    b) _____

c) _____

d) _____

5. *Mao's opposition to Japan*
   a) _____

   b) _____

   c) _____

   d) _____

VI. *The Second World War*
   A. *The War of Movement*
      1. *Advantage to the offensive returned*
         a) _____

         b) _____

         c) _____

      2. *Germany learned first*
         a) _____

         b) _____

         c) _____

      3. *Theaters of operation and civilians*
         a) _____

         b) _____

         c) _____

         d) _____

   B. *War in Europe and North Africa*
      1. *German and Russian territorial gains in Europe*
         a) _____

b) _____

c) _____

d) _____

e) _____

2. *Germans lost the Battle of Britain*
    a) _____

    b) _____

    c) _____

3. *Hitler attacked Russia*
    a) _____

    b) _____

    c) _____

    d) _____

    e) _____

    f) _____

4. *The war moved to Africa*
    a) _____

    b) _____

    c) _____

    d) _____

    e) _____

C. *War in Asia and the Pacific*
    1. *With Europe busy, Japan had its opportunity*
        a) _____

b) _____

c) _____

d) _____

e) _____

f) _____

2.   *The attack on Pearl Harbor*
   a) _____

   b) _____

   c) _____

3.   *The Japanese takeover of Southeast Asia and the U.S. response*
   a) _____

   b) _____

   c) _____

   d) _____

   e) _____

   f) _____

D.   *The End of the War*
   1.   *On the Eastern Front the Russians pushed Germany back*
      a) _____

      b) _____

      c) _____

   2.   *The Allied invasion of Italy and France*
      a) _____

b) _____

c) _____

d) _____

e) _____

f) _____

3. *The Japanese held on*
   a) _____

   b) _____

   c) _____

   d) _____

   e) _____

4. *The United States drops the bombs on Japan*
   a) _____

   b) _____

   c) _____

E. *Chinese Civil War and Communist Victory*
   1. *U.S. support of the Guomindang*
      a) _____

      b) _____

      c) _____

   2. *The Guomindang had the advantage, but too many abuses eroded popular support*
      a) _____

      b) _____

      c) _____

d) _____

3. *The Communists gained weapons and popular support*
    a) _____

    b) _____

    c) _____

    d) _____

4. *The Communists repelled the British and declared a new nation: the People's Republic of China*
    a) _____

    b) _____

    c) _____

    d) _____

VII. *The Character of Warfare*
    A.   *The Price of War*
        1. *Mortality rates and refugees*
            a) _____

            b) _____

            c) _____

        2. *A change in moral values*
            a) _____

            b) _____

            c) _____

    B.   *The War of Science*
        1. *Breakthroughs in chemistry, physics, and code breaking; and pharmaceutical technologies*
            a) _____

b) _____

c) _____

d) _____

e) _____

  2. *Airplanes*

a) _____

b) _____

c) _____

d) _____

  3. *The contributions of civilian inventors—especially atomic bombs*

a) _____

b) _____

c) _____

C. *Bombing Raids*

  1. *German air raids were mostly unsuccessful*

a) _____

b) _____

c) _____

  2. *The British bombing of Germany was devastating but had mixed success*

a) _____

b) _____

c) _____

d) _____

3.   *The American bombing of Japan was devastating*

a) _____

b) _____

c) _____

D.   *The Holocaust*

1.   *The extermination of six million Jews*

a) _____

b) _____

c) _____

d) _____

e) _____

f) _____

2.   *The extermination of three million Polish Catholics, homosexuals, Jehovah's Witnesses, Gypsies, the disabled, and the mentally ill*

a) _____

b) _____

c) _____

d) _____

3.   *Russians exterminated*

a) _____

b) _____

c) _____

E.   *The Home Front in Europe and Asia*

1.   *Bombing, troops, and concentration camps*

a) _____

b) _____

c) _____

d) _____

2. *Civilian contributions*
   a) _____

   b) _____

   c) _____

   d) _____

3. *Women's contributions*
   a) _____

   b) _____

   c) _____

F. ***The Home Front in the United States***
   1. ***High production and economic recovery***
      a) _____

      b) _____

      c) _____

      d) _____

   2. ***Women and minorities entered the work force in larger numbers than ever before***
      a) _____

      b) _____

      c) _____

   3. ***There was ambivalence about women in the workplace***
      a) _____

b) _____

c) _____

d) _____

4. *Racial changes and concerns*
   a) _____

   b) _____

   c) _____

G. *War and the Environment*
   1. *The fighting itself*
      a) _____

      b) _____

      c) _____

   2. *Economic development to support the war*
      a) _____

      b) _____

      c) _____

   3. *Increased need for raw materials*
      a) _____

      b) _____

      c) _____

   4. *Putting the environmental damage into perspective*
      a) _____

      b) _____

      c) _____

d) _____

VIII. *Conclusion*

    A.   *The global order was shattered between 1929 and 1949*

        1. _____

        2. _____

        3. _____

        4. _____

    B.   *Civilian technology was converted to military technology*

        1. _____

        2. _____

        3. _____

    C.   *The rise of the two superpowers: the United States and the Soviet Union*

        1. _____

        2. _____

        3. _____

    D.   *The disappearance of colonial empires*

        1. _____

        2. _____

        3. _____

IDENTIFICATIONS

Define each term and explain why it is significant, including any important dates.

	Identification	**Significance**
"normalcy"		

	Identification	Significance
Franklin D. Roosevelt		
Joseph Stalin		
Depression		
Five-Year Plans		
Benito Mussolini		
Fascist Party		
Adolf Hitler		
Nazi Party		
Chiang Kai-shek		
Mao Zedong		
Long March		

	Identification	Significance
Stalingrad		
El Alamein		
Pearl Harbor		
Battle of Midway		
Hiroshima		
Auschwitz		
bombing raids		
Jews		
appeasement		
Winston Churchill		
Holocaust		

MULTIPLE-CHOICE QUESTIONS

Read the entire question, including *all* the possible answers. Then choose the *one* answer that best fits the question.

1.   The purpose of industrialization in the Soviet Union was to

    a.   produce consumer goods.
    b.   enable communism to spread worldwide.
    c.   overthrow the Russian government.
    d.   prepare for war.
    e.   increase the power of the Communist Party and strengthen the USSR.

2.   What was the most radical social experiment attempted by Stalin?

    a.   Reforming the Russian army
    b.   Giving women the vote
    c.   Collectivizing agriculture
    d.   Turning factories over to the workers
    e.   The Five-Year Plans

3.   Which of the following countries suffered the most in the Depression?

    a.   The United States and Britain
    b.   France and Britain
    c.   The United States and Germany
    d.   Germany and Japan
    e.   Brazil and Turkey

4.   What two regions boomed during the Depression?

    a.   Germany and Japan
    b.   The USSR and the United States
    c.   The United States and Japan
    d.   The USSR and southern Africa
    e.   France and Sweden

5.   The Italian Fascist Party

    a.   was created by Mussolini.
    b.   glorified warfare and the Italian nation.
    c.   supported labor unions and equality for women.
    d.   inspired political movements in Britain and France.
    e.   faded quickly from Italian politics once Mussolini rose to power.

6.   What was Benito Mussolini's genius?

    a.   Making the trains run on time
    b.   Applying the techniques for modern mass communication and advertising to peacetime
    c.   Denouncing Hitler and taking over German holdings in the Pacific
    d.   Industrializing before any other European nation
    e.   Supporting labor unions

7.   Which of the following statements about Hitler's book *Mein Kampf* is *not* true?

   a.   It was written while Hitler was imprisoned after leading an uprising in Munich.
   b.   It contained designs for the atom bomb.
   c.   It outlined Hitler's plans to return Germany to glory.
   d.   It was viewed as so outlandish that no one took it seriously at first.
   e.   It proposed a future time in which a "master race" would rule the world.

8.   Which of the following is *not* a reason that Japan wanted to make China part of its empire?

   a.   All the other good colonies were taken.
   b.   China was an easy victory.
   c.   China had a vast population.
   d.   China had many resources
   e.   Japan did not want to be beholden to the rest of the world.

9.   What was the Manchurian Incident?

   a.   An anti-Stalin propaganda film made in the United States
   b.   A railway explosion that gave Japanese officers an excuse to take over Manchuria
   c.   The first battle of the Second World War
   d.   A diplomatic blunder that nearly cost the Allies the war
   e.   A protest staged by Chinese students

10.   The United States and Europe reacted to the Manchurian Incident by

   a.   boycotting Japanese goods.
   b.   actively opposing Japan's quest for empire.
   c.   praising the Japanese for their initiative.
   d.   condemning Japan's action.
   e.   quickly moving to alleviate the damage done by the French ambassador.

11.   Which of the following was *not* one of the ways Mao and the Communists changed the position of women in the 1920s?

   a.   They organized women textile workers into unions.
   b.   They organized women farmers.
   c.   They allowed women to initiate divorce.
   d.   They banned footbinding.
   e.   They admitted women to leadership positions within the party.

12.   Why did the Western powers not leap immediately to China's aid when the Japanese attacked?

   a.   They did not consider China an ally.
   b.   They knew that it was unwise to fight a ground war in China.
   c.   They were too busy at home with economic problems.
   d.   They were hoping that Japan would share some of the Chinese pie with them.
   e.   They didn't realize how dangerous the situation was.

13.   What fatal mistake did Hitler make that Napoleon had made?

   a.   Both made a secret alliance with Russia/the USSR.
   b.   Both underestimated the strength of European resistance.
   c.   Both tried to take Moscow in the winter.
   d.   Neither thought that the United States would get involved in a European war.
   e.   Both made questionable alliances with Asian countries.

14. Which of the following is *not* one of the ways that women were involved in the war?

    a.   Women went to work in previously male-dominated industrial jobs.

    b.   Women worked on the home front in munitions factories.

    c.   Women served on the front right along with the men, particularly in Germany.

    d.   Women served in non-combative roles to support the military.

    e.   Women went to work in male-dominated agricultural jobs.

SHORT-ANSWER QUESTIONS

Answer each question in one short paragraph, giving the definition, dates, and significance.

1. How did the Depression suffered by the industrialized world affect the colonial world?

2. How did the Japanese respond to the Western actions following the Manchurian Incident? Why?

3. How successful was Japan's attack on China? What did Japan hope to gain?

4. Why did the British prevail in the battle over Egypt?

5. Under what condition would the Japanese surrender to the Allies? What happened before that condition was met?

6. Why did the United States flourish during the Second World War?

7. Compare and contrast the environmental impact during the Depression and during the Second World War.

ESSAY QUESTIONS

Make an outline of each question, listing the major points you want to discuss. Then write your practice essay, following your outline carefully and making sure that you do not skip any of your major points. At this time you will want to add the relevant dates and details that will make your essay persuasive and accurate.

1. Discuss the world economic conditions that led up to the Depression. How did the political leaders react? Did their actions help?

2. Outline Joseph Stalin's plans for the USSR. What were his goals and methods? What were his successes and failures?

3. Compare and contrast both the style and the scope of the warfare in the First and Second World Wars. Give specific examples.

4. What was the Holocaust, and why was it carried out? What have been some of its far-reaching effects? How does it compare with other similar incidents in world history? Give specific examples.

5. What was the home front? Who were the major participants in the war on the home front? How did its legacies change society?

6. Discuss the turmoil that China underwent from the turn of the twentieth century until 1949. Who were the major players? What happened and why? What legacy have those events created?

COMPARISON CHARTS

Using information gathered from the text, fill in the blank areas of each chart with the relevant data pertaining to the regions and categories listed. (Not all blank areas will necessarily be used.)

Chart 30.1

THREE POWERS

	Japan	Italy	Germany
Society			
Resources			
Industry			
Technology			
Economy			
Methods			
Allies			
Land Occupied			
Scapegoats/ Enemies			
War			
Home Front			
Casualties— Military			
Casualties— Civilian			
Failure			

Chart 30.2

TWO DIFFERENT WARS

	Dates	Nations Involved	Technology—Military	Technology—Non-Military	Style of Warfare	Casualties	Home Front	Legacies
First World War								
Second World War								

DIVERSITY AND DOMINANCE

After reading "Diversity and Dominance: Women, Family Values, and the Russian Revolution" in your text, answer the following additional questions.

Do you think that Russian women would agree with Kollontai's assertion that all children were "henceforth *our* children?"

How do you account for the changes in attitude that took place in just sixteen years between what Kollontai and Stalin wrote?

INTERNET ASSIGNMENT

Keywords: **"World War II Propaganda"**

                       "World War II Poster Art"

Wartime propaganda was extensively used by both sides during the Second World War. Using the above keywords, look for examples of propaganda. You might also want to consult the *History WIRED* image library on *The Earth and Its Peoples* web site (refer to the preface of this study guide for information on how to locate the text home page). How is the propaganda from each side characterized? How are they similar? How are they different? Be sure you look for the role of women in the war effort.

INTERNET EXPLORATION

The Maginot Line was supposed to be an unbeatable defense against Hitler's Germany, but the Germans invaded France anyway, and so the Maginot Line has come to symbolize failure. But did it really fail? Use the following site: http://www.maginot-line.com/ to see the impressive fortification built by the French. For anything you have ever wanted to know about the culture of the Second World War, including Bugs Bunny's war efforts, music on the A-bomb, and many other interesting tidbits, try http://www.authentichistory.com/.

MAP EXERCISES

On Outline Map 30.1, shade in these areas:

    Hitler's Germany

    Countries allied with Germany

    Countries occupied by Germany and its allies

    Countries of the Grand Alliance

    Neutral countries

On Outline Map 30.2, mark the farthest advance of Japanese conquests in 1942. Then shade in the following:

    Allied territory

    Territory gained from the Japanese by the Allies

    Territory still held by the Japanese at the end of the war in 1945

Outline Map 30.1

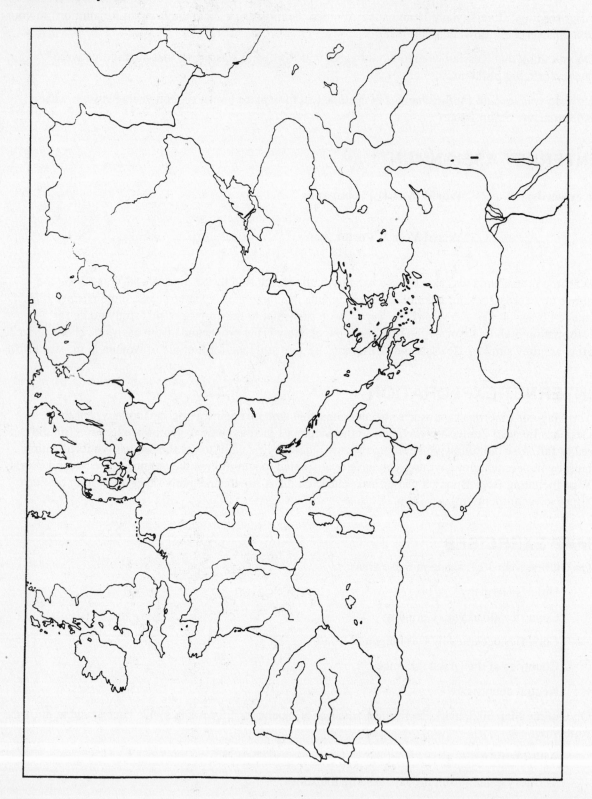

Outline Map 30.2

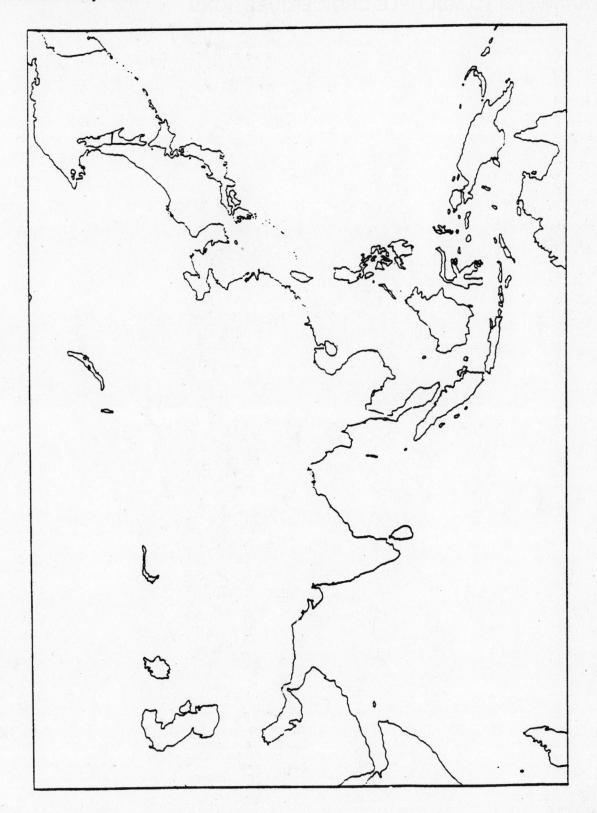

ANSWERS TO MULTIPLE-CHOICE QUESTIONS

1. e p. 806
2. c p. 806
3. d p. 809
4. d p. 812
5. b p. 813
6. b p. 813
7. b p. 813
8. b p. 815
9. b p. 815
10. d p. 815
11. e p. 816
12. c p. 816
13. c p. 819
14. c p. 828

CHAPTER 31

Striving for Independence: Africa, India, and Latin America, 1900–1949

LEARNING OBJECTIVES

After reading Chapter 31 and completing this study chapter, you should be able to explain:

- How African nations experienced imperialism later than most of the world but gained their independence after fewer years of colonialism.

- How the nature of imperialism changed from outright political control to systems in which the colonial economies became dependent on foreign markets.

- What effect nationalism had on the nations of Africa, Asia, and Latin America in their quest for more self-determination.

- What role certain inspirational and able leaders played in the development and course of their nations.

- How different elements within countries both worked toward financial independence for the good of all, and against it for self-interested reasons.

CHAPTER OUTLINE

In the outline below, include important themes, concepts, and details in the blank spaces provided. If you find fewer points than you have space for, leave lines blank. If you find more points, add as many lines as necessary.

I. *Introduction*
    A. *Comparing the styles and goals of Emiliano Zapata and Mahatma Gandhi*
        1. _____

        2. _____

        3. _____

    B. *The legacy of the World Wars in Europe, East Asia, the Middle East, the United States, China, and the USSR*
        1. _____

        2. _____

        3. _____

C.   *Changes in Sub-Saharan Africa, India, and Latin America*
   1. _____

   2. _____

   3. _____

II. *Sub-Saharan Africa, 1900–1945*
   A.   *Colonial Africa: Economic and Social Changes*
      1. *Europeans dominate, Asians benefit from retail, but there were few benefits for Africans*
         a) _____

         b) _____

         c) _____

      2. *When Africans were in charge of their own finances, things went well*
         a) _____

         b) _____

         c) _____

      3. *Most Africans were compelled to work for the benefit of Europeans*
         a) _____

         b) _____

         c) _____

      4. *Health care for Africans*
         a) _____

         b) _____

         c) _____

         d) _____

         e) _____

5. *Urbanization and migrations*
    a) _____

    b) _____

    c) _____

    d) _____

B. *Religious and Political Changes*
    1. *Christianity*
        a) _____

        b) _____

        c) _____

        d) _____

        e) _____

    2. *Islam*
        a) _____

        b) _____

        c) _____

    3. *The rise of nationalism*
        a) _____

        b) _____

        c) _____

    4. *The effect of the Second World War on Africa*
        a) _____

        b) _____

        c) _____

d) _____

e) _____

III. **The Indian Independence Movement, 1905–1947**
    A.   **The Land and the People**
        1.   **Population growth meant less land**
            a) _____

            b) _____

            c) _____

            d) _____

        2.   **The Indian lifestyle**
            a) _____

            b) _____

            c) _____

        3.   **Languages**
            a) _____

            b) _____

            c) _____

        4.   **Hindus and Muslims**
            a) _____

            b) _____

            c) _____

    B.   **British Rule and Indian Nationalism**
        1.   **British Administration**
            a) _____

            b) _____

            c) _____

2. *Technology and acceptance of British rule*

    a) _____

    b) _____

    c) _____

    d) _____

    e) _____

    f) _____

3. *The Indian National Congress and the All-Indian Muslim League*

    a) _____

    b) _____

    c) _____

    d) _____

    e) _____

    f) _____

4. *Many resisted industrialization for India*

    a) _____

    b) _____

    c) _____

    d) _____

    e) _____

5. *Indian support during the First World War, and the end of good relations between India and Britain*

    a) _____

b) _____

c) _____

d) _____

e) _____

f) _____

C.   *Mahatma Gandhi and Militant Nonviolence*
   1.   *Gandhi's early life*
      a) _____

      b) _____

      c) _____

   2.   *Gandhi's political and social ideas*
      a) _____

      b) _____

      c) _____

      d) _____

      e) _____

   3.   *Gandhi's tactics*
      a) _____

      b) _____

      c) _____

      d) _____

      e) _____

      f) _____

D. *India Moves Toward Independence*
    1. *Britain gradually allows some autonomy*
        a) _____

        b) _____

        c) _____

        d) _____

        e) _____

    2. *Many Indians felt ambivalent about supporting the British in the Second World War*
        a) _____

        b) _____

        c) _____

        d) _____

        e) _____

        f) _____

    3. *Famine in Bengal*
        a) _____

        b) _____

        c) _____

E. *Partition and Independence*
    1. *Disputes between Hindus and Muslims*
        a) _____

        b) _____

        c) _____

        d) _____

e) _____

2. **People began to accept the idea of partition**
   a) _____

   b) _____

   c) _____

3. **Independence and more violence**
   a) _____

   b) _____

   c) _____

   d) _____

4. **Kashmir**
   a) _____

   b) _____

   c) _____

   d) _____

IV. **The Mexican Revolution, 1910–1940**
   A. **Mexico in 1910**
      1. **Large division between the rich and the poor**
         a) _____

         b) _____

         c) _____

         d) _____

         e) _____

      2. **The peasants and Indians lost land to wealthy investors**
         a) _____

b) _____

c) _____

d) _____

e) _____

f) _____

g) _____

3. *Mexico under Porfirio Diaz*
   a) _____

   b) _____

   c) _____

   d) _____

   e) _____

   f) _____

B. *Revolution and Civil War, 1911–1920*
   1. *Many different revolutionaries*
     a) _____

     b) _____

     c) _____

   2. *Madero, and the Constitutionalists*
     a) _____

     b) _____

     c) _____

   3. *Emiliano Zapata*
     a) _____

      b) _____

      c) _____

4. *Francisco "Pancho" Villa*
      a) _____

      b) _____

      c) _____

      d) _____

      e) _____

      f) _____

5. *The victory of the Constitutionalists*
      a) _____

      b) _____

      c) _____

      d) _____

      e) _____

      f) _____

C. *The Revolution Institutionalized, 1920–1940*
  1. *The Revolution helped change the social makeup of the governing class*
      a) _____

      b) _____

      c) _____

  2. *The arts*
      a) _____

b) _____

c) _____

3. *Lázaro Cárdenas*
   a) _____

   b) _____

   c) _____

   d) _____

   e) _____

4. *Nationalizing oil and reforms in education and the military*
   a) _____

   b) _____

   c) _____

5. *The legacy of the Mexican Revolution*
   a) _____

   b) _____

   c) _____

V. *Argentina and Brazil, 1900–1949*
   A. *The Transformation of Argentina*
      1. *The land was quite suitable for raising sheep and cattle, and for agriculture*
         a) _____

         b) _____

         c) _____

      2. *Transportation and European preferences*
         a) _____

         b) _____

       c) _____

       d) _____

       e) _____

  3.   *The government represented the wealthy*
       a) _____

       b) _____

       c) _____

       d) _____

B. *Brazil and Argentina, to 1929*
  1.   *Brazil and Argentina's elite tended to focus on their crops and products and not on industry*
       a) _____

       b) _____

       c) _____

  2.   *The middle classes and the poor*
       a) _____

       b) _____

       c) _____

  3.   *The collapse of the rubber market and the First World War caused a disruption of old trade patterns*
       a) _____

       b) _____

       c) _____

       d) _____

  4.   *Protest*
       a) _____

b) _____

c) _____

5. *Outsiders still controlled aviation and radio*
   a) _____

   b) _____

   c) _____

   d) _____

   e) _____

   f) _____

C. *The Depression and the Vargas Regime in Brazil*
   1. *The Depression brought authoritarian regimes*
      a) _____

      b) _____

      c) _____

   2. *Vargas's career and accomplishments*
      a) _____

      b) _____

      c) _____

      d) _____

      e) _____

   3. *The cost of industrialization*
      a) _____

      b) _____

c) _____

d) _____

4.   *Brazil turned to fascism*
   a) _____

   b) _____

   c) _____

   d) _____

D.   *Argentina After 1930*
   1.   *José Uriburu*
      a) _____

      b) _____

      c) _____

   2.   *Juan Perón*
      a) _____

      b) _____

      c) _____

   3.   *Eva Duarte Perón*
      a) _____

      b) _____

      c) _____

   4.   *The demise of the Peróns*
      a) _____

      b) _____

      c) _____

d) _____

E. *Mexico, Argentina, and Brazil: A Comparison*
   1. *Similarities*
      a) _____

      b) _____

      c) _____

      d) _____

   2. *Divergence: Mexico*
      a) _____

      b) _____

      c) _____

   3. *Divergence: Brazil and Argentina*
      a) _____

      b) _____

      c) _____

VI. *Conclusion*
   A. *Colonial and semi-colonial status*
      1. _____

      2. _____

      3. _____

   B. *Different nations responded differently to the stresses*
      1. _____

      2. _____

      3. _____

      4. _____

5. _____

C. *Nationalism*
  1. _____

  2. _____

  3. _____

  4. _____

  5. _____

IDENTIFICATIONS

Define each term and explain why it is significant, including any important dates.

	Identification	Significance
Blaise Daigne		
African National Congress		
Haile Selassie		
Indian National Congress		
Bengal		
All-India Muslim League		

	Identification	Significance

Mohandas K. (Mahatma) Gandhi

Jawaharlal Nehru

Muhammad Ali Jinnah

Pakistan

haciendas

Emiliano Zapata

Francisco "Pancho" Villa

Lázaro Cárdenas

Hipólito Irigoyen

Getulio Vargas

import-substitution industrialization

	Identification	Significance

Juan Perón

Eva Duarte Perón

MULTIPLE-CHOICE QUESTIONS

Read the entire question, including *all* the possible answers. Then choose the *one* answer that best fits the question.

1. Which of the following statements best characterizes Europeans in Africa?

    a. They moved there in large numbers to colonize.
    b. They pushed Africans off most of the land to build cities and housing tracts.
    c. With the exception of a few temperate regions, very few Europeans actually lived in Africa.
    d. No Europeans lived in Africa; they just hired Africans to work the land and send exports to Europe.
    e. Through their actions, they caused massive population decline.

2. Which of the following statements about health in early-twentieth-century Africa is *not* true?

    a. Europeans prided themselves on bringing health care to Africa.
    b. Western medicine greatly improved health in Africa immediately.
    c. Colonialism tended to worsen public health by encouraging migration and the spread of disease.
    d. Labor conscription and European demand for food caused malnutrition.
    e. Eventually, by the 1930s, Europeans finally realized how detrimental their actions were to the health of Africans.

3. Why did the migrations of Africans to the cities damage family life?

    a. Employers would not allow the migrants to go home to visit their families.
    b. Wages were so low that no one could send any money home.
    c. Only men migrated, leaving women behind to raise children and to farm.
    d. Once people migrated, colonial law allowed confiscation of their land, thereby eliminating many family farms.
    e. When women moved to the cities, they often turned to prostitution to survive.

4. What was one of the major attractions of Christian mission schools?

    a. Africans were drawn to Christianity as a way to unify their people.
    b. These schools taught reading, writing, and basic crafts.
    c. Europeans paid Africans to send their children there.
    d. The schools provided free food and clothing.
    e. The schools provided free medical care.

5. Which of the following explains the popularity of Islam among Africans?

    a.   Islam was more similar to African religions than Christianity.
    b.   Most Africans already spoke Arabic, the language of Islam.
    c.   Christians hated Islam because they considered it subversive.
    d.   Islam was less destructive to African traditions such as polygamy.
    e.   Islam was urban, and most Africans lived in cities.

6. Which of the following changes was *not* brought to Africa by the Second World War?

    a.   Hardship
    b.   New political ideas
    c.   Hope
    d.   Despair
    e.   Participation in the global economy

7. The educated middle class of India was awakened to a sense of national dignity that demanded political fulfillment by

    a.   careful guidance by the British.
    b.   the Second World War.
    c.   the economic transformation of India.
    d.   nationalist movements in Africa.
    e.   merging with Afghanistan.

8. The "moral and material progress of India"

    a.   greatly benefited all members if Indian society.
    b.   benefited Indian peasants to the exclusion of the upper classes.
    c.   was mutually beneficial to the Indians and the British.
    d.   hardly benefited the average Indian.
    e.   benefited only the British.

9. Why did English become the common language of India?

    a.   The Indians loved the British so much that they wanted to honor them by making English their official language.
    b.   Because so many different languages were spoken in India, and English was taught to so many Indians for the civil service, it just worked out that way.
    c.   People in the Indian upper class had forgotten their native languages.
    d.   Indians wanted to disassociate themselves from their feudal past and be more modern.
    e.   English was so much easier to learn than any of the Indian languages.

10. In the twentieth century, the majority of Indians practiced

    a.   Hinduism.
    b.   Buddhism.
    c.   Islam.
    d.   Sikhism.
    e.   Christianity, brought by the British.

11. Why did so many poor Mexicans work on haciendas?

    a. They earned more money than they could make on their own land.
    b. The Mexican government nationalized the land.
    c. The United States owned all of the land in Mexico.
    d. Wealthy Mexicans and American companies used unscrupulous means to run the Mexicans off their own land.
    e. The owners of the haciendas promised to protect and educate them.

12. The modernization of Mexico City into a showplace benefited

    a. all of Mexican society.
    b. most of Mexican society.
    c. a handful of well-connected businesspeople.
    d. only Americans.
    e. no one.

13. Why could Zapata and Villa never lead national peasant revolutions?

    a. They did not enjoy popular support.
    b. They had fewer soldiers than the Constitutionalists.
    c. They aligned themselves with the United States, and so lost credibility.
    d. They could not rise above their regional and peasant origins.
    e. They were not good soldiers.

14. From where does the expression "rich as an Argentine" derive?

    a. Argentina was the richest nation in Latin America.
    b. Argentina's per capita income was equal to France's.
    c. Even peasants in Argentina were wealthy.
    d. Argentines spent so lavishly while in Paris, the French started using this expression.
    e. Argentine means "one who is rich in silver," and people throughout South America used it for anyone who had made their fortune from silver mining.

15. Why didn't Brazilians build themselves railroads?

    a. They didn't need them.
    b. They knew that the British would build them and run them for the benefit of all of the Brazilian people.
    c. They couldn't afford to build them.
    d. They felt that each country should do what they were suited for—in Brazil's case that was produce cacao, rubber, and coffee.
    e. They didn't have the technology.

16. Which of the following did *not* occur in Argentina when the Great War began, and the old trade patterns were disrupted?

    a. The landowning class was weakened.
    b. The peasants finally gained land and a piece of the wealth.
    c. A liberal president, Hipólito Irigoyen, was elected.
    d. The United States replaced European countries as Argentina's trading partner.
    e. Great Britain sold off its railroads to Argentina.

SHORT-ANSWER QUESTIONS

Answer each question in one short paragraph, giving the definition, dates, and significance.

1. Why was the African National Congress formed?

2. How did the British serving in India feel about Indians? Did the British deem them as honorable men? Why or why not?

3. Why were the Constitutionalists so successful in Mexico?

4. Discuss the environmental impact of industrialization in Brazil.

5. What was Gandhi's contribution to Indian independence? What were his methods? Did his movement have an influence beyond India?

6. Why was India partitioned into two different states after independence even though it had been a single state under British rule?

7. Describe Mexican society in 1910. How did men like Emiliano Zapata and Pancho Villa change it?

ESSAY QUESTIONS

Make an outline of each question, listing the major points you want to discuss. Then write your practice essay, following your outline carefully and making sure that you do not skip any of your major points. At this time you will want to add the relevant dates and details that will make your essay persuasive and accurate.

1. Discuss nationalist movements in Africa. What elements and philosophies did they include? What goals did they hope to attain and by what means? How successful were they?

2. Describe the system of informal empire that the Europeans had in Latin America. What was its purpose and how did it work? How did it differ from more formal colonialism? How did it affect those colonized?

3. Discuss Hindu-Muslim animosity. How did it come about? What role, if any, did the British play? How did this animosity affect Indian independence?

4. Discuss the Mexican Revolution. What were the goals and methods of the revolutionaries? How successful were they? How does the Mexican Revolution compare with other revolutions that you have learned about?

5. Discuss the role played by elites in Brazil and Argentina.

COMPARISON CHARTS

Using information gathered from the text, fill in the blank areas of each chart with the relevant data pertaining to the regions and categories listed. (Not all blank areas will necessarily be used.)

Chart 31.1

INFORMAL EMPIRE

	Colonizing Countries	Economic Policies	Methods	Technology	Products/ Resources	Military Actions	Revolutions/ Coups
Brazil and Argentina							
Mexico							

Chart 31.2

TWO REVOLUTIONS

	Peasants Before Revolution	Upper and Middle Classes Before Revolution	Classes and Individuals Leading Revolution	Influence from Outside	Economic Troubles	Civil Disturbance	Style of Traditional Governments	Political Philosophy of Revolutionaries	Outcome and Legacy
India									
Mexico									

DIVERSITY AND DOMINANCE

After reading "Diversity and Dominance: A Vietnamese Nationalist Denounces French Colonialism" in your text, answer the following additional questions.

How do the events related by Nguyen Thai Hoc resemble those of the French Revolution? With this in mind, how do you think the French responded to his arguments? Do you think that Nguyen Thai Hoc was an honorable man?

INTERNET ASSIGNMENT

Keywords: **"Mahatma Gandhi"**

          "Juan Perón"

Both Gandhi and Perón appealed to the downtrodden in their countries. Though they had similar goals, their styles and practices were quite different. How can you account for those differences? In addition, explore the role of charismatic leaders on each nation's road to independence.

INTERNET EXPLORATION

Few figures capture the romantic imagination like Pancho Villa. Using this web site http://ist-socrates.berkeley.edu/~border/resource_pages/revolution.html, study pictures from the Mexican Revolution. What can we learn about the leaders of the Revolution from the photographs? Who took the photos? How balanced is this collection? For more information use the keyword "Pancho Villa."

MAP EXERCISES

On Outline Map 31.1, mark the boundary of British India before independence. Shade in the following to indicate their extent after India had gained its independence:

India

Pakistan

Disputed territory controlled by India

Disputed territory controlled by Pakistan

Outline Map 31.1

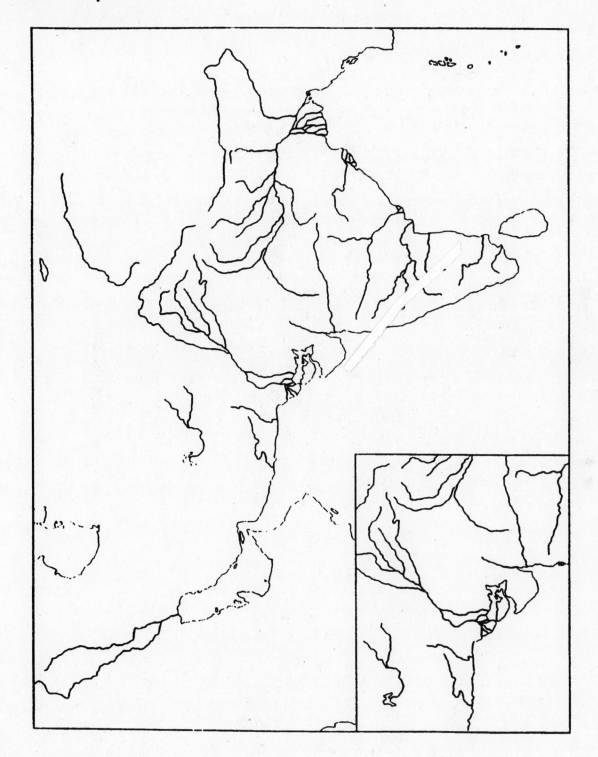

ANSWERS TO MULTIPLE-CHOICE QUESTIONS

1. c   p. 832
2. b   p. 833
3. c   p. 836
4. b   p. 836
5. d   p. 837
6. d   p. 837
7. c   p. 838
8. d   p. 838
9. b   p. 838
10. a   p. 838
11. d   p. 845
12. c   p. 846
13. d   p. 846
14. d   p. 850
15. d   p. 850
16. b   p. 850

CHAPTER 32

The Cold War and Decolonization, 1945–1975

LEARNING OBJECTIVES

After reading Chapter 32 and completing this study chapter, you should be able to explain:

- How difficult decolonization proved, and what challenged fledgling countries as they tried to join the world economy and political arena.

- How allies of the Second World War became bitter enemies within just a few years, and how this animosity turned into the Cold War, which could have been even more devastating than the two world wars that preceded it.

- How the two superpowers maneuvered their resources in an attempt to control the world, and how nonaligned nations took advantage of their rivalry to make gains for themselves.

- What role the Middle East played, both as an oil-producing region and as an area of political and social unrest.

- How the wars of the twentieth century, particularly the Cold War, drained valuable resources, and how this in turn prompted a new worldwide environmental awareness.

CHAPTER OUTLINE

In the outline below, include important themes, concepts, and details in the blank spaces provided. If you find fewer points than you have space for, leave lines blank. If you find more points, add as many lines as necessary.

I. *Introduction*

    A. *The end of the Second World War exposed a world of mutual antagonism rather than one of mutual cooperation*

        1. _____

        2. _____

        3. _____

        4. _____

        5. _____

        6. _____

B. *The business of nation building*
1. _____

2. _____

3. _____

4. _____

C. *Cold War technology and environmental impact*
1. _____

2. _____

3. _____

4. _____

5. _____

II. *The Cold War*
A. *The United Nations*
1. *The formation of the United Nations and its basic structure*
a) _____

b) _____

c) _____

d) _____

e) _____

2. *Beliefs and efficacy of the United Nations*
a) _____

b) _____

c) _____

d) _____

e) _____

f) _____

3. *Early resolutions carried great weight, but later the Western powers came to disregard many of the issues raised by the General Assembly*

a) _____

b) _____

c) _____

d) _____

e) _____

f) _____

B. *Capitalism and Communism*

1. *New monetary systems were developed in the West and the Soviet Union*

a) _____

b) _____

c) _____

d) _____

e) _____

f) _____

2. *New countries often preferred the Soviet approach*

a) _____

b) _____

c) _____

3. *New prosperity and reconstruction*

a) _____

b) _____

c) _____

d) _____

e) _____

f) _____

4. *Western Europe*
   a) _____

   b) _____

   c) _____

   d) _____

   e) _____

5. *The Soviet approach*
   a) _____

   b) _____

   c) _____

   d) _____

   e) _____

   f) _____

C. *West Versus East in Europe and Korea*
   1. *The spread of Communism and Western reaction*
      a) _____

      b) _____

      c) _____

d) _____

e) _____

f) _____

2. *NATO and Soviet competition over Europe*
    a) _____

    b) _____

    c) _____

    d) _____

    e) _____

    f) _____

3. *NATO and Soviet competition over Korea*
    a) _____

    b) _____

    c) _____

    d) _____

    e) _____

    f) _____

D. *United States Defeat in Vietnam*
    1. *Eisenhower said "no" to war in Vietnam, but Kennedy said "yes"*
        a) _____

        b) _____

        c) _____

        d) _____

e) _____

2. *Johnson continued the war*
   a) _____

   b) _____

   c) _____

   d) _____

   e) _____

3. *United States got out in 1973 and U.S. attitudes toward the war*
   a) _____

   b) _____

   c) _____

   d) _____

   e) _____

   f) _____

E. *The Race for Nuclear Supremacy*
   1. *Atomic weapons had ushered in a new era of warfare and diplomacy*
      a) _____

      b) _____

      c) _____

      d) _____

      e) _____

      f) _____

   2. *The Cuban Missile Crisis*
      a) _____

b) _____

c) _____

d) _____

3. *More efficient bombs and delivery systems*
   a) _____

   b) _____

   c) _____

   d) _____

4. *Arms limitation*
   a) _____

   b) _____

   c) _____

5. *Things calmed down in Europe*
   a) _____

   b) _____

   c) _____

   d) _____

6. *The space race*
   a) _____

   b) _____

   c) _____

   d) _____

7. *Restraint*

a) _____

b) _____

c) _____

III. *Decolonization and Nation Building*
   A. *New Nations in South and Southeast Asia*
      1. *India, Pakistan, and Bangladesh*

a) _____

b) _____

c) _____

d) _____

e) _____

      2. *The Japanese role in South Asia and Southeast Asia*

a) _____

b) _____

c) _____

d) _____

      3. *Sukarno*

a) _____

b) _____

c) _____

      4. *Myanmar, Singapore, and the Philippines*

a) _____

b) _____

c) _____

5. *Vietnam*
    a) _____

    b) _____

    c) _____

    d) _____

B. *The Struggle for Independence in Africa*
    1. *Algeria*
        a) _____

        b) _____

        c) _____

        d) _____

        e) _____

        f) _____

    2. *Institutions and factors that made good colonies made poor independent countries*
        a) _____

        b) _____

        c) _____

        d) _____

        e) _____

        f) _____

    3. *Kwame Nkrumah*
        a) _____

        b) _____

c) _____

d) _____

e) _____

f) _____

4. *Jomo Kenyatta*
   a) _____

   b) _____

   c) _____

   d) _____

5. *French Africa and de Gaulle's promises*
   a) _____

   b) _____

   c) _____

   d) _____

6. *The heart versus reason—which colonies would survive?*
   a) _____

   b) _____

   c) _____

   d) _____

   e) _____

   f) _____

7. *The Southern Temperate Zone*
   a) _____

b) _____

c) _____

d) _____

e) _____

f) _____

8.   *South Africa*
    a) _____

    b) _____

    c) _____

    d) _____

    e) _____

    f) _____

C.   *The Quest for Economic Freedom in Latin America*
    1.   *U.S. and Europe dominated Latin American economies*
        a) _____

        b) _____

        c) _____

    2.   *Mexico and Guatemala*
        a) _____

        b) _____

        c) _____

        d) _____

        e) _____

f) _____

3. *U.S. domination in Cuba*
   a) _____

   b) _____

   c) _____

   d) _____

   e) _____

   f) _____

4. *1959 popular rebellion*
   a) _____

   b) _____

   c) _____

   d) _____

5. *The Castro government*
   a) _____

   b) _____

   c) _____

   d) _____

   e) _____

D. *Challenges of Nation Building*
   1. *New nations join the United Nations*
      a) _____

      b) _____

      c) _____

2. *How to organize a government?*
   a) _____

   b) _____

   c) _____

   .d) _____

3. *How to educate the populous?*
   a) _____

   b) _____

   c) _____

   d) _____

IV. *Beyond a Bipolar World*
   A. *The Third World*
      1. *Definition of the terms "non-aligned" and "third world"*
         a) _____

         b) _____

         c) _____

         d) _____

         e) _____

         f) _____

      2. *Many of these countries wanted money from the superpowers*
         a) _____

         b) _____

         c) _____

         d) _____

3. *A balancing act*
   a) _____

   b) _____

   c) _____

   d) _____

   e) _____

   f) _____

B. *Japan and China*
   1. *Japan made amends for the war and rebuilt its industries*
      a) _____

      b) _____

      c) _____

      d) _____

      e) _____

      f) _____

   2. *China very involved in Cold War politics*
      a) _____

      b) _____

      c) _____

      d) _____

   3. *The Great Leap Forward and the Cultural Revolution*
      a) _____

      b) _____

c) _____

d) _____

e) _____

f) _____

4. ***Normalizing United States-China relations***
   a) _____

   b) _____

   c) _____

   d) _____

C. ***The Middle East***
   1. ***Arab politics in the 1950s***
      a) _____

      b) _____

      c) _____

   2. ***British policy on Palestine***
      a) _____

      b) _____

      c) _____

   3. ***The United Nations partitions Palestine into two states***
      a) _____

      b) _____

      c) _____

   4. ***Conflict and refugees***
      a) _____

       b) _____

       c) _____

       d) _____

       e) _____

5.   **The Palestine Liberation Organization (PLO)**
       a) _____

       b) _____

       c) _____

       d) _____

6.   **Organization of Petroleum Exporting Countries (OPEC) and more conflict**
       a) _____

       b) _____

       c) _____

       d) _____

       e) _____

       f) _____

D.   **The Emergence of Environmental Concerns**
   1.   **The beginnings of environmental awareness**
       a) _____

       b) _____

       c) _____

       d) _____

   2.   **High gas prices increased awareness of the scarcity of natural resources**
       a) _____

b) _____

c) _____

V. *Conclusion*
   A. *The "postwar era"*
       1. _____

       2. _____

       3. _____

   B. *U.S. and USSR*
       1. _____

       2. _____

       3. _____

   C. *The end of the postwar era*
       1. _____

       2. _____

       3. _____

IDENTIFICATIONS

Define each term and explain why it is significant, including any important dates.

	Identification	**Significance**
Third World		
Cold War		
iron curtain		

	Identification	Significance

nonaligned nations

United Nations

World Bank

Korean War

Vietnam War

Cuban Missile Crisis

North Atlantic Treaty Organization (NATO)

Warsaw Pact

Cultural Revolution (China)

European Community

Helsinki Accords

	Identification	Significance

Marshall Plan

Organization of Petroleum Exporting Countries (OPEC)

Truman Doctrine

Kwame Nkrumah

apartheid

Fidel Castro

Jawaharlal Nehru

Mao Zedong

Green Revolution

MULTIPLE-CHOICE QUESTIONS

Read the entire question, including *all* the possible answers. Then choose the *one* answer that best fits the question.

1. The Western powers tended to disregard the concerns raised by the UN General Assembly

    a.   as they always had.
    b.   more often as the flood of new member countries was more interested in issues of poverty, racism, and imperialism than with the Cold War.
    c.   because their concerns were invalid.
    d.   because matters concerning the new member countries did not affect the rest of the world.
    e.   because the United States never joined.

2. How long did it take the former allies the United States and the Soviet Union to become suspicious of each other?

    a.   Two years
    b.   Five years
    c.   Seven years
    d.   Ten years
    e.   They ended the war suspicious.

3. Why did the Soviets create the Warsaw Pact?

    a.   In response to the formation of NATO
    b.   In response to the decision to allow West Germany to rearm
    c.   To better utilize money provided by the Marshall Plan
    d.   To defend themselves against U.S. missiles in Turkey
    e.   So they could make Turkey a member to get access to the Mediterranean Sea

4. The United States did not attack China during the Korean War because it did not

    a.   see China as a threat.
    b.   have the military capability.
    c.   want to risk getting the USSR involved.
    d.   really care whether or not it won the war.
    e.   want to anger the Japanese.

5. Which one of the following U.S. presidents began sending military advisers to Vietnam?

    a.   Truman
    b.   Eisenhower
    c.   Kennedy
    d.   Johnson
    e.   Nixon

6. When Nikita Khrushchev said, "We will bury you," he meant

    a.   the Soviets would defeat the United States in a conventional war.
    b.   the Soviets would defeat the United States in a nuclear war.
    c.   the Soviets would beat the United States to the moon.
    d.   the Soviets would beat the United States in an economic competition.
    e.   the Soviet Union would defeat the United States at soccer.

7.   Why did Sukarno, of the Dutch Indies, cooperate with the Japanese in the Second World War?

   a.   He wanted to keep the Dutch from coming back.
   b.   He wanted to be part of the Greater East Asia Co-Prosperity Sphere.
   c.   He had no choice.
   d.   He wanted to become the ruler of all of Southeast Asia.
   e.   He did not cooperate; he led the resistance.

8.   Why did the departure of angry French colonists cause so much trouble in Algeria?

   a.   The French colonists made up the majority of the population.
   b.   The French government then refused to trade with Algeria.
   c.   The Arabs left in Algeria had almost no technical training or managerial experience.
   d.   The Arabs left too because of the famine.
   e.   The departing colonists took all of the national treasury with them.

9.   Which of the following British colonies in West Africa was the first to gain independence in 1957?

   a.   Ghana
   b.   Kenya
   c.   Rhodesia
   d.   South Africa
   e.   Morocco

10.   Which of the following did Charles de Gaulle *not* promise to French colonies in Africa?

   a.   More democratic government and broader suffrage
   b.   Representation in the French National Assembly
   c.   The abolition of forced labor
   d.   The opening of more administrative positions to Africans
   e.   Expansion of French education down to the village levels.

11.   Which of the following did *not* cause problems to newly independent nations?

   a.   The new leaders had to decide what kind of government institutions to use.
   b.   Military coups and regional rebellions were frequent occurrences during the independence process.
   c.   Severe economic challenges faced many new nations.
   d.   A scarcity of raw materials and a surplus of manufactured goods.
   e.   Leaders had to decide which language to choose as their national language for education and government business.

12.   The superpowers dominated the world

   a.   and as time went on, they dominated it more and more.
   b.   but they did not control it.
   c.   economic system, but they had no effect on any other area.
   d.   and used that domination to try to force the world to be peaceful to better serve them.
   e.   for only a decade.

13. Which of the following countries actually benefited from the Cold War?

    a. Japan
    b. The United States
    c. Indonesia
    d. Yugoslavia
    e. China

14. China's Great Leap Forward failed, but it demonstrated that

    a. the Chinese people did not support fiscal reform.
    b. its goals were invalid.
    c. Mao was willing to carry out his own massive economic and social policies.
    d. these types of economic plans never work.
    e. China's economy had recovered.

SHORT-ANSWER QUESTIONS

Answer each question in one short paragraph, giving the definition, dates, and significance.

1. Compare and contrast the independence movements of Ghana and Kenya. What factors made them so different?

2. What was the legacy of the CIA's orchestration of the takeover of the Guatemalan government by the military in 1954?

3. Discuss what happened in Hungary in 1956 and in Czechoslovakia in 1968. What lesson was to be learned from their experiences? Why did Poland not suffer the same fate?

4. How did the nonaligned nations play one superpower against the other? Use Egypt as your example.

5. Discuss how the Vietnam War affected politics in the United States. Why were people angry about President Johnson's restrictions on the military? What were his intentions?

6. What was the relationship like between the People's Republic of China and the USSR?

ESSAY QUESTIONS

Make an outline of each question, listing the major points you want to discuss. Then write your practice essay, following your outline carefully and making sure that you do not skip any of your major points. At this time you will want to add the relevant dates and details that will make your essay persuasive and accurate.

1. Discuss the French view of Algeria. How did this view affect the colonial government there and its treatment of Algerians? Did the French attitude toward Algeria differ from the British attitude toward India? If so, in what ways?

2. What three challenges did newly independent nations face? How did colonialism continue to affect the politics, society, and economy of former colonies long after official imperial control had ended?

3. What was the Cold War, and how did it affect the nations of the world? What methods did the superpowers use to fight the Cold War? What legacy did the Cold War leave, both inside the superpowers and outside them?

4. Discuss the formation of Israel. How did this country come into being? What does Israel mean to Jews? What groups were displaced in the formation of the Jewish state? How have these issues impacted the Middle East in the long term?

5.   How did the nations often termed nonaligned or third world view their international role? What challenges faced them? How did they attempt to overcome these challenges?

6.   How did the environment change due to the wars (including the Cold War) of the twentieth century? What resulted from these changes and how did people react?

COMPARISON CHARTS

Using information gathered from the text, fill in the blank areas of each chart with the relevant data pertaining to the regions and categories listed. (Not all blank areas will necessarily be used.)

Chart 32.1
AFRICAN INDEPENDENCE

	Colonizer	Date	New Name	Leader of Independence Movement	Resources/ Products	Government System	Stability	Special Issues
Gold Coast								
East Africa								
Ivory Coast								
French Equatorial Africa								
Algeria								
Niger								
Angola/ Mozambique								
Guinea								
Rhodesia								
South Africa								

Chart 32.2

CHOOSING SIDES

	Superpower Influence/ Intervention	Wars/Conflicts	Goods/Services Received from Superpower	Motivating Factors	Results
Korea					
Vietnam					
Cuba					
Eastern Europe					
Indonesia					
Japan					
China					
Egypt					
Guatemala					

DIVERSITY AND DOMINANCE

After reading "Diversity and Dominance: Race and the Struggle for Justice in South Africa" in your text, answer the following additional questions.

How do you account for Steve Biko's anger, and Bishop Tutu's understanding? Wouldn't you think that it would be the other way around?

INTERNET ASSIGNMENT

Keywords: **"Israel, history" and "Jerusalem Archives"**

                    "Palestine, history" and "Palestinian Liberation Organization"

The conflict between Israelis and Palestinians over a very small piece of (non-oil-rich) real estate has dominated Middle Eastern diplomacy since the formation of the state of Israel in 1947. Use the above keywords to learn the history of the relationship between Israelis and Palestinians. Be sure you look for maps and photographs. Why did the British decide to partition Palestine into Jewish and Arab sectors? Why was this action so unsuccessful? Is this one conflict really to blame for all, or even most, of the problems in the Middle East? Why or why not? How close are we to resolving this dispute?

INTERNET EXPLORATION

In response to the threat of nuclear attack, and even nuclear annihilation, many people built bomb shelters in their backyards. Even various governments were not immune to the fear caused by the Cold War, and they built their own Cold War bunkers. Visit a recently declassified bunker in the United States at http://www.pbs.org/wgbh/amex/bomb/sfeature/bunker.html. How were the accommodations after "the end of the world as we know it"? For whom was the bunker built? Would you want to live underground until the radiation subsided? For further exploration, use the keyword "Cold War Bunker."

MAP EXERCISES

On Outline Map 32.1, shade in the countries that belonged to NATO and those that belonged to the Warsaw Pact.

On Outline Map 32.2, shade in the OPEC nations.

Outline Map 32.1

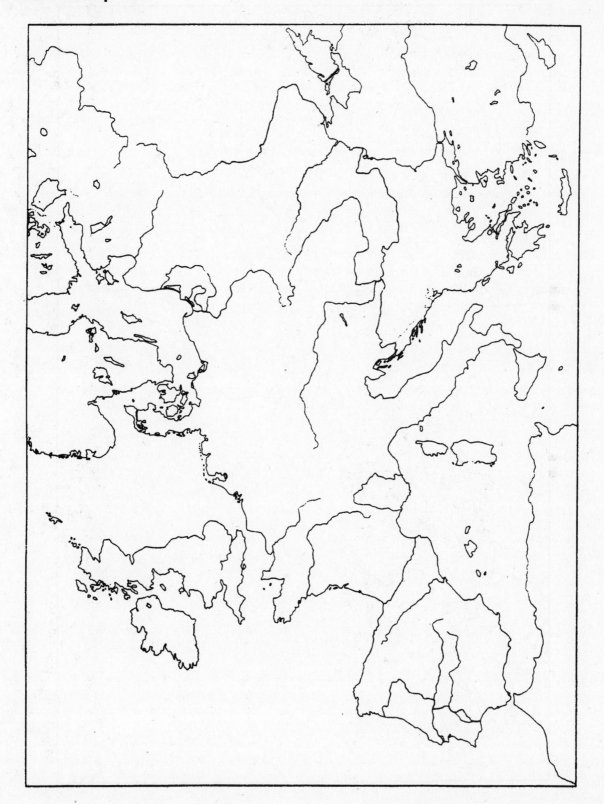

Outline Map 32.2

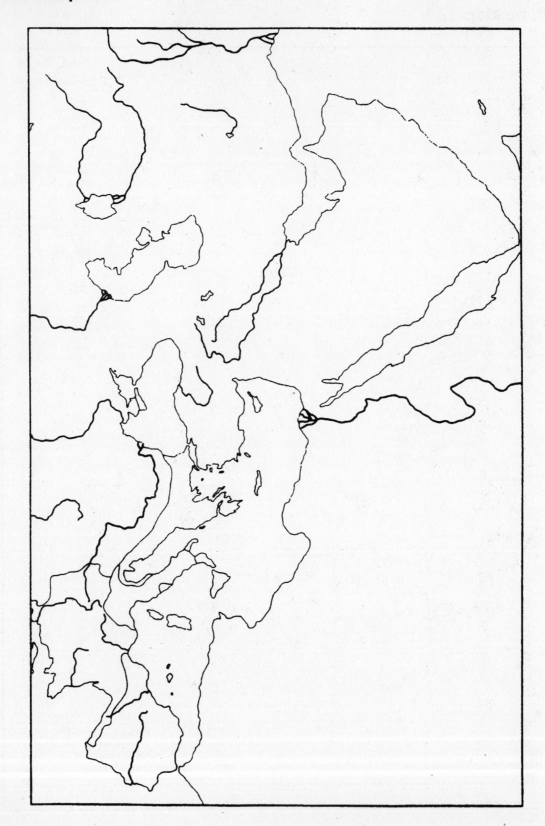

ANSWERS TO MULTIPLE-CHOICE QUESTIONS

1.   a   p. 862
2.   c   p. 866
3.   c   p. 866
4.   b   p. 866
5.   a   p. 868
6.   c   p. 869
7.   b   p. 872
8.   a   p. 872
9.   b   p. 873
10.   c   p. 874
11.   b   p. 879
12.   c   p. 879
13.   b   p. 881
14.   a   p. 881

CHAPTER 33

Crisis, Realignment, and the Dawn of the Post-Cold War World, 1975–1991

LEARNING OBJECTIVES

After reading Chapter 33 and completing this study chapter, you should be able to explain:

- How the state of the world in the late twentieth century was influenced by the Cold War, new technology, population growth, and changes in the worldwide economic system.

- How population has grown worldwide in the last 150 years, leveling out in industrialized countries but escalating in developing nations, and what impact population levels have had on the economies of countries, as well as on their use of resources.

- How people have migrated both within their own countries and to new countries, and how cities have continued to grow as part of this process.

- How, although technology brings benefits to peoples and nations, it does not always do so equally, and how technology can both help and hinder the growth of society.

- What role people and governments are taking to mitigate damage done to the environment by industrialization, and how they may approach sharing the world's remaining resources.

CHAPTER OUTLINE

In the outline below, include important themes, concepts, and details in the blank spaces provided. If you find fewer points than you have space for, leave lines blank. If you find more points, add as many lines as necessary.

I. *Introduction*
   A. *Street kids in Rio de Janeiro*
      1. _____

      2. _____

      3. _____

      4. _____

   B. *Symptoms of social breakdown in the developing industrial world*
      1. _____

      2. _____

3. _____

4. _____

C. *Population growth*
   1. _____

   2. _____

   3. _____

II. *Postcolonial Crises and Asian Economic Expansion, 1975–1991*
   A. *Revolutions, Repression, and Democratic Reform in Latin America*
      1. *Cuba*
         a) _____

         b) _____

         c) _____

      2. *Brazil*
         a) _____

         b) _____

         c) _____

      3. *Chile*
         a) _____

         b) _____

         c) _____

         d) _____

         e) _____

      4. *Argentina*
         a) _____

         b) _____

c) _____

d) _____

5. *Nicaragua*
    a) _____

    b) _____

    c) _____

    d) _____

6. *Jimmy Carter's conciliation*
    a) _____

    b) _____

    c) _____

7. *Ronald Reagan's return to U.S. intervention*
    a) _____

    b) _____

    c) _____

    d) _____

    e) _____

    f) _____

8. *The end of the dictatorships*
    a) _____

    b) _____

    c) _____

    d) _____

e) _____

f) _____

9. *Economic trouble and debt*
   a) _____

   b) _____

   c) _____

   d) _____

10. *More U.S. domination*
    a) _____

    b) _____

    c) _____

    d) _____

B. *Islamic Revolutions in Iran and Afghanistan*
   1. *The Iranian Revolution*
      a) _____

      b) _____

      c) _____

      d) _____

   2. *Ayatollah Ruhollah Khomeini and the Republic of Iran*
      a) _____

      b) _____

      c) _____

   3. *Hostages, humiliation, and the shift toward Iraq*
      a) _____

b) _____

c) _____

d) _____

e) _____

f) _____

4. *Soviets in Afghanistan*

a) _____

b) _____

c) _____

d) _____

e) _____

C. *Asian Transformation*

1. *Japanese growth, corporate structure, and success*

a) _____

b) _____

c) _____

d) _____

e) _____

f) _____

g) _____

2. *South Korean industry*

a) _____

b) _____

      c) _____

      d) _____

      e) _____

  3. *Taiwan*

      a) _____

      b) _____

      c) _____

      d) _____

  4. *Hong Kong and Singapore*

      a) _____

      b) _____

      c) _____

      d) _____

  5. *Why were the Newly Industrialized Economies (NIEs) so successful?*

      a) _____

      b) _____

      c) _____

      d) _____

      e) _____

D. *China Rejoins the World Economy*
  1. *Relaxed state control of the economy*

      a) _____

      b) _____

      c) _____

d) _____

e) _____

2. *China's per capita output grew*
   a) _____

   b) _____

   c) _____

   d) _____

3. *The Tiananmen Square incident*
   a) _____

   b) _____

   c) _____

   d) _____

III. *The End of the Bipolar World, 1989–1991*
   A. *Crisis in the Soviet Union*
      1. *Decay and inequity*
         a) _____

         b) _____

         c) _____

         d) _____

      2. *Dissent and banishment*
         a) _____

         b) _____

         c) _____

3. *Mikhail Gorbachev*
   a) _____

   b) _____

   c) _____

B. *The Collapse of the Socialist Bloc*
   1. *Solidarity in Poland*
      a) _____

      b) _____

      c) _____

      d) _____

   2. *Combination of religion and nationalism*
      a) _____

      b) _____

      c) _____

      d) _____

   3. *1989, the Eastern Bloc fell*
      a) _____

      b) _____

      c) _____

      d) _____

   4. *Germany reunified*
      a) _____

      b) _____

      c) _____

d) _____

5. ***Ethnic tensions and the end of the Soviet Union***
   a) _____

   b) _____

   c) _____

   d) _____

   e) _____

   f) _____

6. ***Yugoslavia and Czechoslovakia***
   a) _____

   b) _____

   c) _____

C. ***The Persian Gulf War, 1990–1991***
   1. ***Iraq decided to invade Kuwait***
      a) _____

      b) _____

      c) _____

   2. ***Saudi Arabia, the United States, and the United Nations***
      a) _____

      b) _____

      c) _____

   3. ***Boost to U.S. morale***
      a) _____

      b) _____

c) _____

IV.   *The Challenge of Population Growth*
   A.   *Demographic Transition*
      1.   *Population growth in the nineteenth century*
         a) _____

         b) _____

         c) _____

         d) _____

      2.   *Population rate begins to decrease in the twentieth century*
         a) _____

         b) _____

         c) _____

      3.   *The Third World*
         a) _____

         b) _____

         c) _____

         d) _____

      4.   *World population explosion*
         a) _____

         b) _____

         c) _____

      5.   *HIV/AIDS*
         a) _____

         b) _____

         c) _____

d) _____

B.   *The Industrialized Nations*
   1.   *Falling birthrates*
      a) _____

      b) _____

      c) _____

   2.   *Improved life expectancy*
      a) _____

      b) _____

      c) _____

      d) _____

      e) _____

   3.   *The potential support ration (PSR) crisis*
      a) _____

      b) _____

      c) _____

      d) _____

      e) _____

   4.   *The former socialist nations*
      a) _____

      b) _____

      c) _____

      d) _____

      e) _____

C. *The Developing Nations*
   1. *Africa*
      a) _____

      b) _____

      c) _____

      d) _____

      e) _____

   2. *Muslim countries and Latin America*
      a) _____

      b) _____

      c) _____

      d) _____

   3. *Asia*
      a) _____

      b) _____

      c) _____

      d) _____

      e) _____

D. *Old and Young Populations*
   1. *Pakistan*
      a) _____

      b) _____

      c) _____

2. *Sweden*

   a) _____

   b) _____

   c) _____

3. *South Korea*

   a) _____

   b) _____

   c) _____

4. *Japan*

   a) _____

   b) _____

   c) _____

V. *Unequal Development and the Movement of Peoples*
   A. *The Problem of Growing Inequality*
      1. *Abundance and poverty*

         a) _____

         b) _____

         c) _____

         d) _____

         e) _____

      2. *Per capita GNIs*

         a) _____

         b) _____

         c) _____

         d) _____

e) _____

3. *Wealth inequity within nations*
    a) _____

    b) _____

    c) _____

4. *United States: haves and have-nots*
    a) _____

    b) _____

    c) _____

    d) _____

    e) _____

B. *Internal Migration: The Growth of Cities*
    1. *A move to an urban center usually positive*
        a) _____

        b) _____

        c) _____

    2. *But population pressure began to compromise quality of life*
        a) _____

        b) _____

        c) _____

    3. *Rural resettlement*
        a) _____

        b) _____

        c) _____

C.   *Global Migration*
1.   **People from developing nations moved to industrialized nations from 1960s to 1990s**
   a) _____

   b) _____

   c) _____

2.   **Characteristics of immigrants**
   a) _____

   b) _____

   c) _____

   d) _____

3.   **Immigrants and population**
   a) _____

   b) _____

   c) _____

   d) _____

VI.   ***Technological and Environmental Change***
A.   *New Technologies and the World Economy*
1.   **Improvements in existing technologies**
   a) _____

   b) _____

   c) _____

2.   **Computers**
   a) _____

   b) _____

   c) _____

d) _____

e) _____

f) _____

3.   *The transnational corporation*
  a) _____

  b) _____

  c) _____

  d) _____

  e) _____

  f) _____

B.   *Conserving and Sharing Resources*
  1.   *Response to abuse of the environment*
    a) _____

    b) _____

    c) _____

    d) _____

  2.   *Response to population pressure and resources*
    a) _____

    b) _____

    c) _____

    d) _____

    e) _____

    f) _____

3. *Population and environmental problems combined*
   a) _____

   b) _____

   c) _____

C. *Responding to Environmental Threats*
   1. *Efforts to protect the environment*
      a) _____

      b) _____

      c) _____

      d) _____

   2. *Results of these efforts*
      a) _____

      b) _____

      c) _____

      d) _____

   3. *Still problems in former Soviet Union and China*
      a) _____

      b) _____

      c) _____

   4. *Global action to protect the environment*
      a) _____

      b) _____

      c) _____

      d) _____

VII. *Conclusion*
    A.   *The price of the Cold War*
        1. _____

        2. _____

        3. _____

        4. _____

        5. _____

        6. _____

    B.   *Economic growth and integration*
        1. _____

        2. _____

        3. _____

        4. _____

    C.   *Population growth, migration, and technology*
        1. _____

        2. _____

        3. _____

        4. _____

        5. _____

        6. _____

IDENTIFICATIONS

Define each term and explain why it is significant, including any important dates.

	Identification	**Significance**
proxy wars		
Salvador Allende		
Dirty War		
Sandinistas		
Neo-liberalism		
Ayatollah Ruhollah Khomeini		
Saddam Husain		
keiretsu		
Asian Tigers		
newly industrialized economies (NIEs)		

	Identification	Significance

Deng Xiaoping

Tiananmen Square

Mikhail Gorbachev

perestroika

Solidarity

Thomas Malthus

demographic transition

MULTIPLE-CHOICE QUESTIONS

Read the entire question, including *all* the possible answers. Then choose the *one* answer that best fits the question.

1. The dramatic economic growth and rapid technological progress of the post–World War II era has

   a. coincided with greater peace and security worldwide.
   b. benefited only the industrialized nations.
   c. coincided with growing social dislocation and inequality.
   d. coincided with a generalized rise in the standard of living of all the world's peoples.
   e. finally allowed developing countries to "catch up with the West."

2.   What is a "proxy war?"

    a.   Another name for limited nuclear war

    b.   A war in which only two combatants are chosen out of many factions

    c.   A style of one-on-one combat favored by Second World nations

    d.   Conflicts in which the rival super powers financed and armed competing local factions

    e.   An economic rather than military war

3.   Which of the following programs pursued by Fidel Castro caused conflict with the United States?

    a.   He sought to end U.S. domination of Cuba, and uplift the Cuban masses by changing the economy.

    b.   He wanted to create a Pan-South American league to keep U.S. investors and military from interfering in South American politics.

    c.   He wanted to escape Soviet domination, but he also resented U.S. attempts at annexation.

    d.   He wanted extensive financial aid from both the United States and U.S.S.R.

    e.   He sought more aid from China.

4.   What is the "Brazilian solution?"

    a.   The great success story of South America

    b.   A combination of entrepreneurialism, humanitarianism, and industrialization

    c.   A combination of dictatorship, violent repression, and government promotion of industrialization

    d.   A process by which gold refining became more environmentally responsible

    e.   A secret plan by the United States to control the economy of Brazil

5.   How did the Ayatollah Khomeini view the United States?

    a.   As a big brother that would lead Iran to economic prosperity

    b.   As a partner in promoting Middle Eastern peace

    c.   As a competitor in OPEC oil production

    d.   As an unbiased ally in the United Nations

    e.   As a "Great Satan" opposed to Islam

6.   Which of the following *cannot* be said to have contributed to the success of the Newly Industrialized Economies (NIEs)?

    a.   They all have disciplined, hard-working work forces.

    b.   The governments invest heavily in education.

    c.   Their people have a high rate of personal savings.

    d.   They all have a hands-off policy regarding government control and regulation.

    e.   They emphasize outward-looking export strategies.

7.   From 1850 to 1914, European population

    a.   fell by half.

    b.   almost doubled.

    c.   increased slightly.

    d.   remained constant.

    e.   decreased.

8.   How many people in Africa live with HIV?

   a.   1 million
   b.   4 million
   c.   12 million
   d.   20 million
   e.   28 million

9.   Which of the following factors is *not* thought to be particularly helpful in controlling the birthrate of any country?

   a.   Government controls
   b.   Education levels, especially of women
   c.   The material values of consumer culture
   d.   Availability of contraception
   e.   Female employment outside of the home

10.   Regarding the monetary situation of the poor of the world in 2003,

   a.   they are much better off than they were in 1960.
   b.   they are as poor or poorer than they were in 1960.
   c.   most are much worse off than they were in 1960.
   d.   only industrialized nations have benefited during the twentieth century.
   e.   little change has occurred in poor countries since 1960.

11.   Which of the following has generally encouraged people to migrate to urban areas in the twentieth century?

   a.   Employment brokers canvass the countryside to recruit laborers.
   b.   The cities offer good opportunities.
   c.   Urban areas often have good social services.
   d.   More money can be made in the cities.
   e.   The countryside can no longer support them.

12.   Environmental protection has progressed furthest in societies

   a.   that are ideologically closest to nature.
   b.   that have the most to lose.
   c.   with the most economic resources.
   d.   with the most outspoken environmentalists.
   e.   with the most stringent environmental laws.

13.   Why has the United States introduced robots more slowly into its factories than Europe or Japan?

   a.   Labor costs are lower in the United States.
   b.   Strong labor unions have prevented it.
   c.   U.S. robotics technology lags far behind that of Europe and Japan.
   d.   Robots would bring the price of goods down too far for profitability.
   e.   The United States is ideologically against mechanization.

14.   Modern economies are driven by

   a.   production of goods for domestic and foreign markets.
   b.   high levels of personal savings.
   c.   high levels of consumption.
   d.   low levels of consumer debt.
   e.   low levels of national debt.

15.   In the United States by the year 2000, smog levels were
    a.   down nearly one third from 1970 levels.
    b.   down nearly one half from 1970 levels.
    c.   roughly the same as in 1970.
    d.   up twenty percent from 1970 levels.
    e.   the highest ever.

16.   Who may eventually have to fund global environmental improvements?
    a.   The United States
    b.   The United Nations
    c.   Third World nations
    d.   All the industrialized nations
    e.   Independent entrepreneurs

SHORT-ANSWER QUESTIONS

Answer each question in one short paragraph, giving the definition, dates, and significance.

1.   Briefly discuss U.S. intervention in Latin America in the 1970s and 1980s; what were U.S. goals, and what were the results of that intervention?

2.   What kinds of economic policies were pursued by countries trying to build up their economies in the twentieth century? Give specific examples.

3.   How can demographics positively or negatively affect a country's economy? Use specific examples.

4.   What caused the Persian Gulf War?

5.   Characterize the world's environment in the 1970s. How does it compare with the environment of 2003?

6.   Discuss the forces behind the fall of the USSR. What events took place, and what were the results?

ESSAY QUESTIONS

Make an outline of each question, listing the major points you want to discuss. Then write your practice essay, following your outline carefully and making sure that you do not skip any of your major points. At this time you will want to add the relevant dates and details that will make your essay persuasive and accurate.

1.   Discuss the challenges that faced the peoples of the world in the late twentieth century. Why did these problems arise, and what options do we have for solving them?

2.   How did the U.S. economy change after the initial boom brought by the Second World War? What caused these changes, and how did the United States react? Discuss similar changes going on in the Soviet Union at the same time. What could account for the similarity?

3.   Discuss the success of South Korea, Taiwan, Hong Kong, and Singapore. What fueled their achievements, what were their methods, and how has their success affected the world economy?

4.   The twentieth century saw a spreading gap between the rich and the poor, both on a national level and on an individual level. Discuss this income gap. How did it come about? What methods have been used to try to narrow the gap? What has been the result of a world of haves and have-nots?

5.   Discuss population growth in the twentieth century. In what countries does population seem to grow the most and why? What policies do certain countries pursue to either encourage or discourage population increase? How does population growth affect resource use? Do people in all parts of the world use the same amount of resources? How does this issue affect international relations?

COMPARISON CHARTS

Using information gathered from the text, fill in the blank areas of each chart with the relevant data pertaining to the regions and categories listed. (Not all blank areas will necessarily be used.)

Chart 33.1
THE HAVES AND HAVE-NOTS

	Industrialized Nations	Industrializing Nations
Population		
Birthrate		
Mortality Rate		
Age Distribution		
Population Controls		
Role of Women		
Products/Resources		
Per Capita GNP		
Trading Partners		
Examples of Nations		

Chart 33.2

THE FALL OF THE SOVIET UNION AND THE SOCIALIST BLOC

	Leaders of the Movement	Local Response	Financial Repercussion	Population Growth or Decline	Environmental Impact	Pollution
USSR/Russia						
Germany						
Yugoslavia						
Poland						
Romania						
Czechoslovakia						

DIVERSITY AND DOMINANCE

After reading "Diversity and Dominance: The Struggle for Women's Rights in an Era of Global Political and Economic Change" in your text, answer the following additional questions.

What do you think Gladys Acosta means by "the end of ideologies"?

Why does she say that national identities play a different role now than they used to?

What role do women play in the economy of today, and how does she contrast women's needs and goals with Neo-liberalism and other economic policies?

INTERNET ASSIGNMENT

Keywords: **"Fall of the Berlin Wall" and "Berlin Wall"**

                   "Tiananmen Square"

The fall of the Berlin Wall and the student protest at Tiananmen Square both occurred in 1989. Use the above keywords to find web sites about these two events. Why did each happen? What did each event mean to Communism in Germany and China? Why did the fall of the Berlin Wall and the student protest at Tiananmen Square receive so much attention worldwide? What do they mean today, over a decade later?

INTERNET EXPLORATION

In the 1970s, much of the world began to awaken to the reality that the earth did not possess inexhaustible resources, and did not have the ability to recover continually from environmental damage. Few people have been as influential in the movement to preserve our planet, and even reverse the process of degradation than Jacques Cousteau. His actions made the public aware of the mysterious undersea world, and of the essential role played by our oceans. Visit the official Cousteau Society web site at http://www.cousteausociety.org/. For further exploration use the keyword "Cousteau Society."

MAP EXERCISE

On Outline Map 33.1, using different colors, shade in the regions of the world that have the following population growth rates:

    3% or more

    2%-2.9%

    1%-1.9%

    0%-0.9%

    population loss

Outline Map 33.1

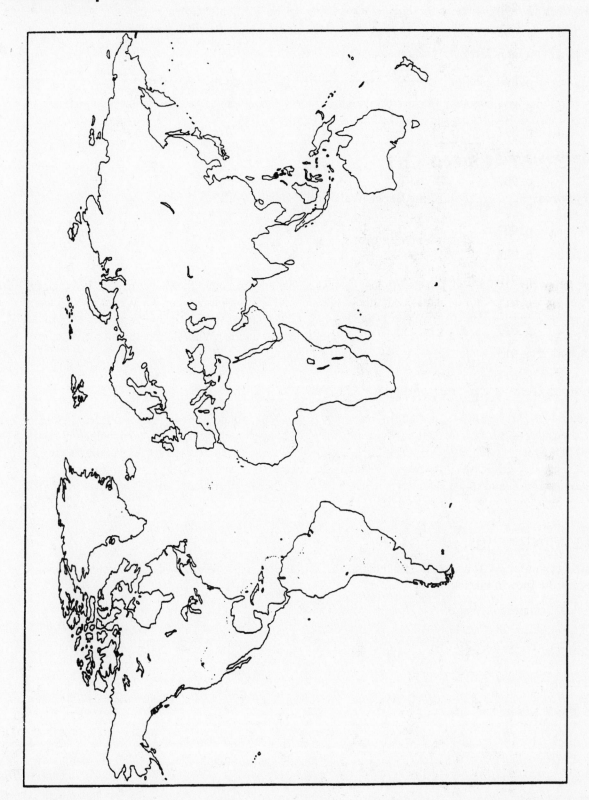

ANSWERS TO MULTIPLE-CHOICE QUESTIONS

1.   c   p. 888
2.   d   p. 888
3.   a   p. 890
4.   c   p. 890
5.   e   p. 893
6.   d   p. 897
7.   b   p. 902
8.   e   p. 903
9.   a   p. 903, 904
10. b   p. 907
11. a   p. 908
12. c   p. 910
13. a   p. 911
14. c   p. 913
15. a   p. 915
16. d   p. 915

CHAPTER 34

Globalization at the Turn of the Millennium

LEARNING OBJECTIVES

After reading Chapter 34 and completing this study chapter, you should be able to explain:

- How global integration has influenced the economy, politics, technology, and cultures of the world, including those who have resisted this globalization.

- How popular culture has spread through the media of film, video, sound recording, and computers to become a global phenomenon, and what specific role Western culture has played in this process.

- How world leaders have created international organizations such as the United Nations and the World Trade Organization to help the world face the challenges of the twentieth century and beyond.

- How linguistic, ethnic, and religious differences have inspired nationalist movements, which have benefited some nations and nearly destroyed others.

- How cultural traditions endure in the face of change.

CHAPTER OUTLINE

In the outline below, include important themes, concepts, and details in the blank spaces provided. If you find fewer points than you have space for, leave lines blank. If you find more points, add as many lines as necessary.

I. *Introduction*
    A. *The attack on the World Trade Center and the Pentagon*
        1. _____

        2. _____

        3. _____

        4. _____

        5. _____

        6. _____

     B.   *The hijackers*

         1. _____

         2. _____

         3. _____

         4. _____

         5. _____

         6. _____

     C.   *Understanding 9/11*

         1. _____

         2. _____

         3. _____

         4. _____

         5. _____

II.   *Global Political Economies*

     A.   *The Spread of Democracy*

         1.   *Democracies in the United States and Europe*

            a) _____

            b) _____

            c) _____

            d) _____

            e) _____

         2.   *Democracies in Latin America*

            a) _____

            b) _____

c) _____

d) _____

3. ***Democracies in Asia***
    a) _____

    b) _____

    c) _____

    d) _____

    e) _____

4. ***Democracies in Africa***
    a) _____

    b) _____

    c) _____

    d) _____

    e) _____

5. ***Democracies in the Middle East***
    a) _____

    b) _____

    c) _____

    d) _____

B. ***Global Politics***
    1. ***Autonomy and Intervention***
        a) _____

        b) _____

        c) _____

d) _____

e) _____

2. **Peacekeeping Successes**
    a) _____

    b) _____

    c) _____

3. **Disagreements on how to stop civil conflicts**
    a) _____

    b) _____

    c) _____

    d) _____

    e) _____

    f) _____

4. **The cost of intervention, and conflicts that resolved themselves**
    a) _____

    b) _____

    c) _____

    d) _____

    e) _____

C. **Arms Control and Terrorism**
    1. **Nuclear proliferation**
        a) _____

        b) _____

c) _____

d) _____

e) _____

f) _____

2.   *Chemical and biological weapons*
   a) _____

   b) _____

   c) _____

3.   *Terrorism and Usama bin Laden*
   a) _____

   b) _____

   c) _____

   d) _____

   e) _____

   f) _____

4.   *Preemptive strikes and the "coalition of the willing"*
   a) _____

   b) _____

   c) _____

   d) _____

   e) _____

   f) _____

5. *Opposition to the new Persian Gulf War*
   a) _____

   b) _____

   c) _____

   d) _____

D. *The Global Economy*
   1. *After socialist economic experiments ended, capitalism—with all of its advantages and problems—became standard*
      a) _____

      b) _____

      c) _____

      d) _____

      e) _____

   2. *Reservations about investing*
      a) _____

      b) _____

      c) _____

      d) _____

   3. *Historic disparities in economies and per capita incomes continued*
      a) _____

      b) _____

      c) _____

E. *Managing the Global Economy*
   1. *Regional Trade Associations*
      a) _____

b) _____

c) _____

d) _____

2. *The World Trade Organization (WTO)*
   a) _____

   b) _____

   c) _____

3. *The International Monetary Fund (IMF) and the World Bank*
   a) _____

   b) _____

   c) _____

4. *The amount of aid reduced, but new attention focused on economic backwardness*
   a) _____

   b) _____

   c) _____

   d) _____

   e) _____

5. *Agricultural interests*
   a) _____

   b) _____

   c) _____

III. *Trends and Visions*
   A. *A New Age?*
      1. *The Lexus and the Olive Tree*
         a) _____

b) _____

c) _____

d) _____

e) _____

2. *The wake of 9/11*
    a) _____

    b) _____

    c) _____

3. *Distinct regions?*
    a) _____

    b) _____

    c) _____

    d) _____

B. *Christian Millenarianism*
    1. *The meaning of the year 2000*
        a) _____

        b) _____

        c) _____

        d) _____

        e) _____

    2. *Attempts to gain more converts*
        a) _____

        b) _____

        c) _____

3. ***Cult movements***
    a) _____

    b) _____

    c) _____

    d) _____

C. ***Militant Islam***
    1. ***Jewish beliefs about the year 2000***
        a) _____

        b) _____

        c) _____

    2. ***From empires to colonies***
        a) _____

        b) _____

        c) _____

    3. ***Results of disappointment in economic advancement***
        a) _____

        b) _____

        c) _____

        d) _____

    4. ***Frustration toward Israel and the United States***
        a) _____

        b) _____

        c) _____

        d) _____

e) _____

f) _____

5. *The ideological vision of Muslims under attack*

a) _____

b) _____

c) _____

d) _____

e) _____

f) _____

D. *Universal Rights and Values*
1. *Enlightenment origins*

a) _____

b) _____

c) _____

d) _____

2. *The Universal Declaration of Human Rights*

a) _____

b) _____

c) _____

d) _____

e) _____

f) _____

3. *Some people had reservations about the principles of the Declaration*
    a) _____

    b) _____

    c) _____

4. *Nongovernmental Organizations (NGOs)*
    a) _____

    b) _____

    c) _____

    d) _____

5. *AIDS*
    a) _____

    b) _____

    c) _____

    d) _____

6. *Other international agreements and the United States*
    a) _____

    b) _____

    c) _____

    d) _____

E. *Women's Rights*
    1. *The women's movement in the West*
        a) _____

        b) _____

        c) _____

d) _____

2. *Non-Western women's perceptions and their views on women's rights*
   a) _____

   b) _____

   c) _____

   d) _____

3. *Efforts to bring unity and continuing diversity*
   a) _____

   b) _____

   c) _____

   d) _____

   e) _____

   f) _____

   g) _____

IV. *Global Culture*
   A. *The Media and the Message*
      1. *Cultural imperialism—or not?*
         a) _____

         b) _____

         c) _____

         d) _____

         e) _____

      2. *Movies and jazz*
         a) _____

b) _____

c) _____

3. *Transistors*
   a) _____

   b) _____

   c) _____

4. *Television*
   a) _____

   b) _____

   c) _____

   d) _____

   e) _____

   f) _____

5. *The Internet*
   a) _____

   b) _____

   c) _____

   d) _____

   e) _____

B. *The Spread of Pop Culture*
   1. *Elite culture*
      a) _____

      b) _____

      c) _____

2. *Global pop culture mostly American*

    a) _____

    b) _____

    c) _____

    d) _____

3. *Other cultures are becoming contributors*

    a) _____

    b) _____

    c) _____

    d) _____

C. *Emerging Global Culture*

    1. *Reopened intellectual and cultural contacts*

        a) _____

        b) _____

        c) _____

    2. *The rising importance of English as a second language*

        a) _____

        b) _____

        c) _____

        d) _____

        e) _____

        f) _____

        g) _____

3. *Science and technology*
    a) _____

    b) _____

    c) _____

    d) _____

4. *The University*
    a) _____

    b) _____

    c) _____

    d) _____

D. *Enduring Cultural Diversity*
    1. *Japanese success*
        a) _____

        b) _____

        c) _____

        d) _____

        e) _____

    2. *Threats to cultural diversity*
        a) _____

        b) _____

        c) _____

        d) _____

V. *Conclusion*
    A. *A Golden Age?*
        1. _____

      2. _____

      3. _____

  B.   *Change and the nature of change*
      1. _____

      2. _____

      3. _____

      4. _____

      5. _____

      6. _____

  C.   *Responses to uncertainty*
      1. _____

      2. _____

      3. _____

IDENTIFICATIONS

Define each term and explain why it is significant, including any important dates.

	Identification	**Significance**
globalization		
ethnic cleansing		
weapons of mass destruction		
terrorism		

	Identification	Significance
Usama bin Laden		
World Trade Organization (WTO)		
millenarianism		
nuclear nonproliferation		
Universal Declaration of Human Rights		
nongovernmental organizations (NGOs)		
cultural imperialism		
pop culture		
global culture		

MULTIPLE-CHOICE QUESTIONS

Read the entire question, including *all* the possible answers. Then choose the *one* answer that best fits the question.

1. The Bosnia crisis

    a. was averted by the fall of communism.
    b. encouraged the unification of Yugoslavia.
    c. was the sole cause of the breakup of the Balkan Republic.
    d. challenged the homogeneity of Yugoslavian religion.
    e. challenged the international community to question whether or not disinterested countries should interfere in civil conflicts.

2. By 2003, most people lived

    a. in democracies.
    b. in dictatorships.
    c. in cities.
    d. in safe housing.
    e. in developed countries.

3. The greatest single beneficiary of post–Cold War foreign investment was

    a. Mexico.
    b. Iran.
    c. India.
    d. Russia.
    e. China.

4. Which of the following religions has the most adherents?

    a. Christianity
    b. Islam
    c. Judaism
    d. Hinduism
    e. Buddhism

5. Which of the following has *not* resulted from the failure of modernization to materialize in many Muslim countries as promised?

    a. Many Muslims have begun to look to their sacred past.
    b. Many Muslims feel hostility toward the seduction of the modern world.
    c. A rekindling of the Islamic struggle against non-Muslim infidels.
    d. Feelings of resentment toward Israel.
    e. Despair that will probably result in the loss of Muslim cultural identity.

6. Why did many countries, including the United States, pull out of some international agreements in the early twenty-first century?

    a. Many feared a one-world government.
    b. Many realized that these large international agreements just do not work.
    c. Many felt that these agreements threatened their national interests.
    d. Business is generally against international treaties.
    e. The agreements were just too expensive to maintain.

7.   Which of the following is *not* a reason that Muslim women cover their hair and conceal their bodies?

   a.   Defense against coarse male behavior
   b.   Expression of personal belief
   c.   Resistance to secular dictatorship
   d.   Dictate of the Quran
   e.   Laws of some Middle Eastern governments

8.   Many people interpreted the spread of American products

   a.   as a sign that the worldwide economy was failing.
   b.   as a sign that the worldwide economy was thriving.
   c.   as an attempt by the United States to dominate the world.
   d.   as an attempt by corporations to exploit the entire world for their benefit.
   e.   as proof that American culture is superior.

9.   What was the key invention that made popular culture available to global audiences?

   a.   The television
   b.   The radio
   c.   The phonograph
   d.   The printing press
   e.   The Internet

10.   Which of the following did *not* help to make English a global second language?

   a.   The British took English to every continent during the age of imperialism.
   b.   Diplomacy, business, and academic conferences tend to be conducted in English.
   c.   Because of its global use, English is a link to the outside world.
   d.   English often provides unity to diverse peoples within a country.
   e.   The United States pays Third World governments to teach English to their people.

11.   Global culture

   a.   is the means by which American industry promotes its products overseas.
   b.   is completely dominated by the United States.
   c.   is quickly wiping out cultural diversity.
   d.   is a second culture that dominates in some contexts, but does not displace other traditions.
   e.   is on the decline in the twenty-first century in the face of the rising tide of nationalism and religious fundamentalism.

12.   Japan's economic success in the modern industrial world calls into question which of the following assumptions?

   a.   Only Europeans or Americans had the capability to perform at high economic levels.
   b.   Only Marxists are good industrialists.
   c.   Asian countries are best at agriculture.
   d.   The spread of industrialization to different parts of the world would require the adoption of Western culture as well.
   e.   That worldwide recession is inevitable.

SHORT-ANSWER QUESTIONS

Answer each question in one short paragraph, giving the definition, dates, and significance.

1.   What is global integration, and how might it affect the peoples of the world?

2.   Discuss the threat posed by terrorism and weapons of mass destruction. How have people reacted to this potential threat?

3.   What have Western advocates of women's rights learned from women in other parts of the world?

4.   How do many Muslims view Muslim terrorism against the West?

ESSAY QUESTIONS

Make an outline of each question, listing the major points you want to discuss. Then write your practice essay, following your outline carefully and making sure that you do not skip any of your major points. At this time you will want to add the relevant dates and details that will make your essay persuasive and accurate.

1.   Trace the spread and development of democracy outside of the West. Be sure you address the diversity that democracy can take, and the challenges it often faces.

2.   Discuss the role of technology in the development of the world in the twenty-first century, paying particular attention to economy and culture. Who have been the major players, and how have some people responded to this?

3.   What is the structure and purpose of the United Nations? How did it develop, and why do countries belong to it even if they are suspicious of world government? What has been its role in world politics? What are some of the weaknesses of this organization?

4.   What is the Universal Declaration of Human Rights? What are its aims, and who wrote it? Although most countries support the concept of human rights, some have disagreed with the aims outlined in the Declaration. Why? Give specific examples.

5.   Discuss how ethnic, religious, and linguistic diversity can negatively affect a region. Use three examples.

COMPARISON CHARTS

Using information gathered from the text, fill in the blank areas of each chart with the relevant data pertaining to the regions and categories listed. (Not all blank areas will necessarily be used.)

Chart 34.1

UNITY: INTERNATIONALIZATION

	United States	Latin America	Europe	Muslim World	Africa	Asia	Australia/ Pacific
Popular Culture							
Industrialization							
Human Rights							
Feminism							
Religion							

Chart 34.2

EXPRESSIONS OF CULTURE

	Origins	Effects in Asia	Effects in Africa	Effects in Middle East	Effects in Latin America
Elite Global Culture					
Global Pop Culture					
Resistance to Cultural Change					

DIVERSITY AND DOMINANCE

After reading "Diversity and Dominance: World Literature in English" in your text, please answer the following additional questions.

Why does Shashi Tharoor assert that writing in English is consistent with the multiplicity of Indian society? What do you think of his critics' assertions that he is somehow less Indian for writing in English?

Do you think that Shashi Tharoor's job as Under-Secretary-General for Communications and Public Information for the United Nations influences his decision to write in English?

INTERNET ASSIGNMENT

Keywords: **"Religious Fundamentalism"**

                   "Doctors Without Borders"

Religious fundamentalism has been blamed for many of the world's ills. What religions and regions are experiencing religious fundamentalism today? What does the term "religious fundamentalism" mean? Look for examples of Christian, Muslim, and Jewish fundamentalism. How do these movements affect their countries and the world? Now look for lesser-known cases of fundamentalism among Hindus, Buddhists, and Sikhs. What do all of these groups have in common?

Doctors Without Borders is a volunteer organization formed to alleviate illness caused by war, poverty, and disaster. This phenomenon is a positive force in the world today, and won the Nobel Peace Prize in 1999. Can you think of other world movements that are major forces in the world today? How are they helpful or hurtful to the peoples of the world?

INTERNET EXPLORATION

The end of the twentieth century has been marked by revived interest in time and the calendar. Was 2000 the first year of the new Millennium? Is there Biblical significance to the year 2000? Is there a year zero? Have we always used the calendar we use today (the Gregorian calendar)? Are calendars all over the world the same as ours? Is there a better calendar out there somewhere? What can we learn about the measurement of time from this great debate about the calendar? For exploration use the keywords "Calendar Studies" or "History of the Calendar."

MAP EXERCISE

On Outline Map 34.1, shade in the areas where the following religions are practiced:

Christianity

Islam

Hinduism

Buddhism

Tribal/Chinese folk religion

Also shade in the areas that are non-religious or atheist.

On Outline Map 34.2, shade in the areas where the following GDPs are earned:

Over $20,000

$10,000-20,000

$2,000-$10,000

Under $2,000

Outline Map 34.1

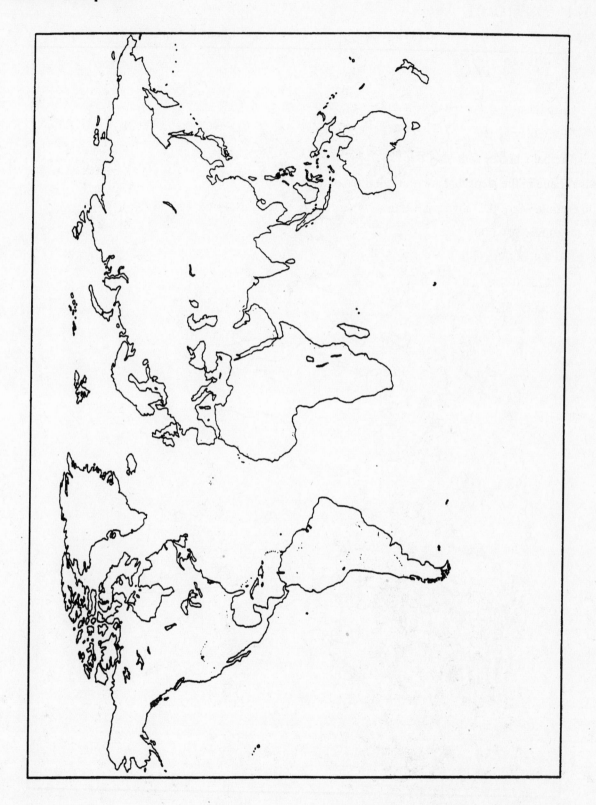

Outline Map 34.2

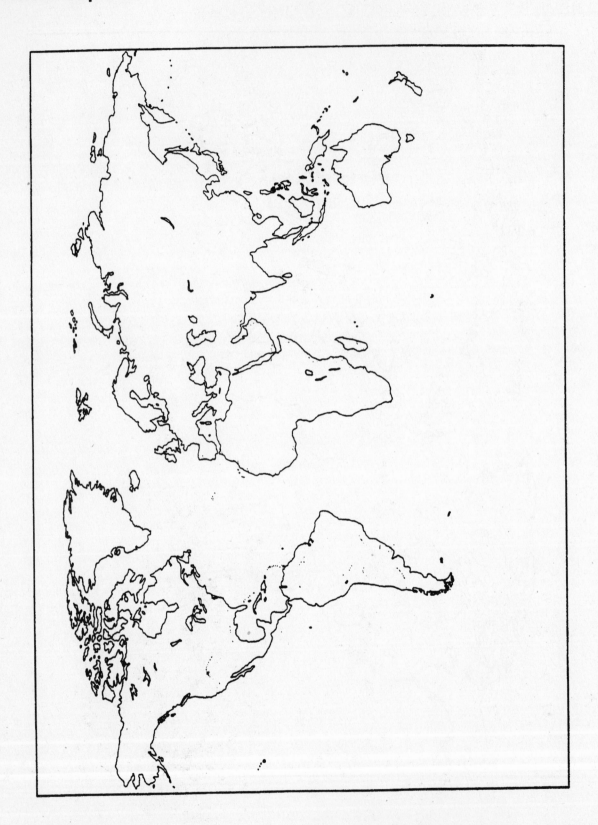

ANSWERS TO MULTIPLE-CHOICE QUESTIONS

1. e   p. 922
2. a   p. 920
3. e   p. 925
4. a   p. 930
5. e   p. 933
6. c   p. 934
7. d   p. 936
8. c   p. 937
9. a   p. 938
10. e   p. 939, 940
11. d   p. 941
12. d   p. 941